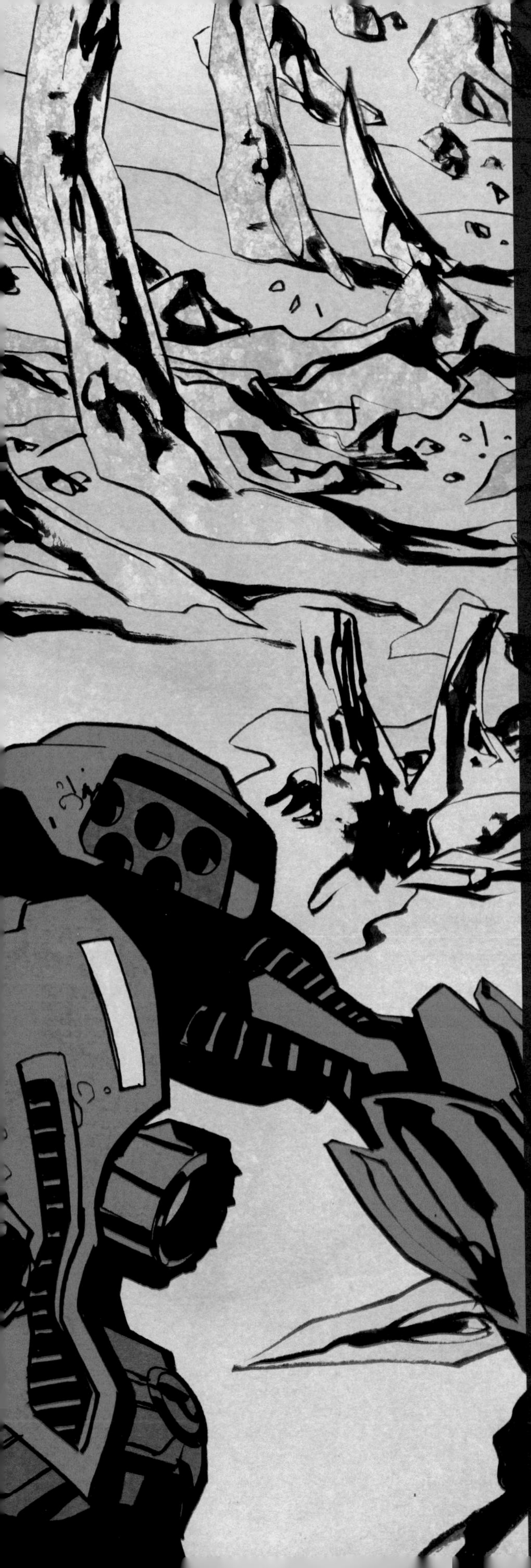

BATMAN – DETECTIVE COMICS

VOLUME 8

BLOOD OF HEROES

WRITTEN BY
BRIAN BUCCELLATO
RAY FAWKES
FRANCIS MANAPUL
PETER J. TOMASI

ART BY
FERNANDO BLANCO
FRANCIS MANAPUL
STEVE PUGH
MARCIO TAKARA

COLOR BY
BRIAN BUCCELLATO
CHRIS SOTOMAYOR

LETTERS BY
WES ABBOTT
JARED K. FLETCHER

COLLECTION COVER ART BY
FRANCIS MANAPUL

BATMAN CREATED BY
BOB KANE WITH **BILL FINGER**

SUPERMAN CREATED BY
JERRY SIEGEL AND
JOE SHUSTER
BY SPECIAL ARRANGEMENT
WITH THE JERRY SIEGEL FAMILY

BATMAN – DETECTIVE COMICS VOLUME 8: BLOOD OF HEROES

Published by DC Comics. Compilation and all new material Copyright © 2016 DC Comics. All Rights Reserved. Originally published online as
DETECTIVE COMICS Sneak Peek and in single magazine form as DETECTIVE COMICS 41-47. Copyright © 2015, 2016 DC Comics.
All Rights Reserved. All characters, their distinctive likenesses and related elements featured in this publication are trademarks of
DC Comics. The stories, characters and incidents featured in this publication are entirely fictional. DC Comics does not read or
accept unsolicited ideas, stories or artwork.

DC Comics, 2900 West Alameda Ave., Burbank, CA 91505
Printed by LSC Communications, Salem, VA. 10/28/16. First Printing.
ISBN: 978-1-4012-6924-1

Library of Congress Cataloging-in-Publication Data

Names: Tomasi, Peter, author. | Buccellato, Brian, author, illustrator. |
Manapul, Francis, author, illustrator.
Title: Batman/Detective Comics. Volume 8, Blood of heroes / Peter J. Tomasi,
writer ; Brian Buccellato, writer, colorist ; Francis Manapul, writer,
cover artist, interior artist.
Other titles: Blood of heroes
Description: Burbank, CA : DC Comics, [2016]
Identifiers: LCCN 2016017003 | ISBN 9781401263553 (hardback)
Subjects: LCSH: Comic books, strips, etc. | BISAC: COMICS & GRAPHIC NOVELS /
Superheroes.
Classification: LCC PN6728.B36 T6 2016 | DDC 741.5/973—dc23
LC record available at https://lccn.loc.gov/2016017003

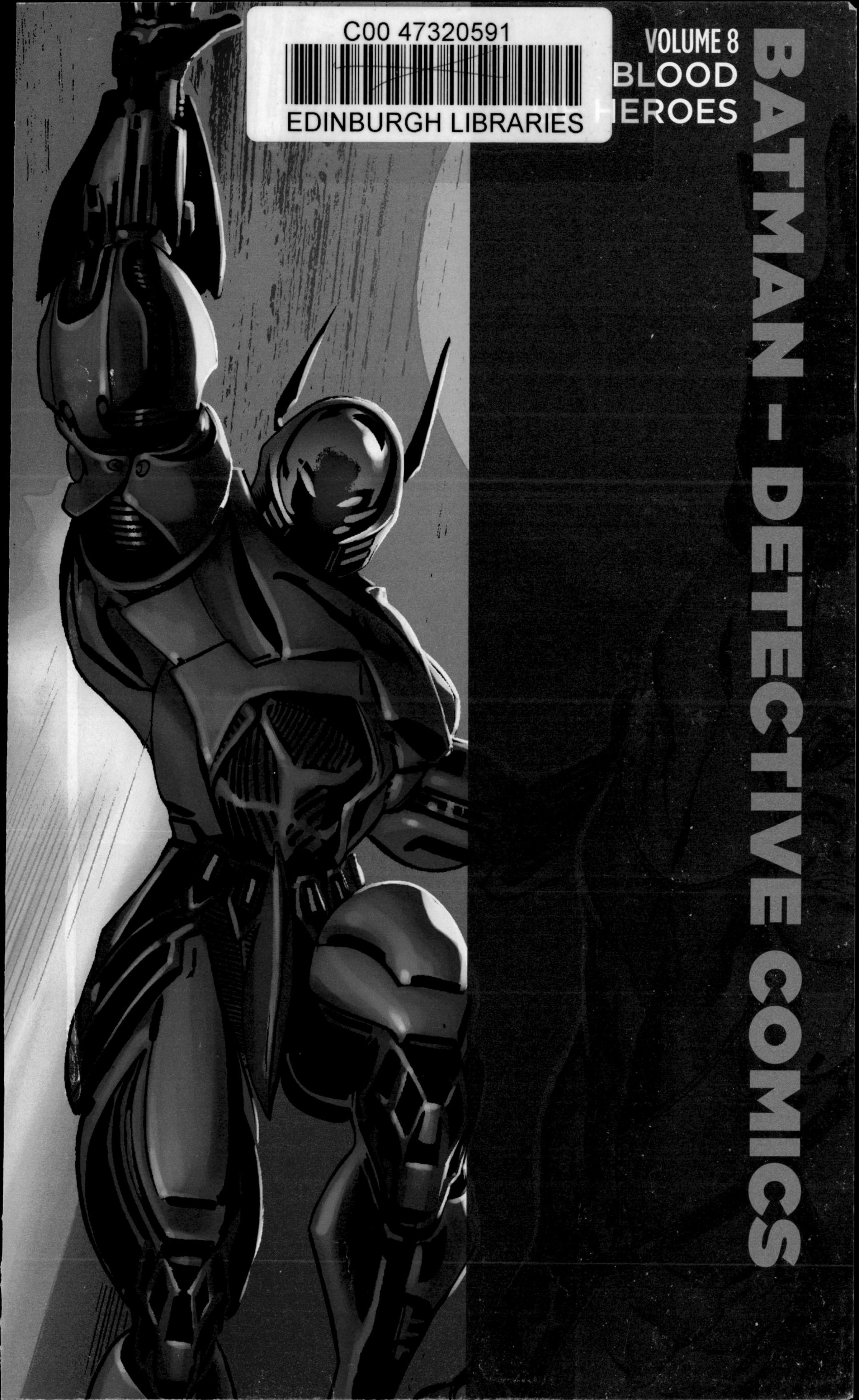
VOLUME 8
BLOOD
HEROES
BATMAN - DETECTIVE COMICS

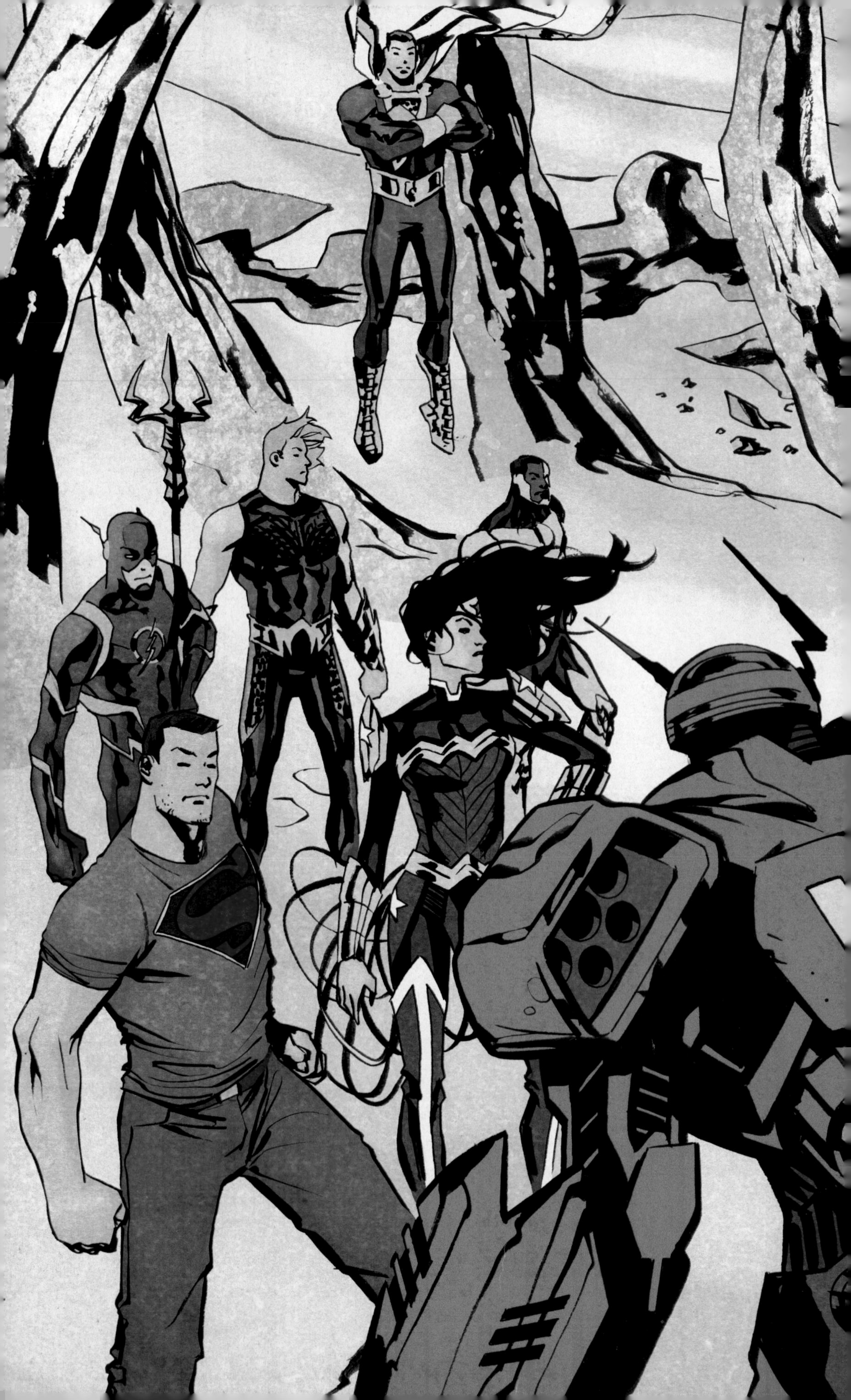

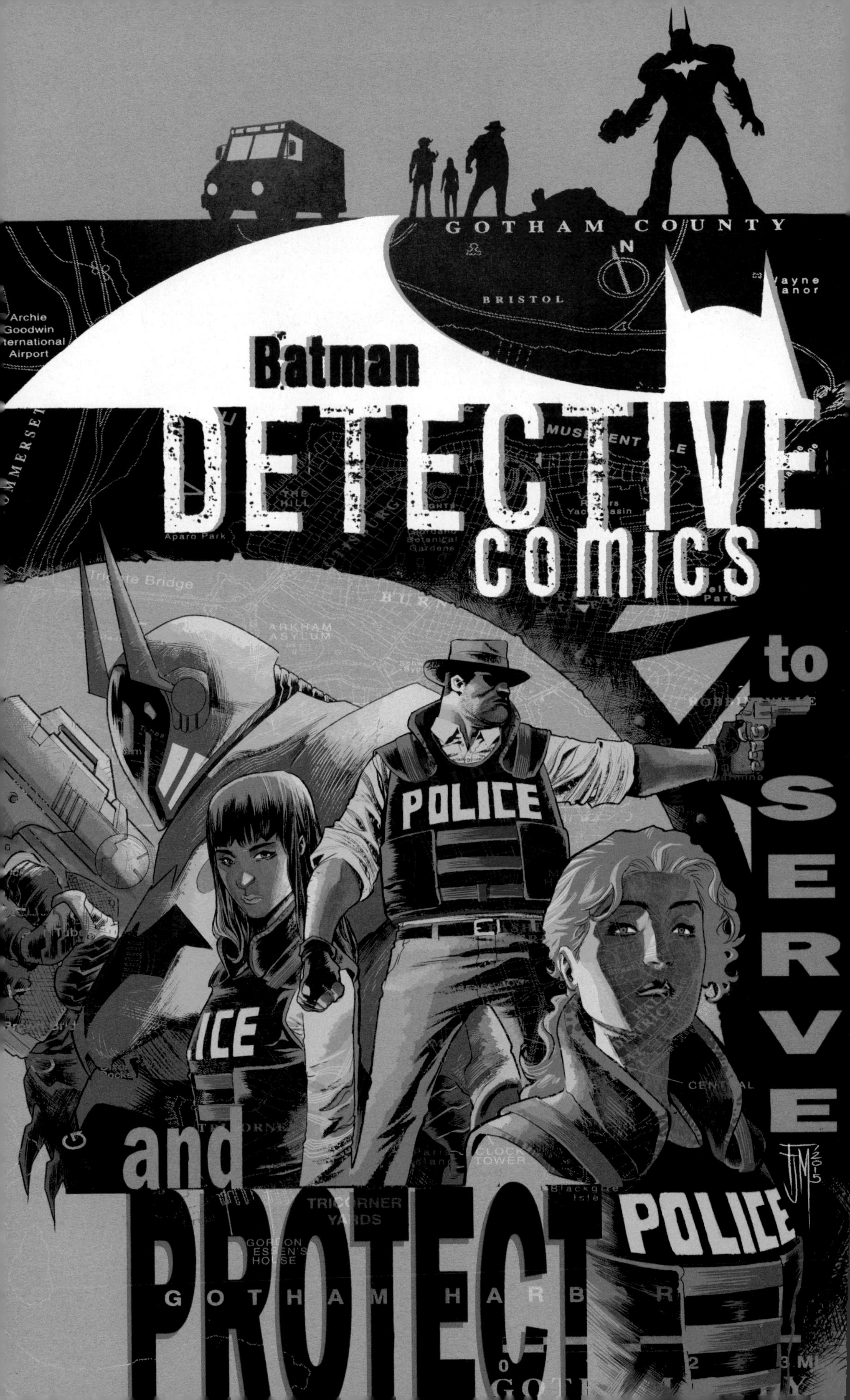
Batman
DETECTIVE
COMICS
GOTHAM COUNTY
N
BRISTOL
Archie
Goodwin
Airport
Aparo Park
ARKHAM
ASYLUM
POLICE
ICE
POLICE
to
SERVE
and
PROTECT
TRICORNER
YARDS
CLOCK
TOWER
CENTRAL

FRANCIS MANAPUL & BRIAN BUCCELLATO writers FRANCIS MANAPUL artist BRIAN BUCCELLATO colorist JARED K. FLETCHER letterer

REUNION

FRANCIS MANAPUL & BRIAN BUCCELLATO plot BRIAN BUCCELLATO writer FERNANDO BLANCO artist BRIAN BUCCELLATO colorist JARED K. FLETCHER letterer FRANCIS MANAPUL cover

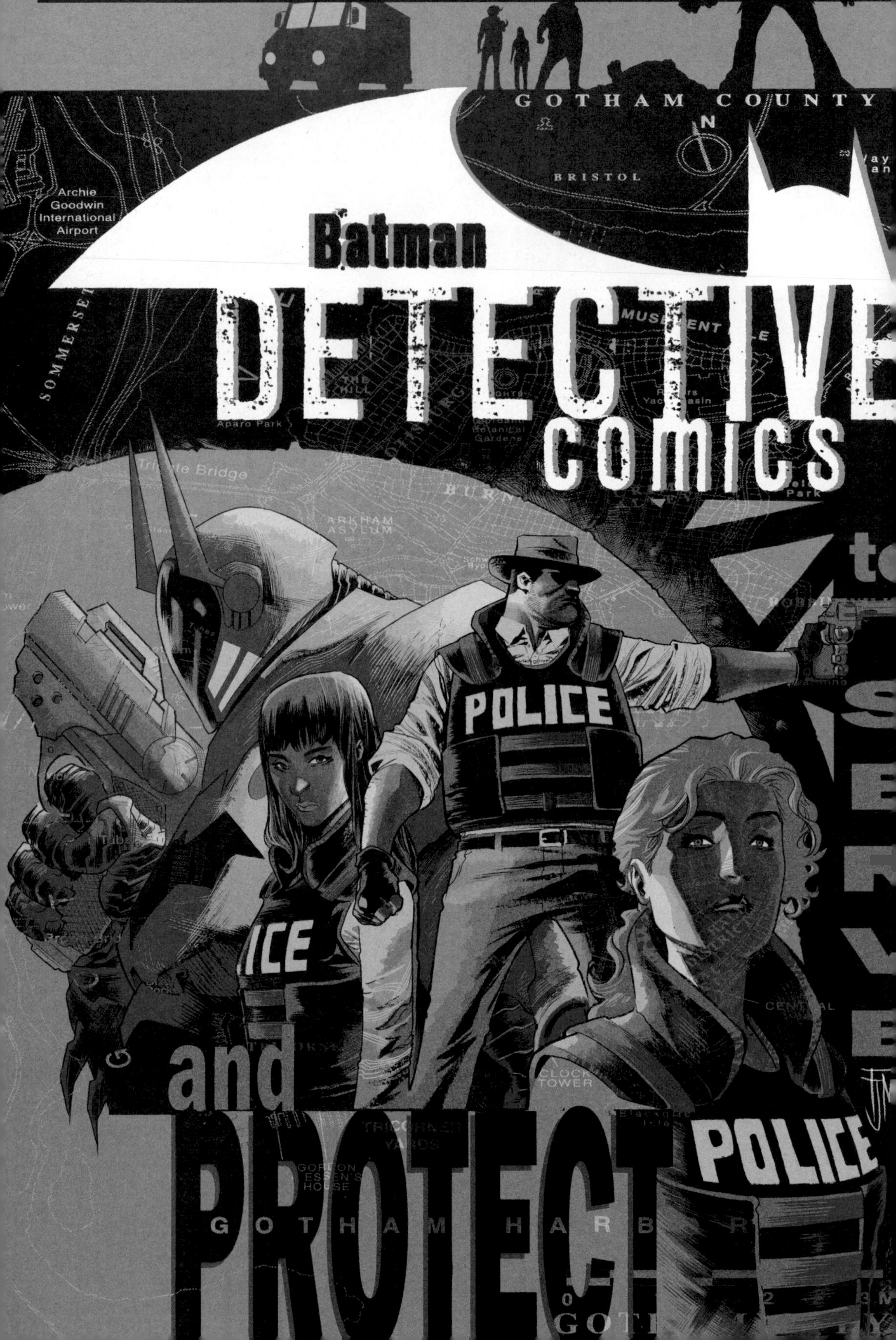

GOTHAM COUNTY
N
BRISTOL
Archie Goodwin International Airport
Batman
DETECTIVE
COMICS
SOMMERSET
Aparo Park
Trigate Bridge
ARKHAM ASYLUM
to
SERVE
and
PROTECT
POLICE
ICE
POLICE
CLOCK TOWER
TRICORNER YARDS
GOTHAM HARB
CENTRAL

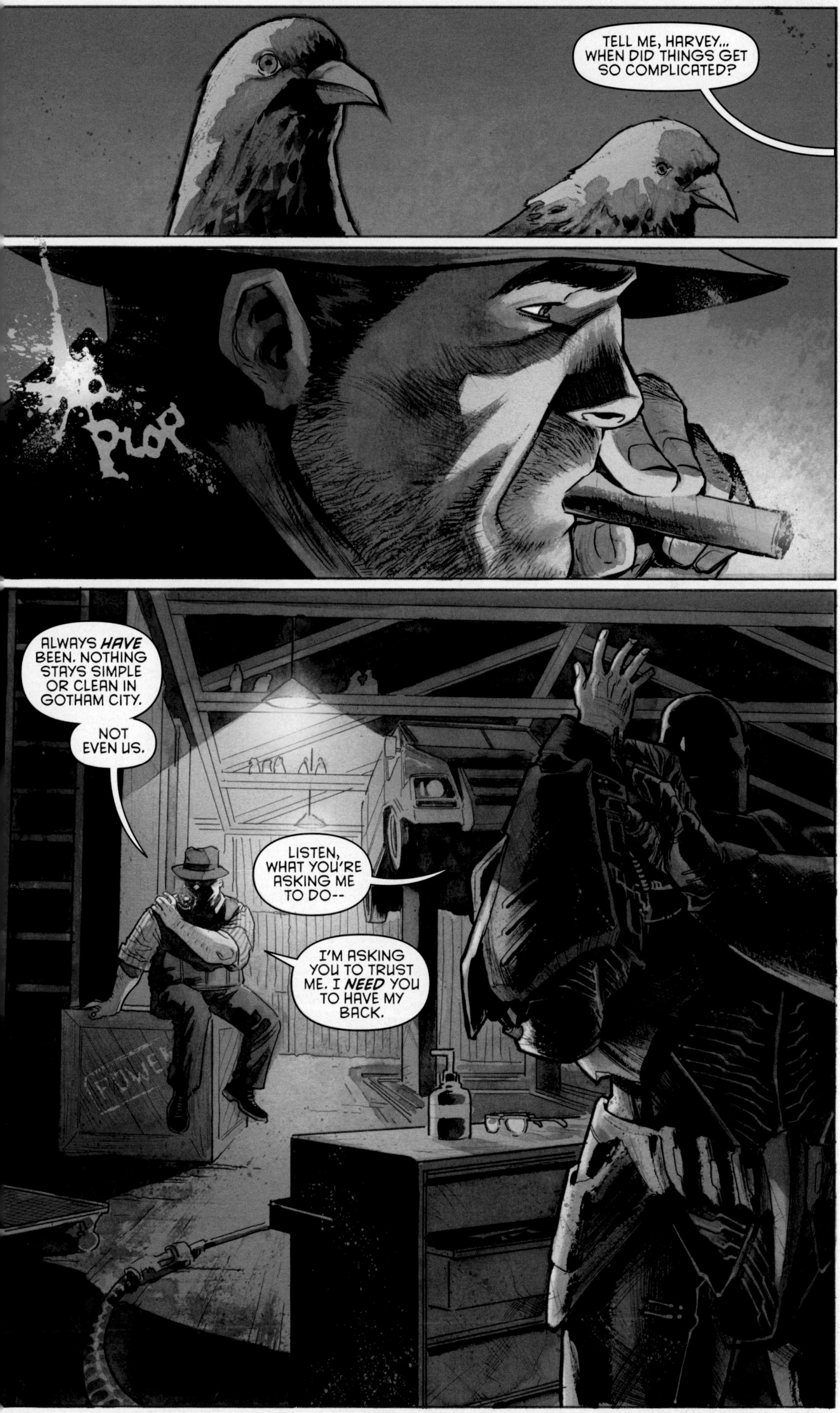

TELL ME, HARVEY... WHEN DID THINGS GET SO COMPLICATED?
PLOP
ALWAYS *HAVE* BEEN. NOTHING STAYS SIMPLE OR CLEAN IN GOTHAM CITY.
NOT EVEN US.
LISTEN, WHAT YOU'RE ASKING ME TO DO--
I'M ASKING YOU TO TRUST ME. I *NEED* YOU TO HAVE MY BACK.
POWER

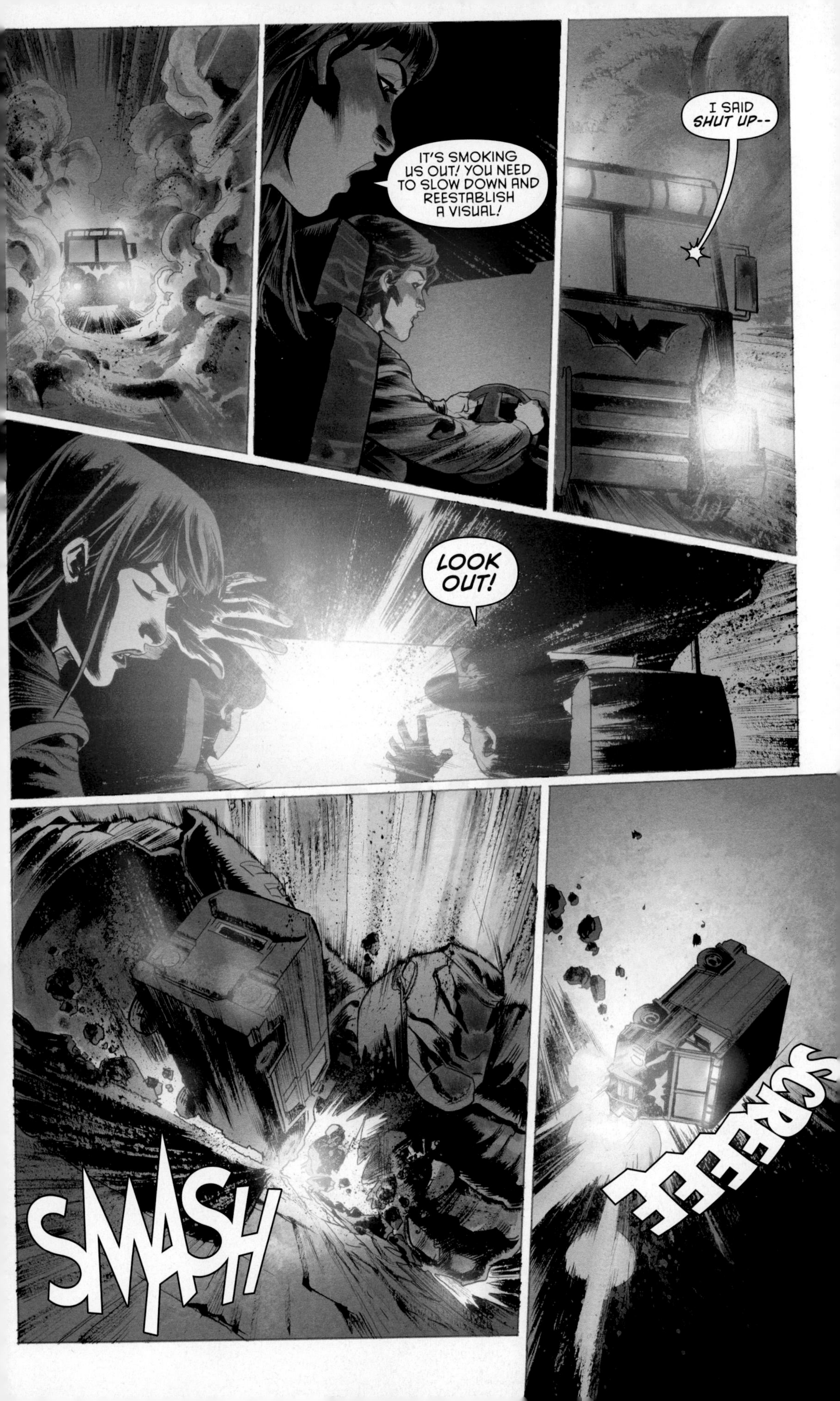

IT'S SMOKING US OUT! YOU NEED TO SLOW DOWN AND REESTABLISH A VISUAL!
I SAID SHUT UP--
LOOK OUT!
SMASH
SCREEEE

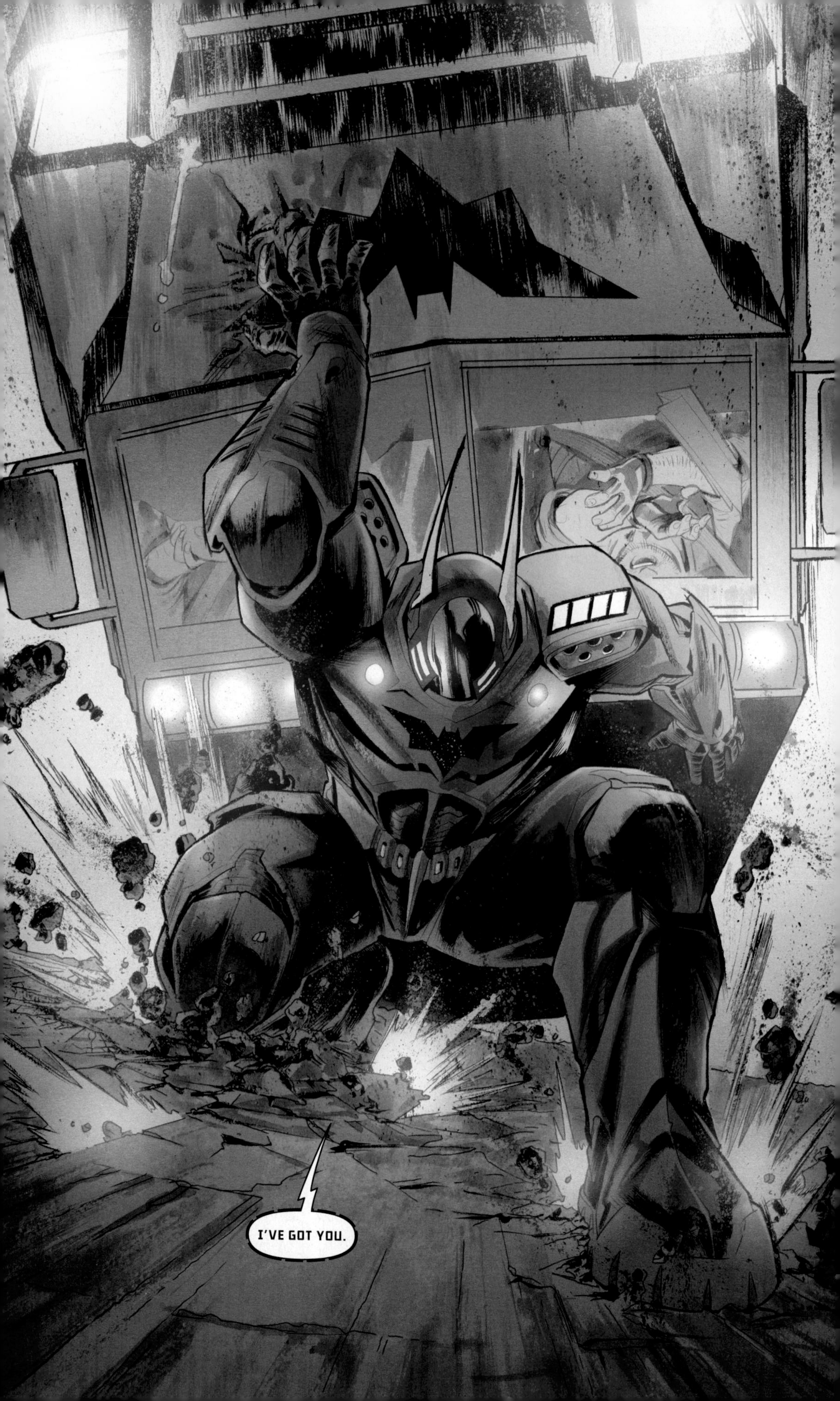
I'VE GOT YOU.

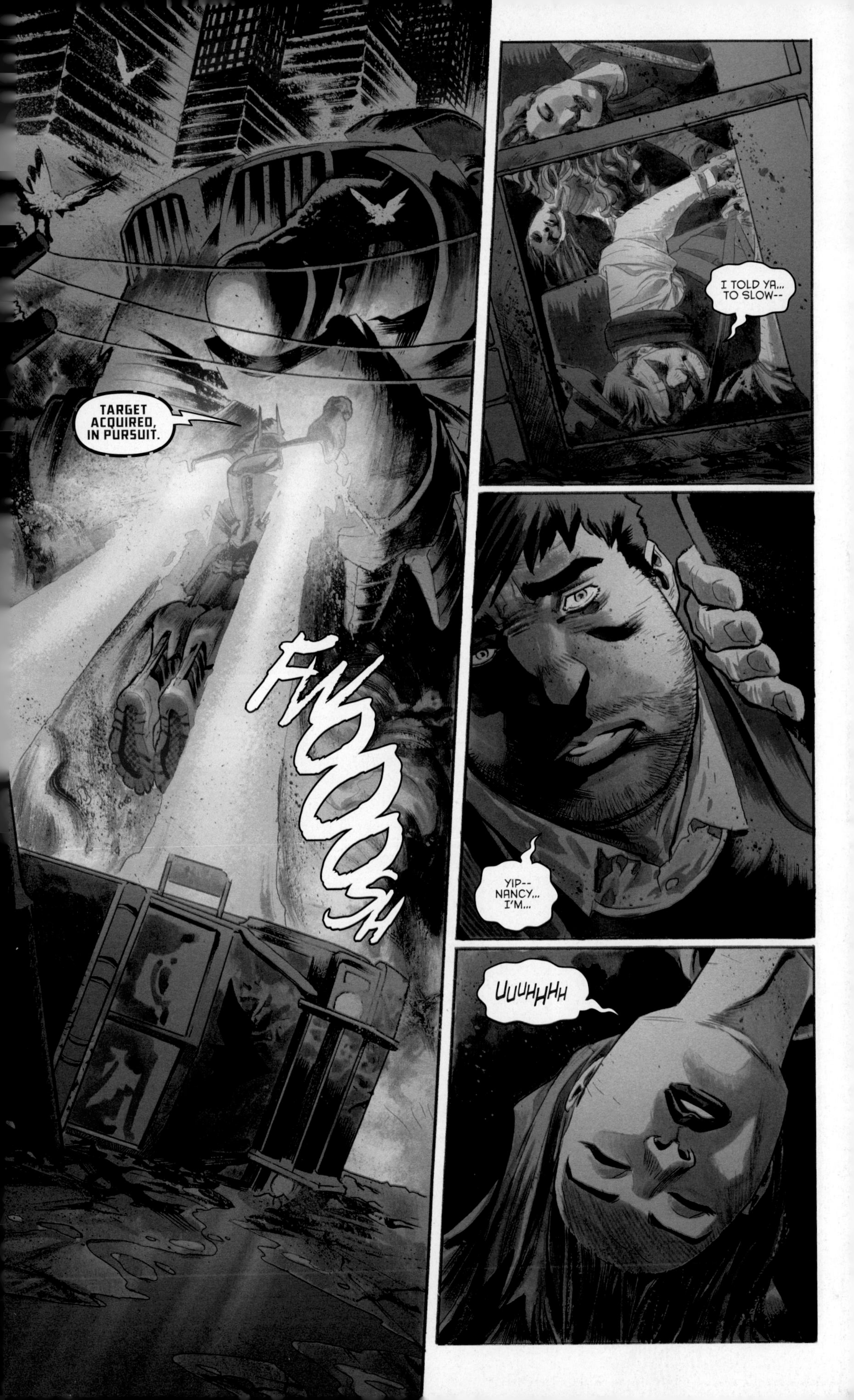
TARGET ACQUIRED, IN PURSUIT.
FWOOOOSH
I TOLD YA... TO SLOW--
YIP-- NANCY... I'M...
UUUHHHH

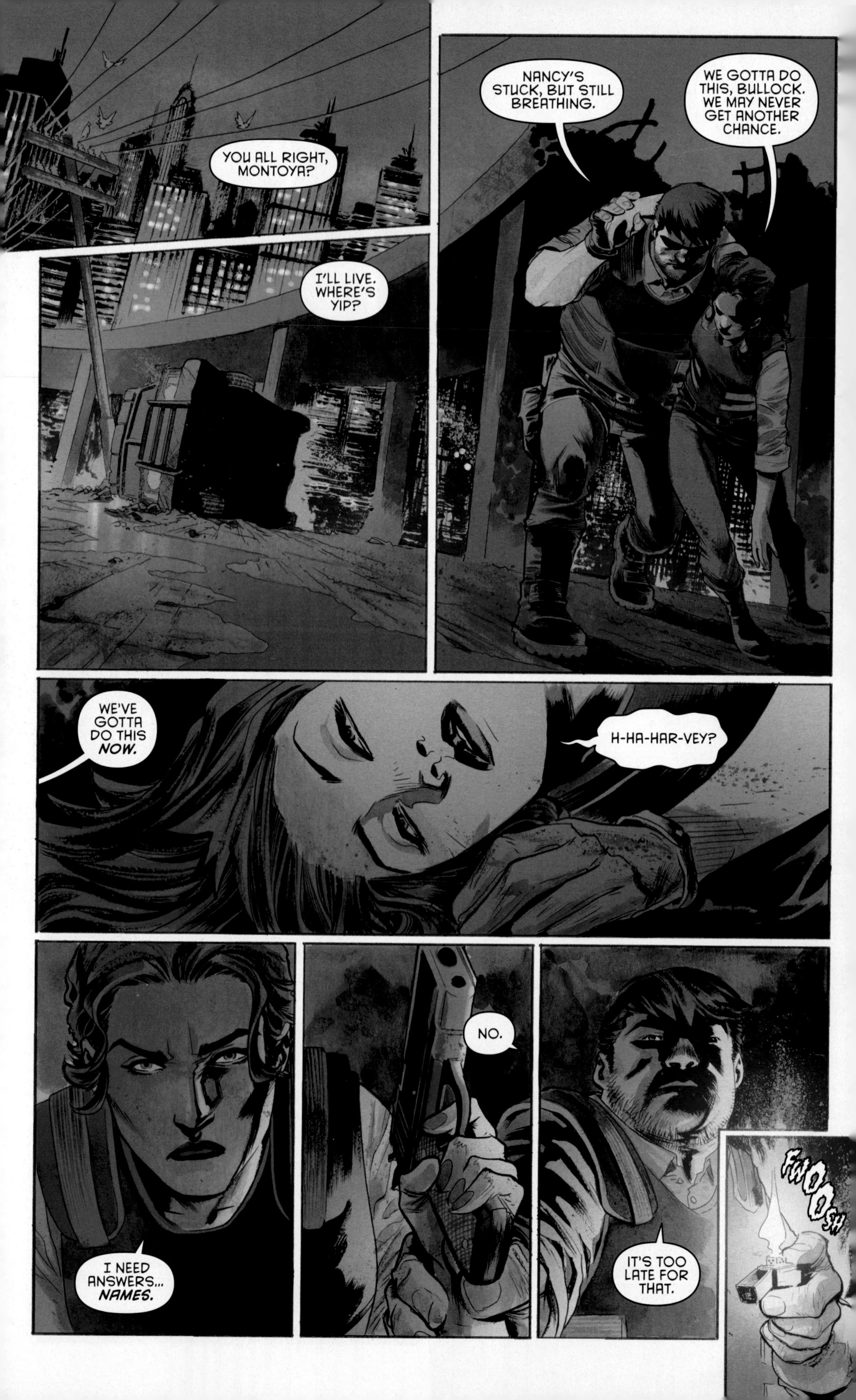

YOU ALL RIGHT, MONTOYA?
I'LL LIVE. WHERE'S YIP?
NANCY'S STUCK, BUT STILL BREATHING.
WE GOTTA DO THIS, BULLOCK. WE MAY NEVER GET ANOTHER CHANCE.
WE'VE GOTTA DO THIS *NOW.*
H-HA-HAR-VEY?
I NEED ANSWERS... ***NAMES.***
NO.
IT'S TOO LATE FOR THAT.
FWOOSH

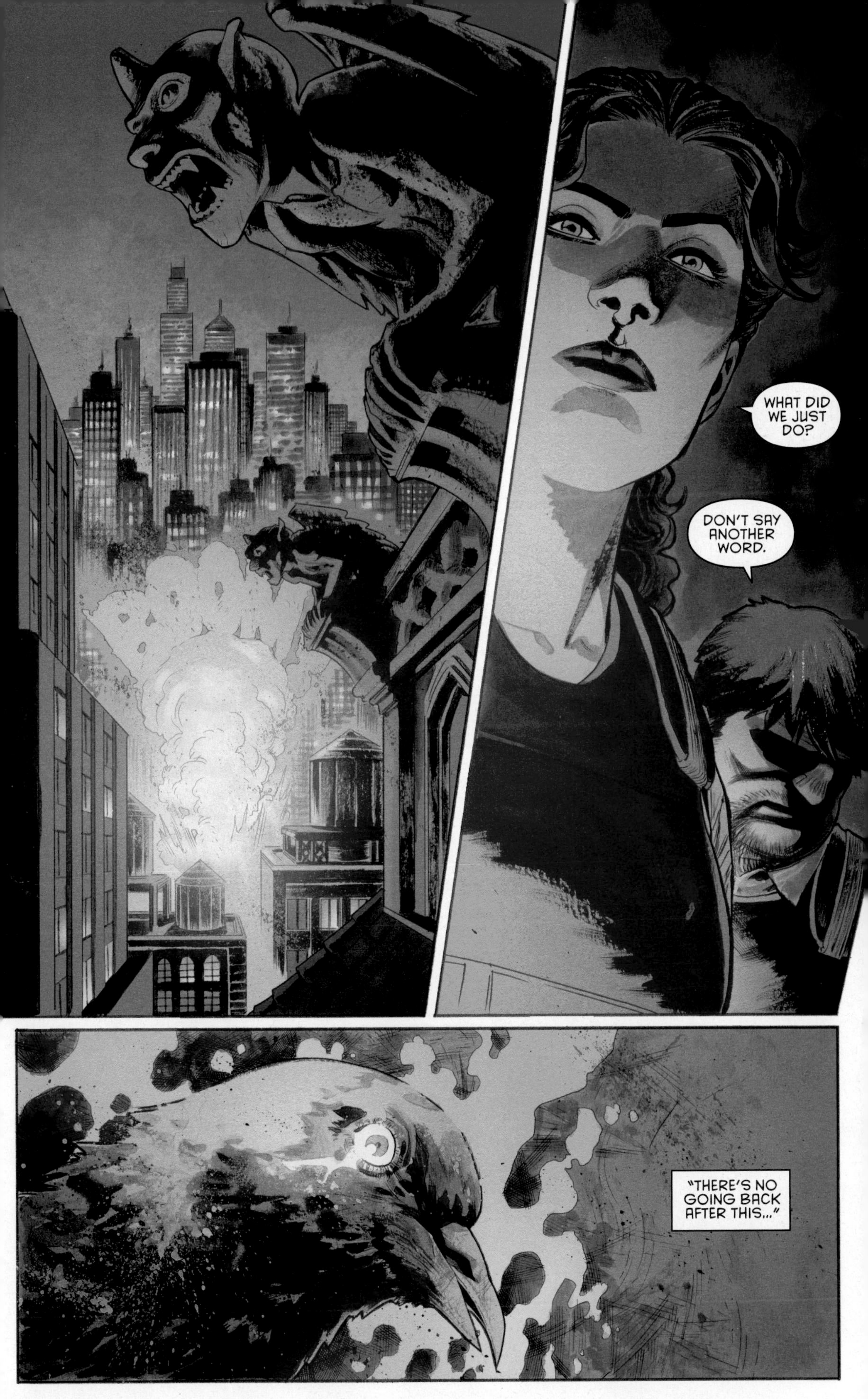
WHAT DID WE JUST DO?
DON'T SAY ANOTHER WORD.
"THERE'S NO GOING BACK AFTER THIS..."

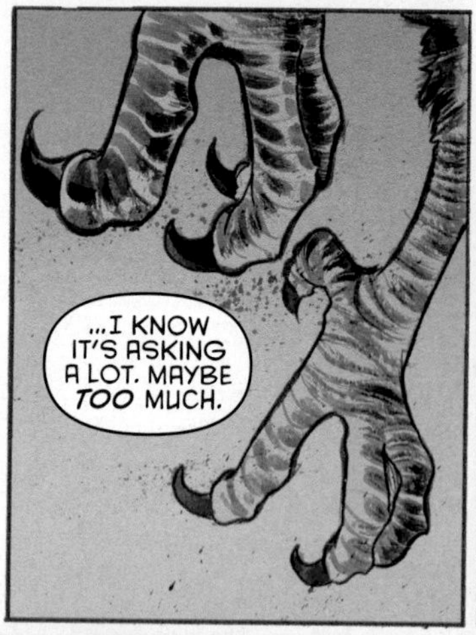
...I KNOW IT'S ASKING A LOT. MAYBE *TOO* MUCH.
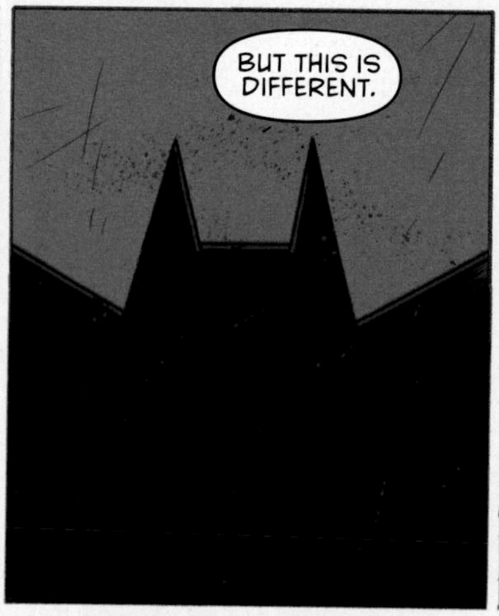
BUT THIS IS DIFFERENT.
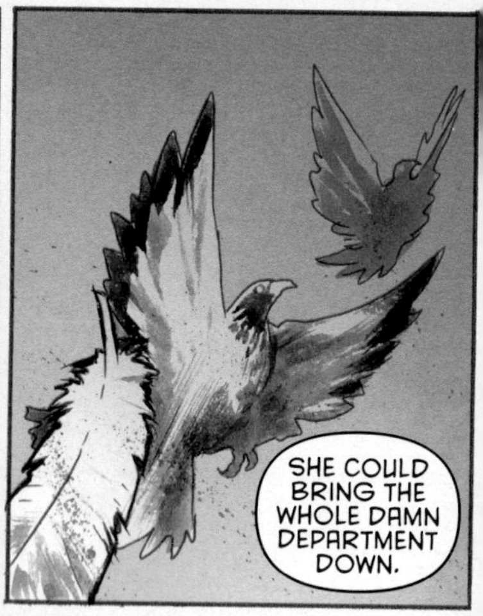
SHE COULD BRING THE WHOLE DAMN DEPARTMENT DOWN.
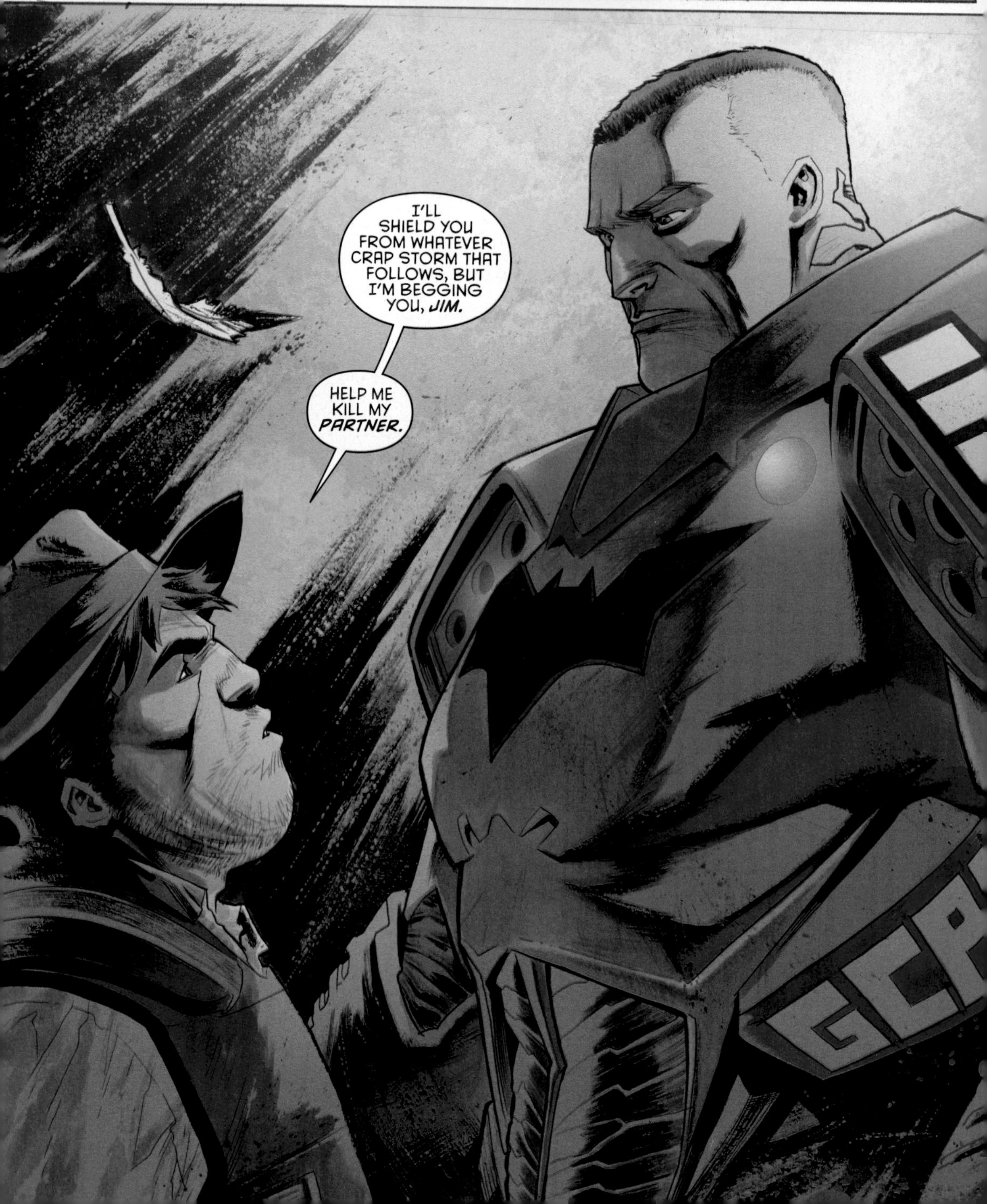
I'LL SHIELD YOU FROM WHATEVER CRAP STORM THAT FOLLOWS, BUT I'M BEGGING YOU, *JIM.*
HELP ME KILL MY *PARTNER.*
GCP

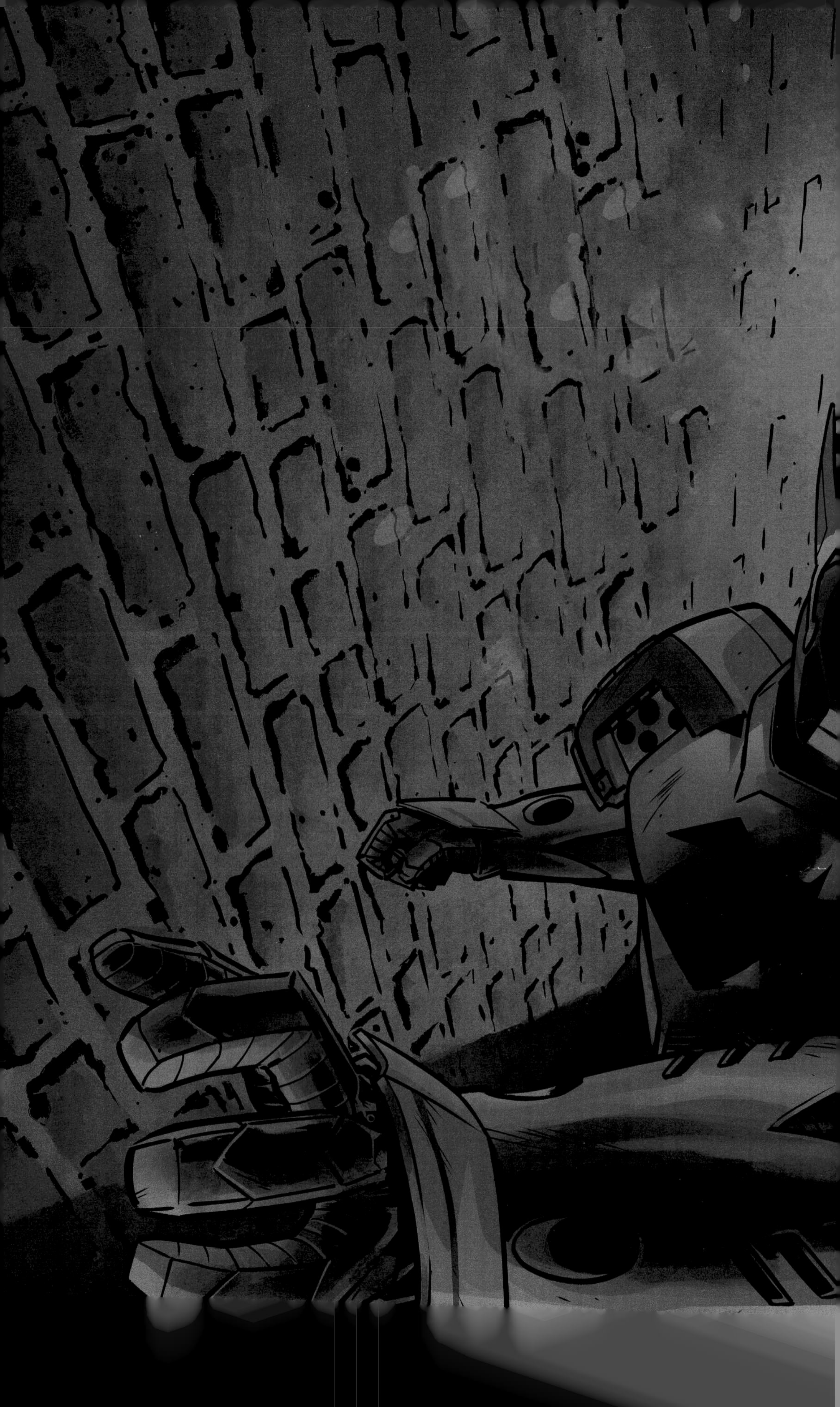

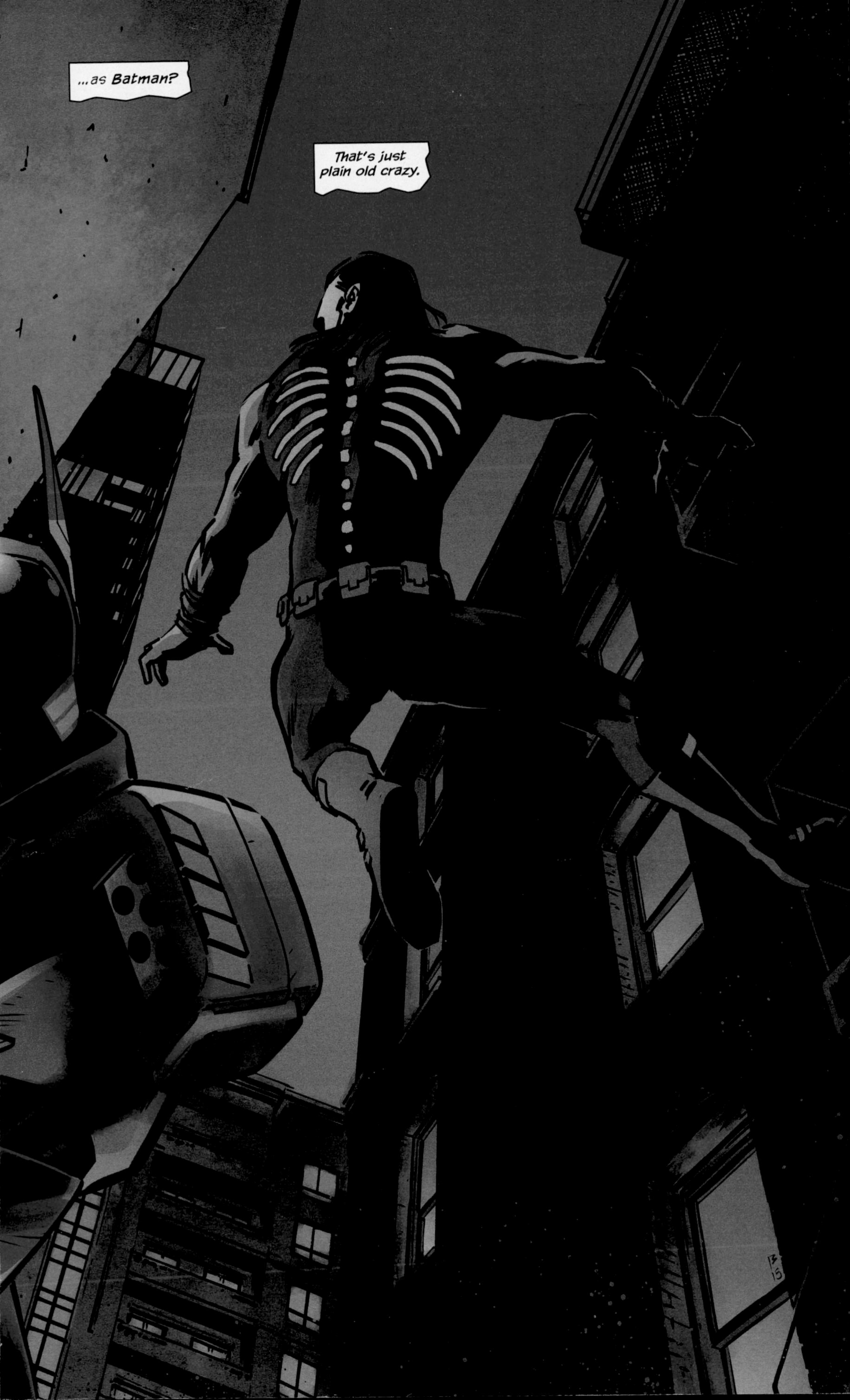
...as Batman?
That's just plain old crazy.

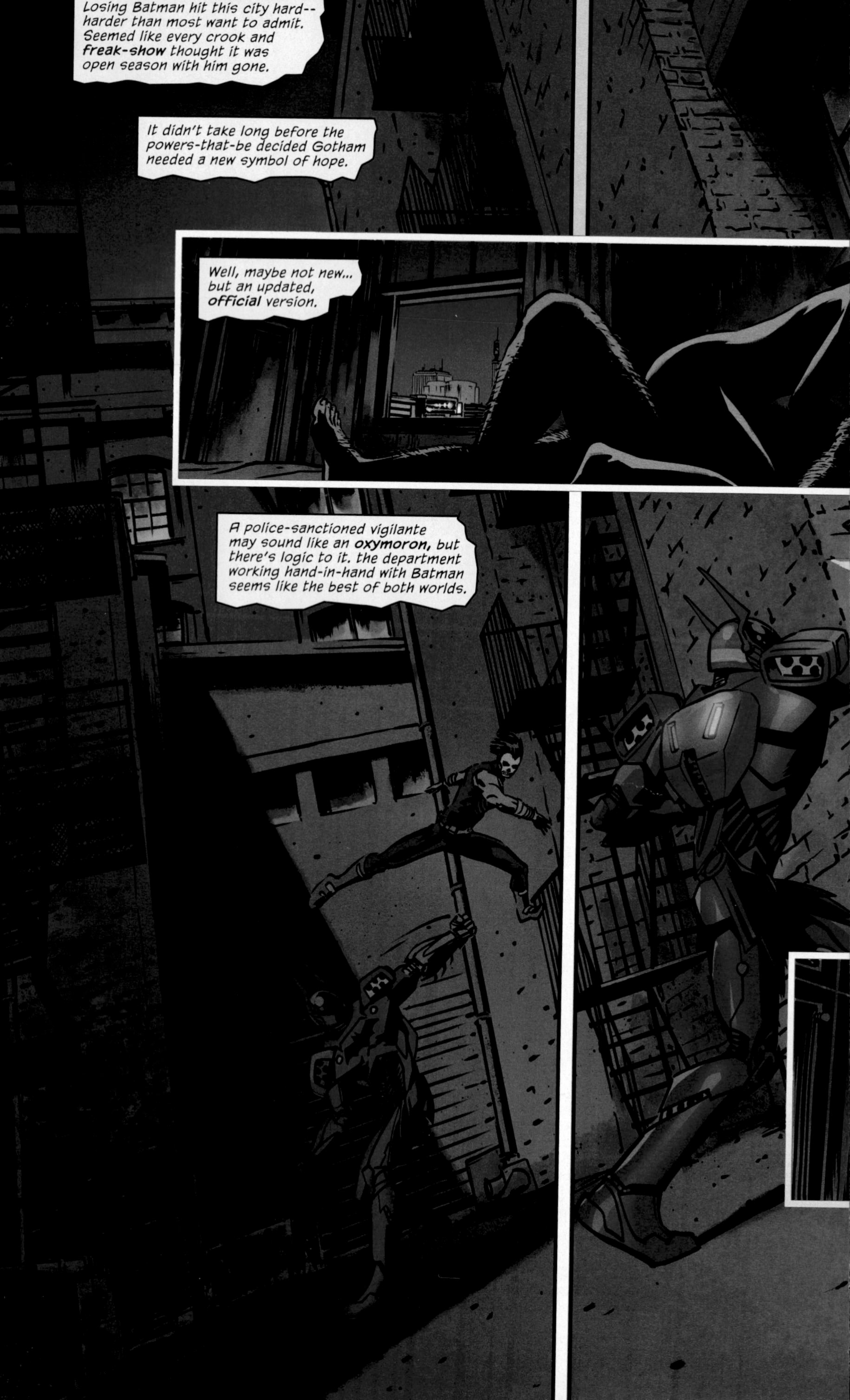
Losing Batman hit this city hard--harder than most want to admit. Seemed like every crook and **freak-show** thought it was open season with him gone.
It didn't take long before the powers-that-be decided Gotham needed a new symbol of hope.
Well, maybe not new... but an updated, **official** version.
A police-sanctioned vigilante may sound like an **oxymoron,** but there's logic to it. the department working hand-in-hand with Batman seems like the best of both worlds.

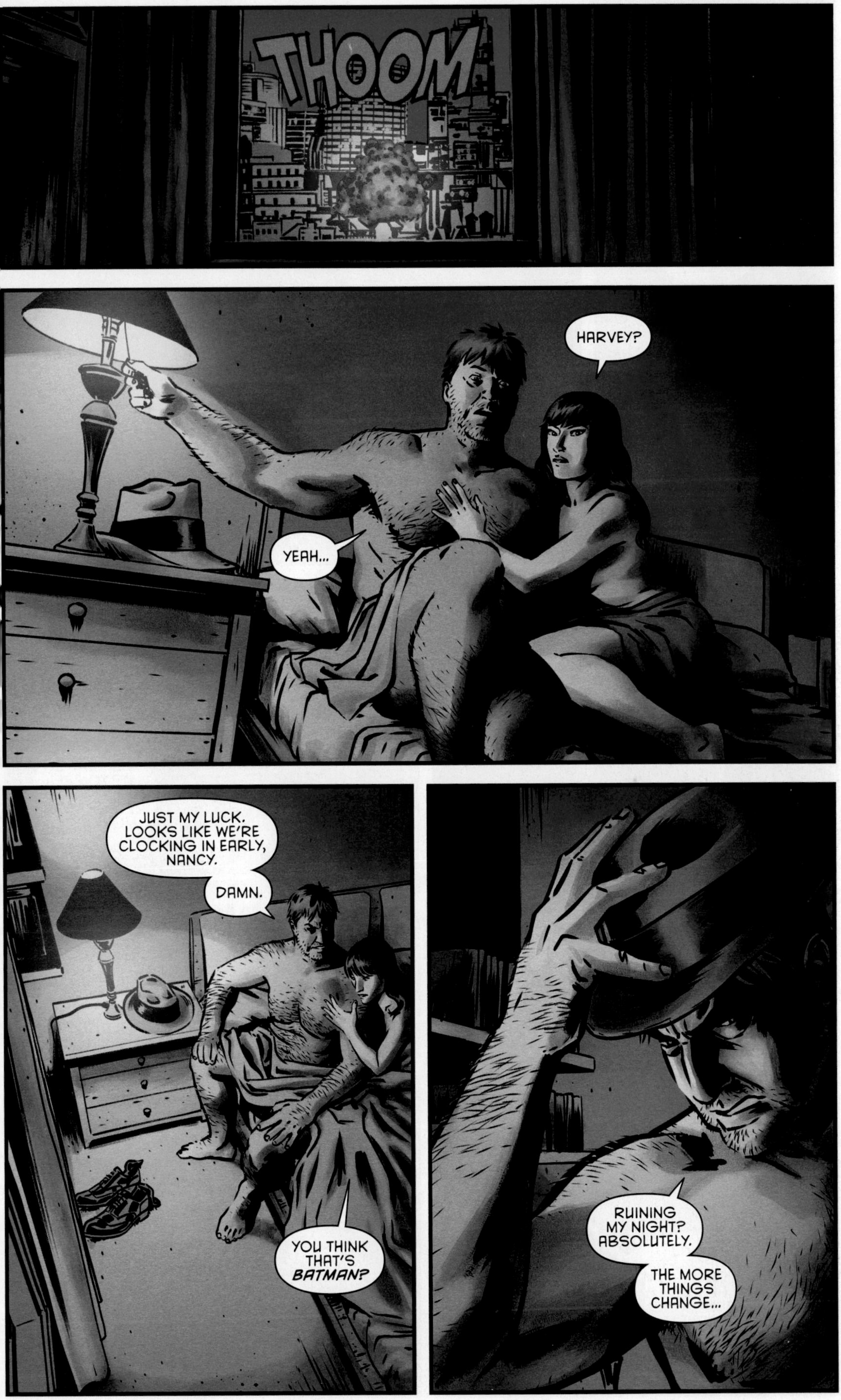
THOOM
HARVEY?
YEAH...
JUST MY LUCK. LOOKS LIKE WE'RE CLOCKING IN EARLY, NANCY.
DAMN.
YOU THINK THAT'S *BATMAN?*
RUINING MY NIGHT? ABSOLUTELY.
THE MORE THINGS CHANGE...

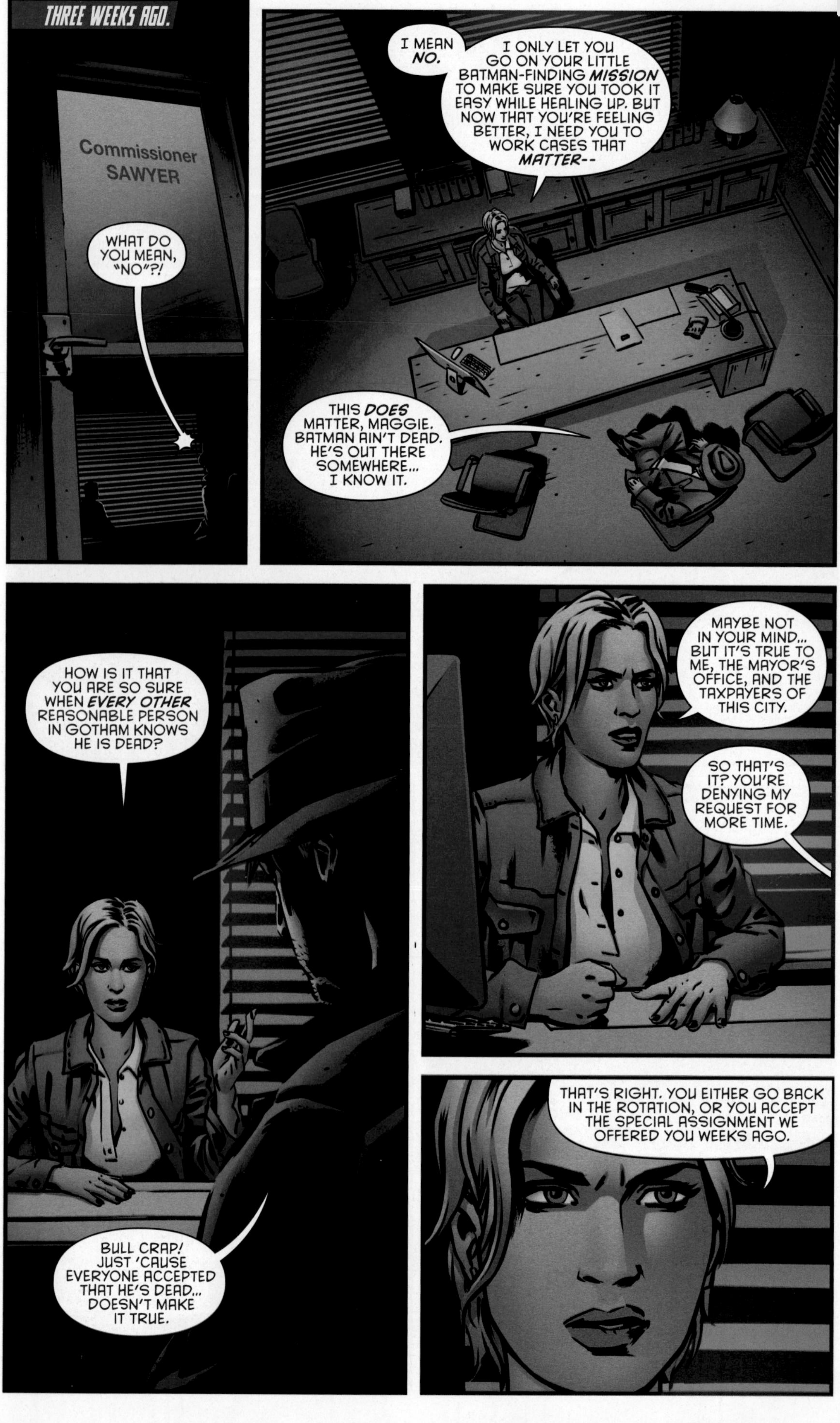
THREE WEEKS AGO.
Commissioner SAWYER
WHAT DO YOU MEAN, "NO"?!
I MEAN NO.
I ONLY LET YOU GO ON YOUR LITTLE BATMAN-FINDING MISSION TO MAKE SURE YOU TOOK IT EASY WHILE HEALING UP. BUT NOW THAT YOU'RE FEELING BETTER, I NEED YOU TO WORK CASES THAT MATTER--
THIS DOES MATTER, MAGGIE. BATMAN AIN'T DEAD. HE'S OUT THERE SOMEWHERE... I KNOW IT.
HOW IS IT THAT YOU ARE SO SURE WHEN EVERY OTHER REASONABLE PERSON IN GOTHAM KNOWS HE IS DEAD?
BULL CRAP! JUST 'CAUSE EVERYONE ACCEPTED THAT HE'S DEAD... DOESN'T MAKE IT TRUE.
MAYBE NOT IN YOUR MIND... BUT IT'S TRUE TO ME, THE MAYOR'S OFFICE, AND THE TAXPAYERS OF THIS CITY.
SO THAT'S IT? YOU'RE DENYING MY REQUEST FOR MORE TIME.
THAT'S RIGHT. YOU EITHER GO BACK IN THE ROTATION, OR YOU ACCEPT THE SPECIAL ASSIGNMENT WE OFFERED YOU WEEKS AGO.

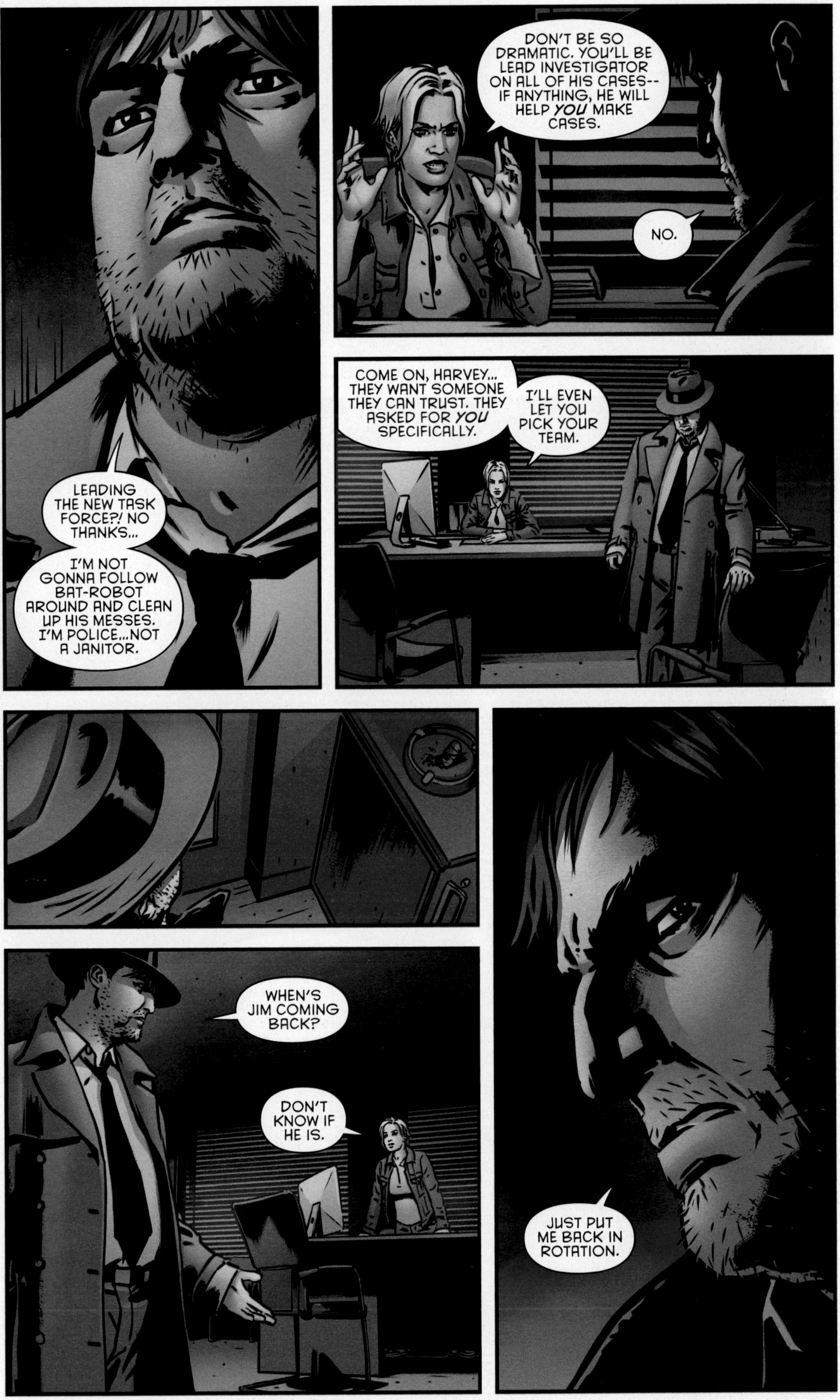
LEADING THE NEW TASK FORCE?! NO THANKS...
I'M NOT GONNA FOLLOW BAT-ROBOT AROUND AND CLEAN UP HIS MESSES. I'M POLICE...NOT A JANITOR.
DON'T BE SO DRAMATIC. YOU'LL BE LEAD INVESTIGATOR ON ALL OF HIS CASES-- IF ANYTHING, HE WILL HELP *YOU* MAKE CASES.
NO.
COME ON, HARVEY... THEY WANT SOMEONE THEY CAN TRUST. THEY ASKED FOR *YOU* SPECIFICALLY.
I'LL EVEN LET YOU PICK YOUR TEAM.
WHEN'S JIM COMING BACK?
DON'T KNOW IF HE IS.
JUST PUT ME BACK IN ROTATION.

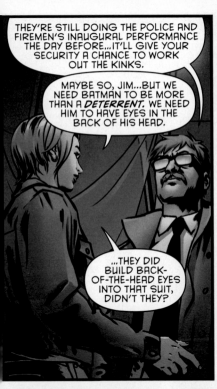

THEY'RE STILL DOING THE POLICE AND FIREMEN'S INAUGURAL PERFORMANCE THE DAY BEFORE...IT'LL GIVE YOUR SECURITY A CHANCE TO WORK OUT THE KINKS.

MAYBE SO, JIM...BUT WE NEED BATMAN TO BE MORE THAN A *DETERRENT*. WE NEED HIM TO HAVE EYES IN THE BACK OF HIS HEAD.

...THEY DID BUILD BACK-OF-THE-HEAD EYES INTO THAT SUIT, DIDN'T THEY?

I WOULDN'T KNOW.

TRANSLATION... "YOU STILL HAVEN'T DECIDED IF YOU'RE GOING TO DO IT."

AM I WRONG?

YOU'RE NOT WRONG.

WELL *SOMEBODY* NEEDS TO GET INTO THAT SUIT, JIM. MAYBE I'LL ASK BULLOCK...IF HE CAN GET INTO IT.

I THINK THE BATMAN TASK FORCE IS A BETTER "FIT."

TELL *HIM* THAT... HE WON'T COME ON BOARD. HE'S CONVINCED THAT THE *REAL* BATMAN IS STILL ALIVE...

...AND HE WANTS TO FIND HIM. I CAN TALK TO HIM.

THEY DON'T WANT YOU TALKING TO ANYONE ABOUT IT. REGARDLESS OF WHAT YOU DECIDE.

THAT'S STUPID... I TRUST HIM.

THE POWERS-THAT-BE DON'T. ESPECIALLY WITH HIS PARTNER, *YIP*, UNDER SUSPENSION FOR THAT SHOOTING.

SO DO ME A FAVOR AND DON'T TELL HIM.

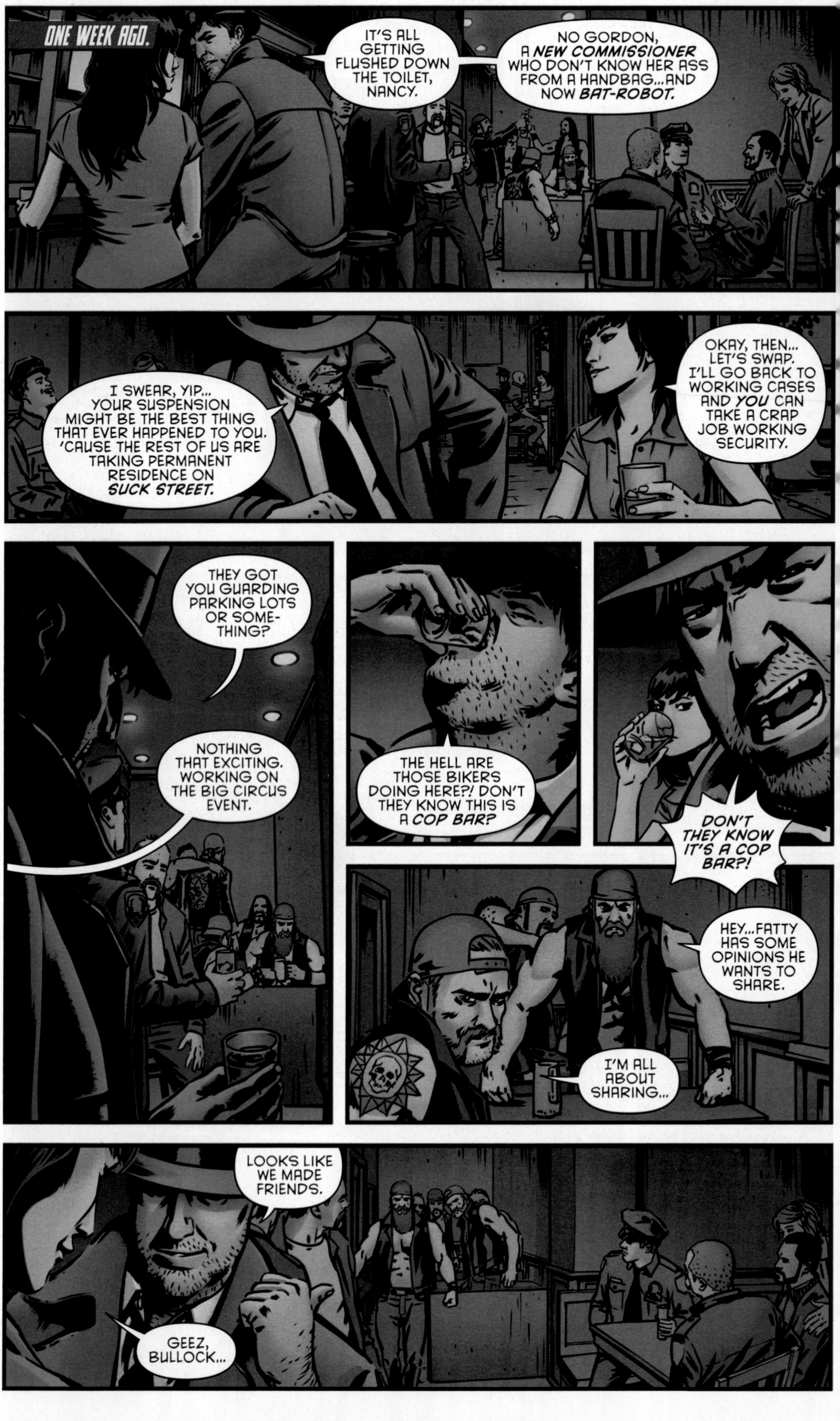
ONE WEEK AGO.
IT'S ALL GETTING FLUSHED DOWN THE TOILET, NANCY.
NO GORDON, A NEW COMMISSIONER WHO DON'T KNOW HER ASS FROM A HANDBAG...AND NOW BAT-ROBOT.
I SWEAR, YIP... YOUR SUSPENSION MIGHT BE THE BEST THING THAT EVER HAPPENED TO YOU. 'CAUSE THE REST OF US ARE TAKING PERMANENT RESIDENCE ON SUCK STREET.
OKAY, THEN... LET'S SWAP. I'LL GO BACK TO WORKING CASES AND YOU CAN TAKE A CRAP JOB WORKING SECURITY.
THEY GOT YOU GUARDING PARKING LOTS OR SOME-THING?
NOTHING THAT EXCITING. WORKING ON THE BIG CIRCUS EVENT.
THE HELL ARE THOSE BIKERS DOING HERE?! DON'T THEY KNOW THIS IS A COP BAR?
DON'T THEY KNOW IT'S A COP BAR?!
HEY...FATTY HAS SOME OPINIONS HE WANTS TO SHARE.
I'M ALL ABOUT SHARING...
LOOKS LIKE WE MADE FRIENDS.
GEEZ, BULLOCK...

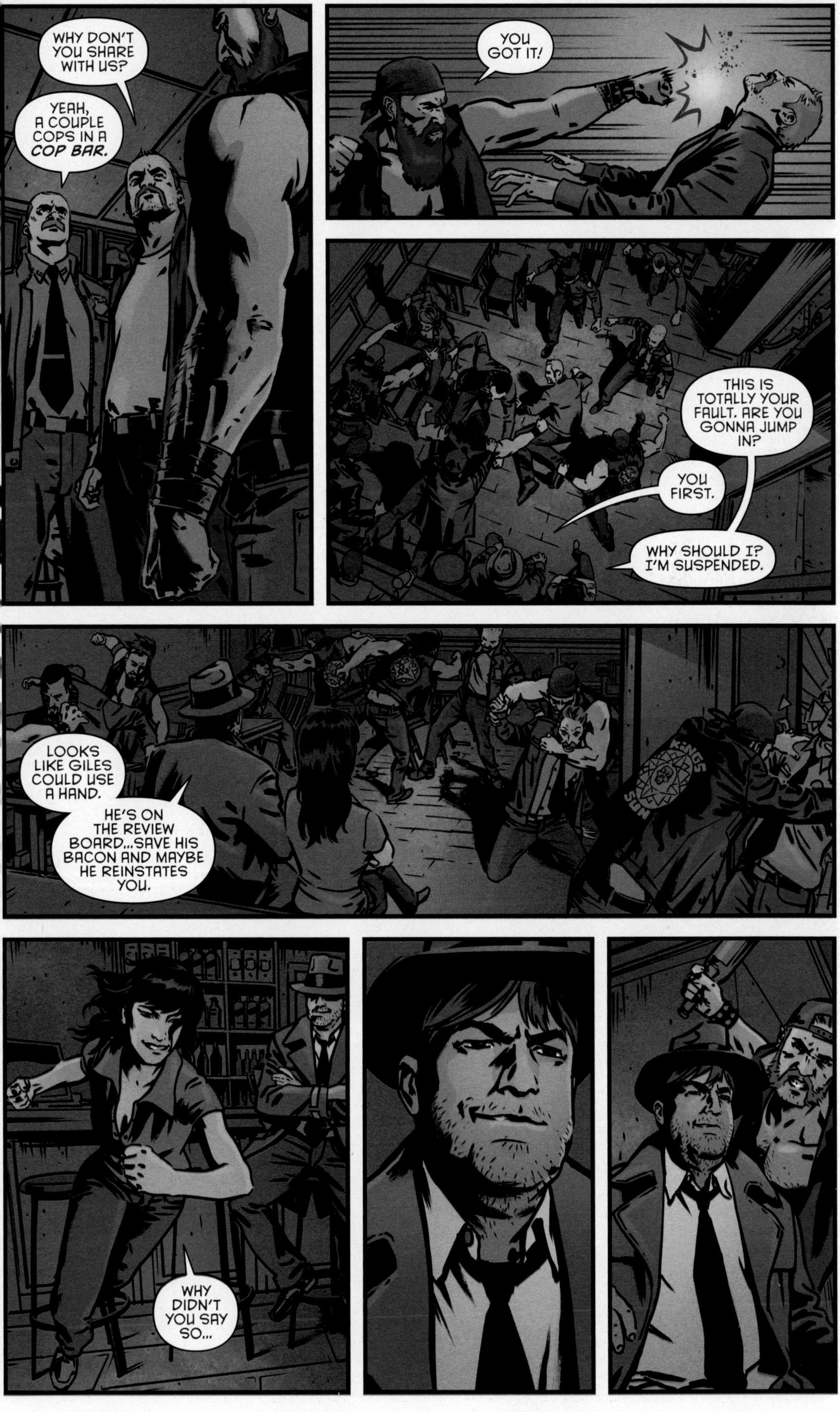
WHY DON'T YOU SHARE WITH US?
YEAH, A COUPLE COPS IN A *COP BAR.*
YOU GOT IT!
THIS IS TOTALLY YOUR FAULT. ARE YOU GONNA JUMP IN?
YOU FIRST.
WHY SHOULD I? I'M SUSPENDED.
LOOKS LIKE GILES COULD USE A HAND.
HE'S ON THE REVIEW BOARD...SAVE HIS BACON AND MAYBE HE REINSTATES YOU.
WHY DIDN'T YOU SAY SO...

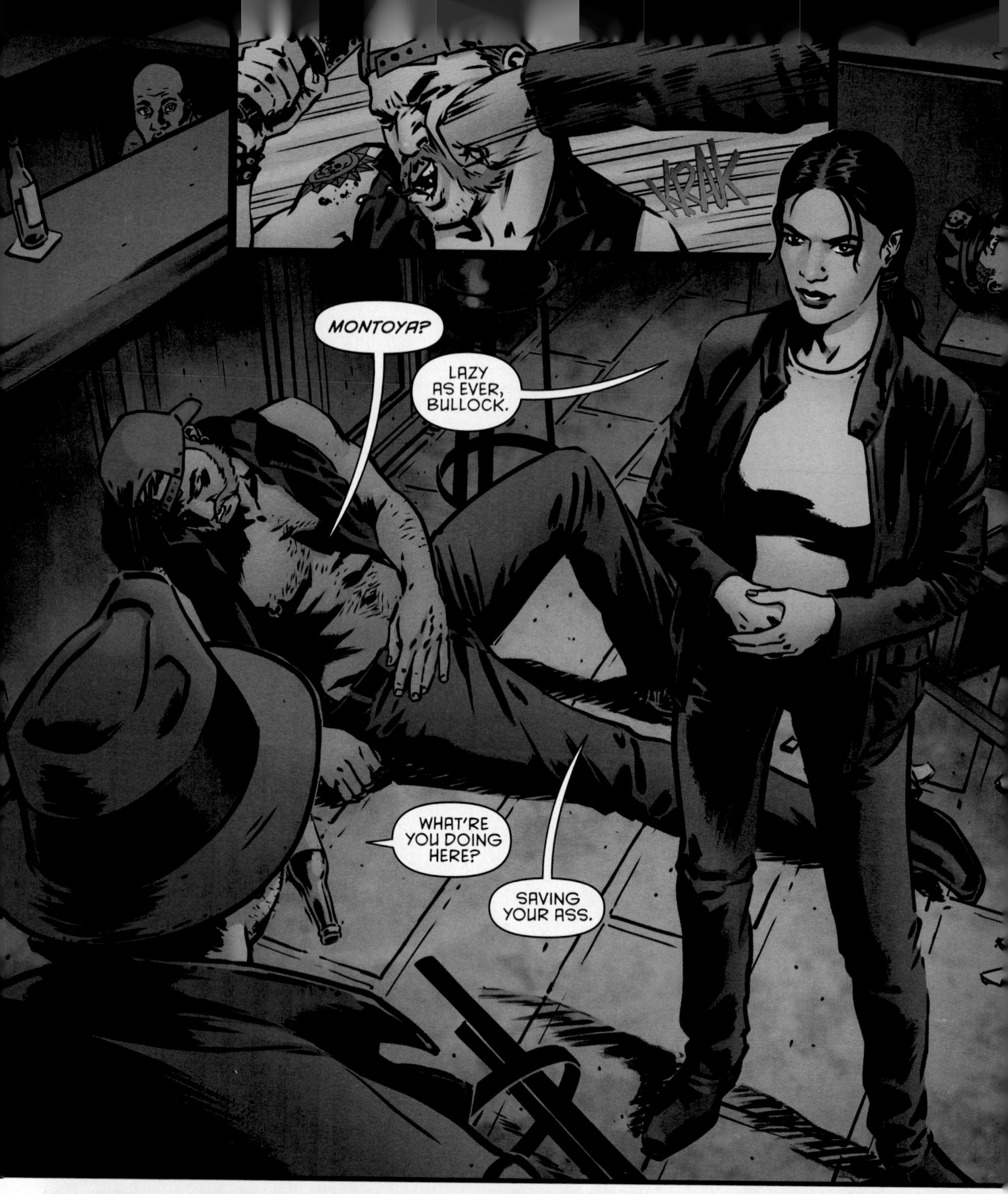
KRAK
MONTOYA?
LAZY AS EVER, BULLOCK.
WHAT'RE YOU DOING HERE?
SAVING YOUR ASS.

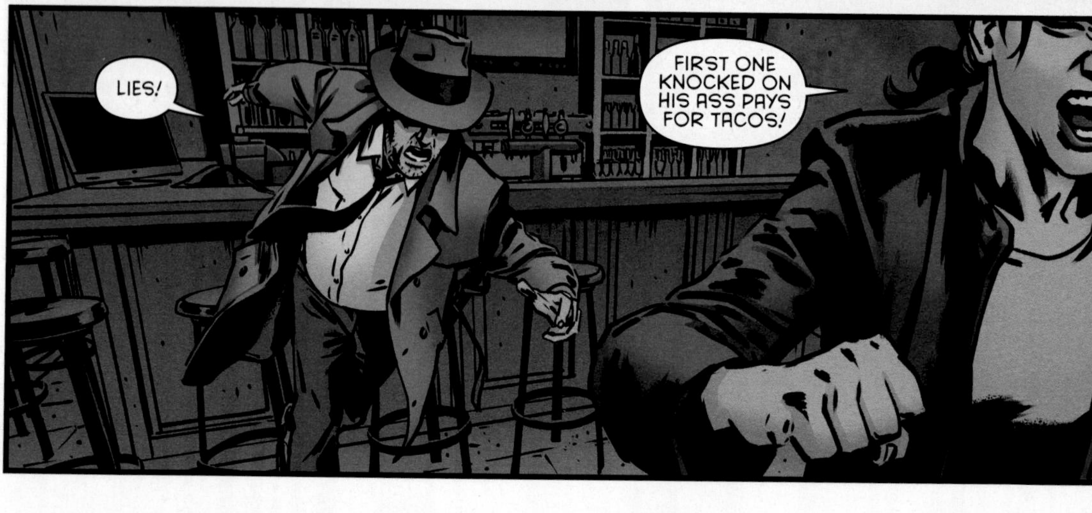
LIES!
FIRST ONE KNOCKED ON HIS ASS PAYS FOR TACOS!

THANKS FOR THE *EATS*, HARV.

WHATEVER.

GLASS JAW.

MAN HANDS.

SO...HOW DO YOU KNOW HARVEY?

BULLOCK WAS MY TRAINING OFFICER, IF YOU CAN BELIEVE THAT...BUT HE WAS A LOT THINNER THEN.

AND SHE WAS A LOT NICER. BLÜDHAVEN MUST'VE DONE SOMETHING TO HER.

WELL, I'M BACK IN GOTHAM NOW. NEW ASSIGNMENT.

JUST LIKE I SAID YOU'D BE.

WHEN? FIVE YEARS AGO?

STILL COUNTS.

FIRST OF ALL, NO IT DOESN'T...

SECOND OF ALL...WHY'D YOU TURN DOWN THE BATMAN TASK FORCE?

THEY OFFERED YOU THE TASK FORCE? WHY DIDN'T YOU TELL ME?

BECAUSE SCREW THAT JOB. I AIN'T HOLDING FAKE BATMAN'S HAND--

I AM.

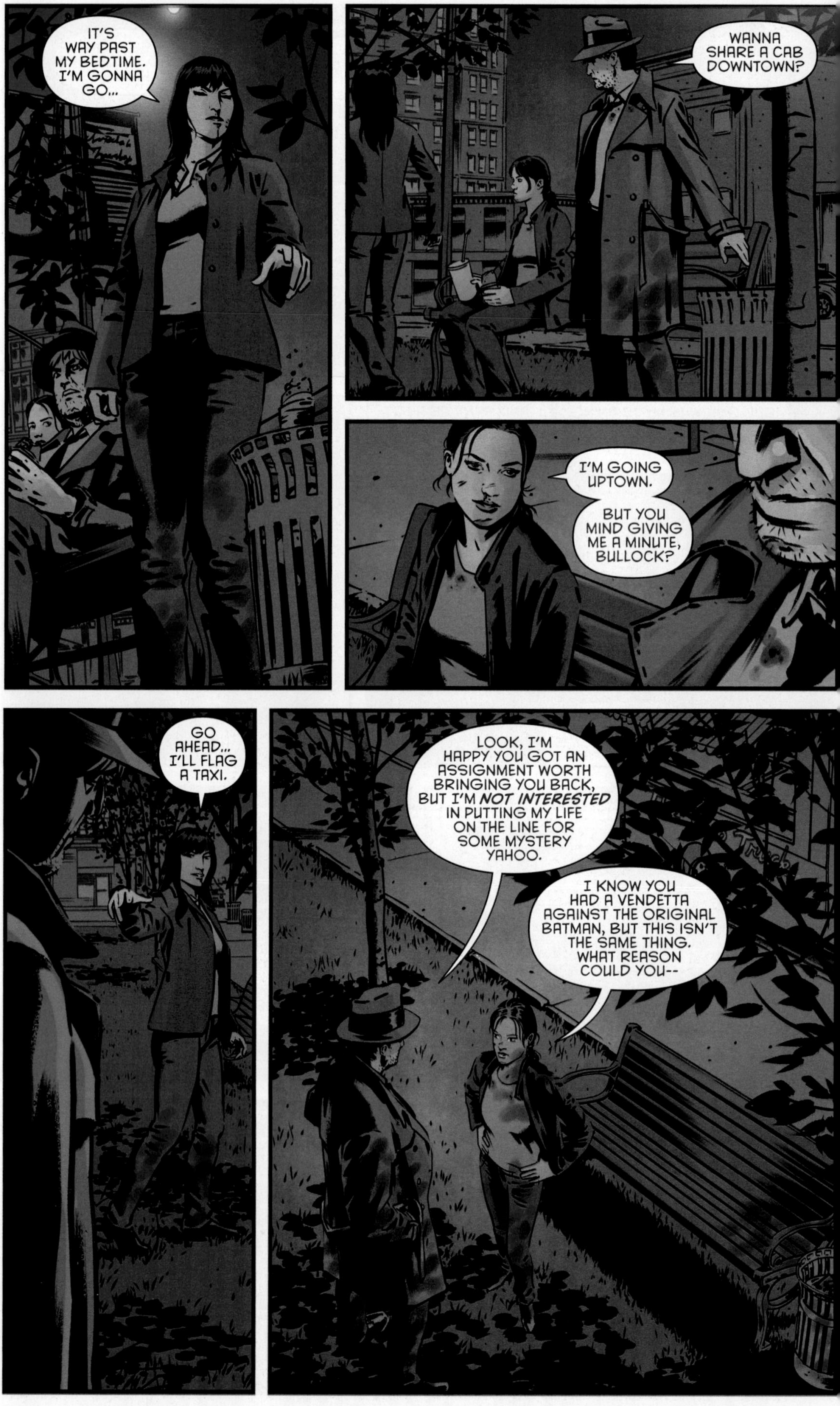
IT'S WAY PAST MY BEDTIME. I'M GONNA GO...
WANNA SHARE A CAB DOWNTOWN?
I'M GOING UPTOWN.
BUT YOU MIND GIVING ME A MINUTE, BULLOCK?
GO AHEAD... I'LL FLAG A TAXI.
LOOK, I'M HAPPY YOU GOT AN ASSIGNMENT WORTH BRINGING YOU BACK, BUT I'M NOT INTERESTED IN PUTTING MY LIFE ON THE LINE FOR SOME MYSTERY YAHOO.
I KNOW YOU HAD A VENDETTA AGAINST THE ORIGINAL BATMAN, BUT THIS ISN'T THE SAME THING. WHAT REASON COULD YOU--

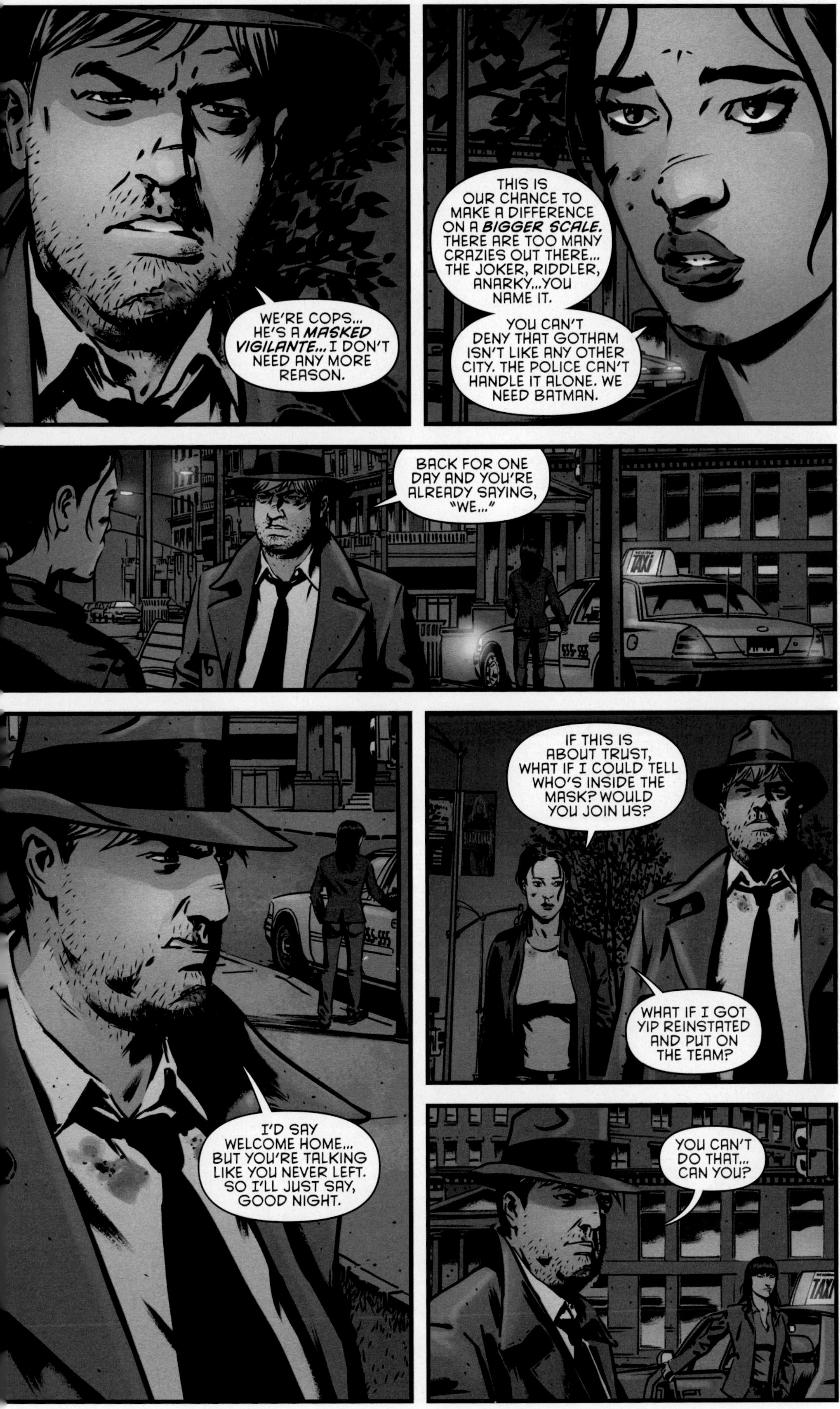
WE'RE COPS... HE'S A *MASKED VIGILANTE*... I DON'T NEED ANY MORE REASON.
THIS IS OUR CHANCE TO MAKE A DIFFERENCE ON A *BIGGER SCALE.* THERE ARE TOO MANY CRAZIES OUT THERE... THE JOKER, RIDDLER, ANARKY...YOU NAME IT.
YOU CAN'T DENY THAT GOTHAM ISN'T LIKE ANY OTHER CITY. THE POLICE CAN'T HANDLE IT ALONE. WE NEED BATMAN.
BACK FOR ONE DAY AND YOU'RE ALREADY SAYING, "WE..."
TAXI
I'D SAY WELCOME HOME... BUT YOU'RE TALKING LIKE YOU NEVER LEFT. SO I'LL JUST SAY, GOOD NIGHT.
IF THIS IS ABOUT TRUST, WHAT IF I COULD TELL WHO'S INSIDE THE MASK? WOULD YOU JOIN US?
WHAT IF I GOT YIP REINSTATED AND PUT ON THE TEAM?
YOU CAN'T DO THAT... CAN YOU?
TAXI

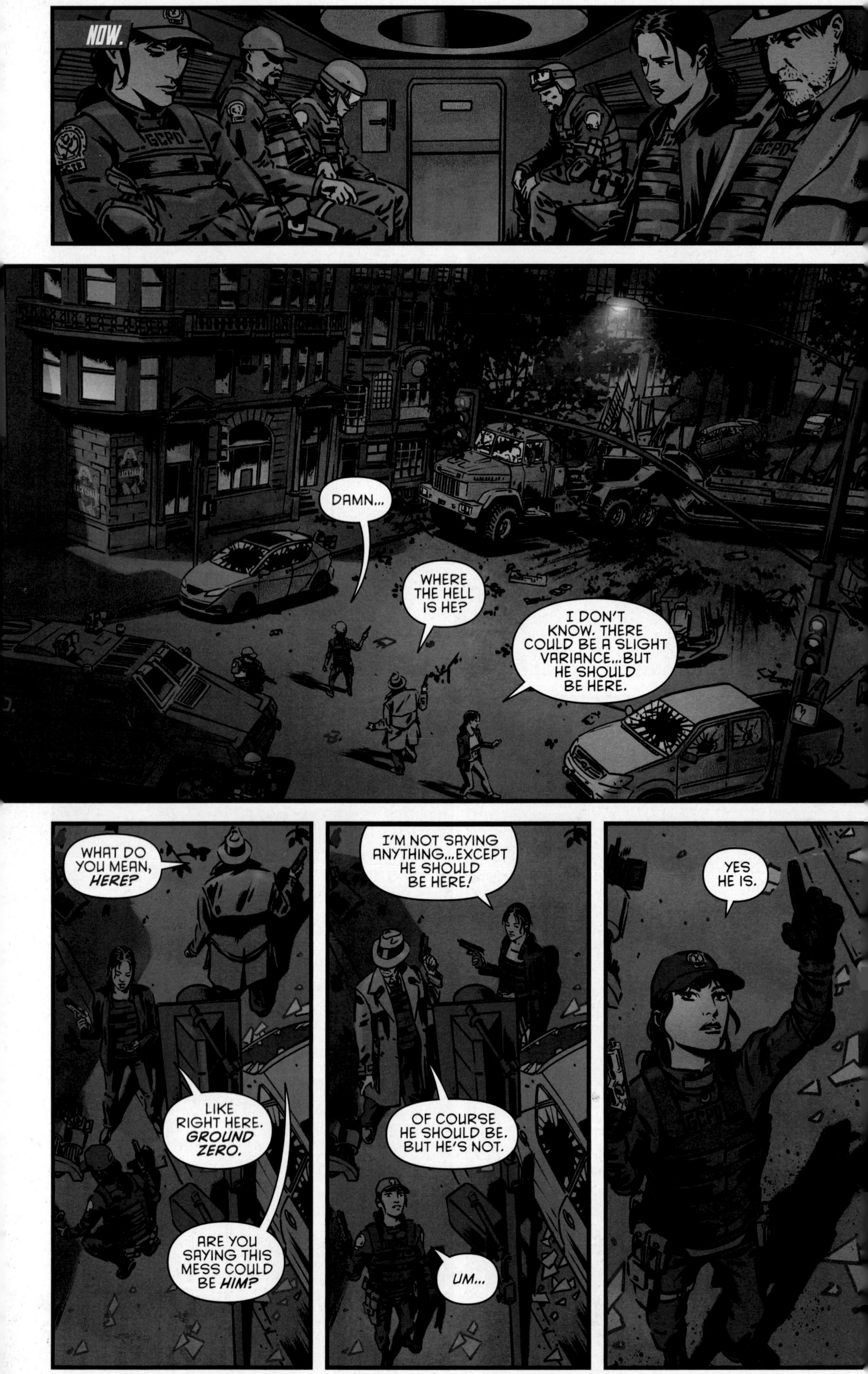
NOW.
DAMN...
WHERE THE HELL IS HE?
I DON'T KNOW. THERE COULD BE A SLIGHT VARIANCE...BUT HE SHOULD BE HERE.
WHAT DO YOU MEAN, *HERE?*
LIKE RIGHT HERE. ***GROUND ZERO.***
ARE YOU SAYING THIS MESS COULD BE *HIM?*
I'M NOT SAYING ANYTHING...EXCEPT HE SHOULD BE HERE!
OF COURSE HE SHOULD BE. BUT HE'S NOT.
UM...
YES HE IS.

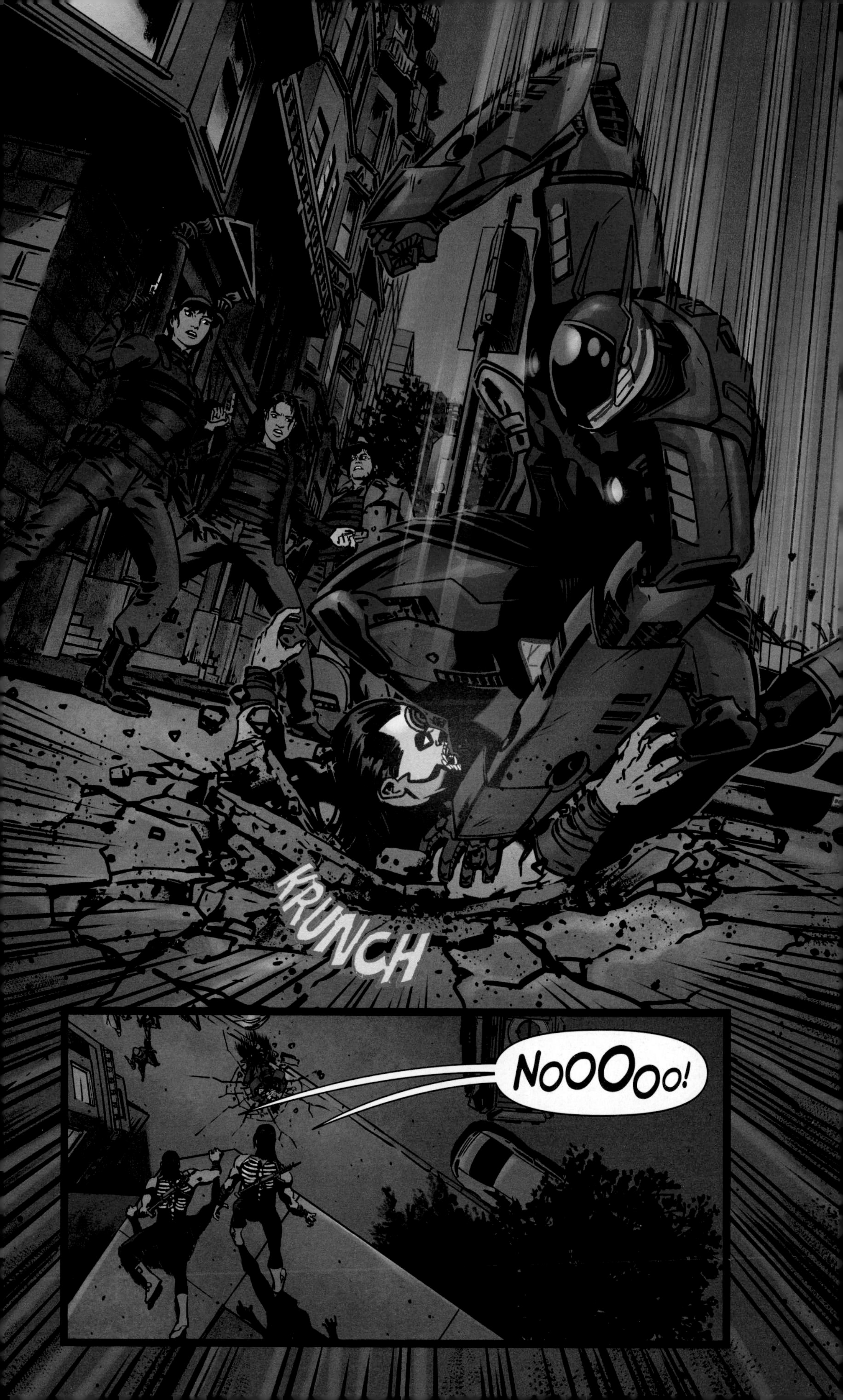
KRUNCH
NoOOoo!

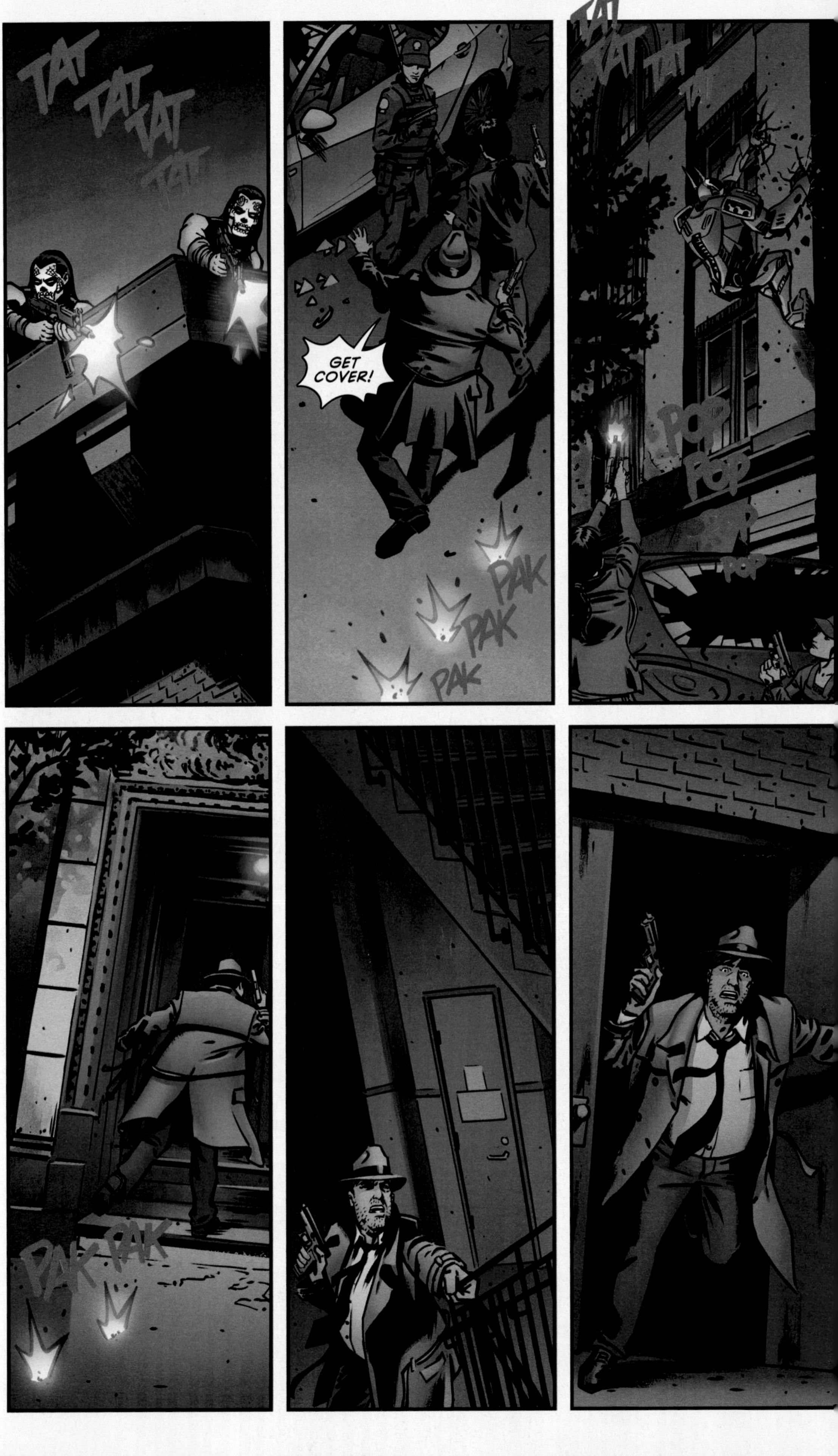
TAT TAT TAT TAT
GET COVER!
PAK PAK PAK
TAT TAT TAT TAT
POP POP POP POP
PAK PAK

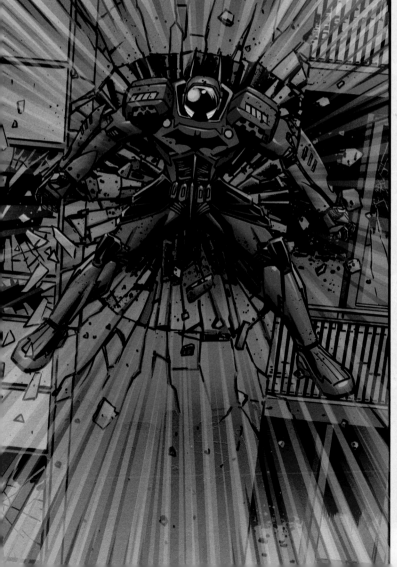

NO!

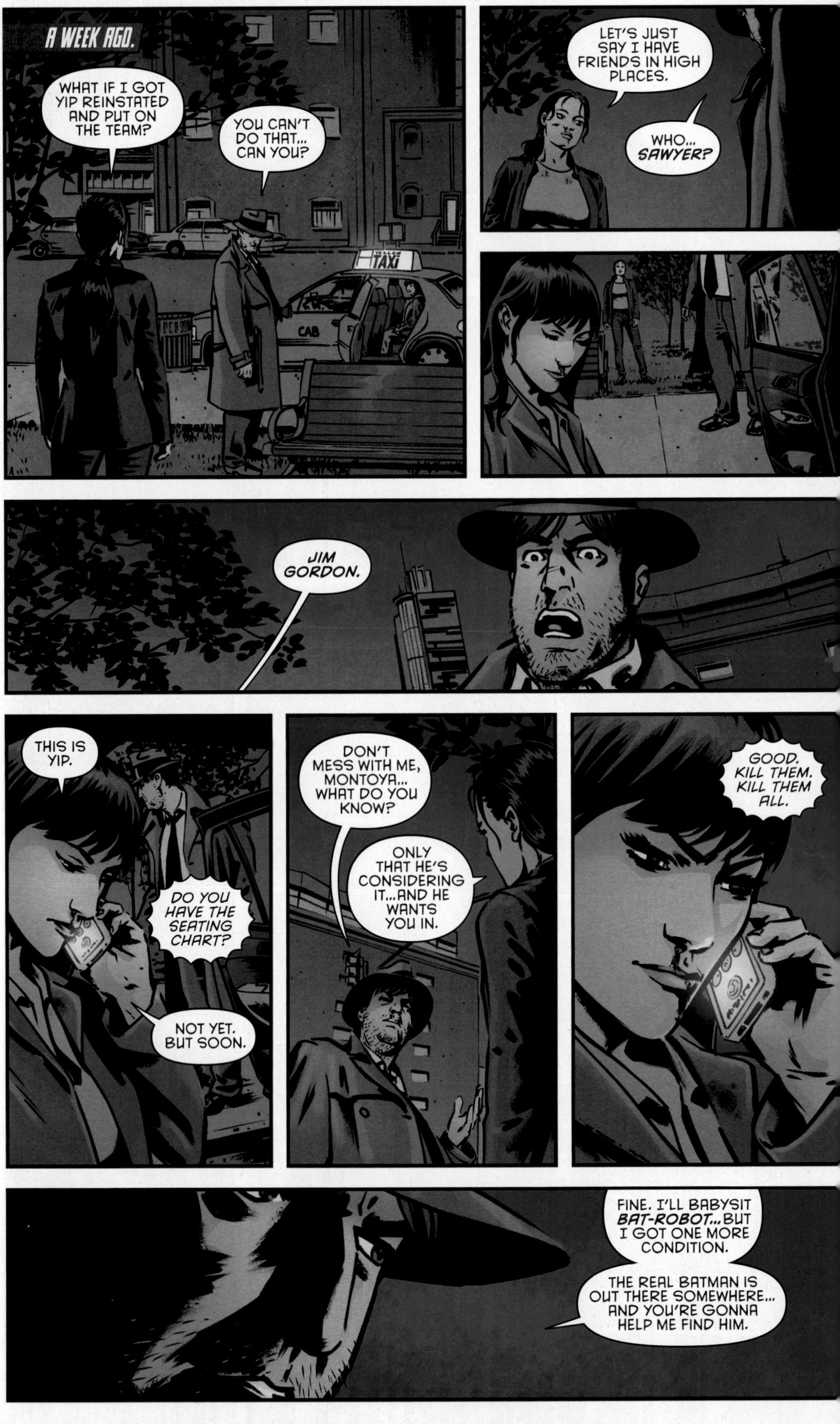
A WEEK AGO.
WHAT IF I GOT YIP REINSTATED AND PUT ON THE TEAM?
YOU CAN'T DO THAT... CAN YOU?
LET'S JUST SAY I HAVE FRIENDS IN HIGH PLACES.
WHO... SAWYER?
YELLOW TAXI
CAB
JIM GORDON.
THIS IS YIP.
DO YOU HAVE THE SEATING CHART?
NOT YET. BUT SOON.
DON'T MESS WITH ME, MONTOYA... WHAT DO YOU KNOW?
ONLY THAT HE'S CONSIDERING IT...AND HE WANTS YOU IN.
GOOD. KILL THEM. KILL THEM ALL.
FINE. I'LL BABYSIT BAT-ROBOT...BUT I GOT ONE MORE CONDITION.
THE REAL BATMAN IS OUT THERE SOMEWHERE... AND YOU'RE GONNA HELP ME FIND HIM.

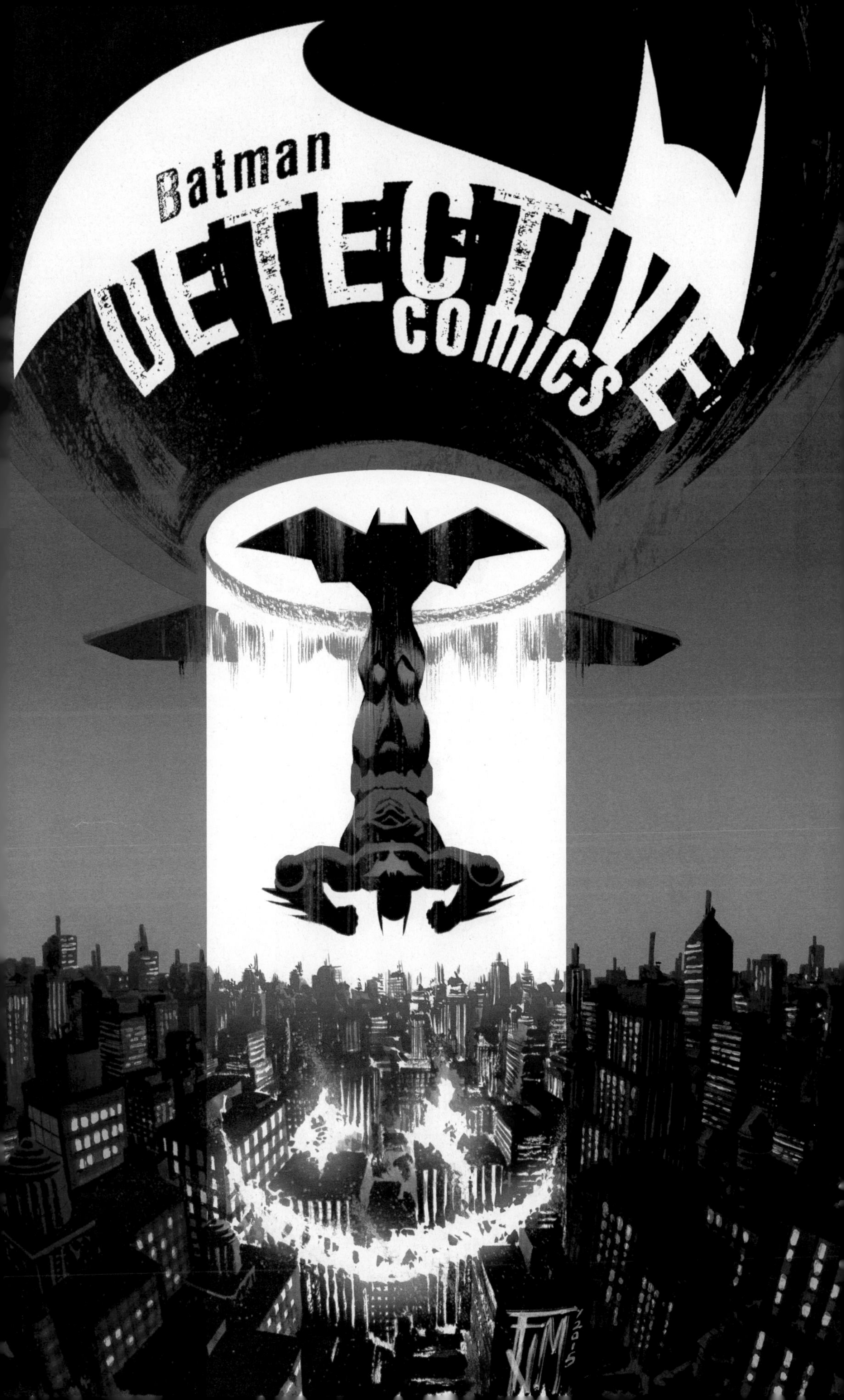
Batman
DETECTIVE
COMICS
FM 2015

PARTNERSHIPS

FRANCIS MANAPUL & BRIAN BUCCELLATO plot BRIAN BUCCELLATO writer FERNANDO BLANCO artist BRIAN BUCCELLATO colorist
WES ABBOTT letterer FRANCIS MANAPUL cover

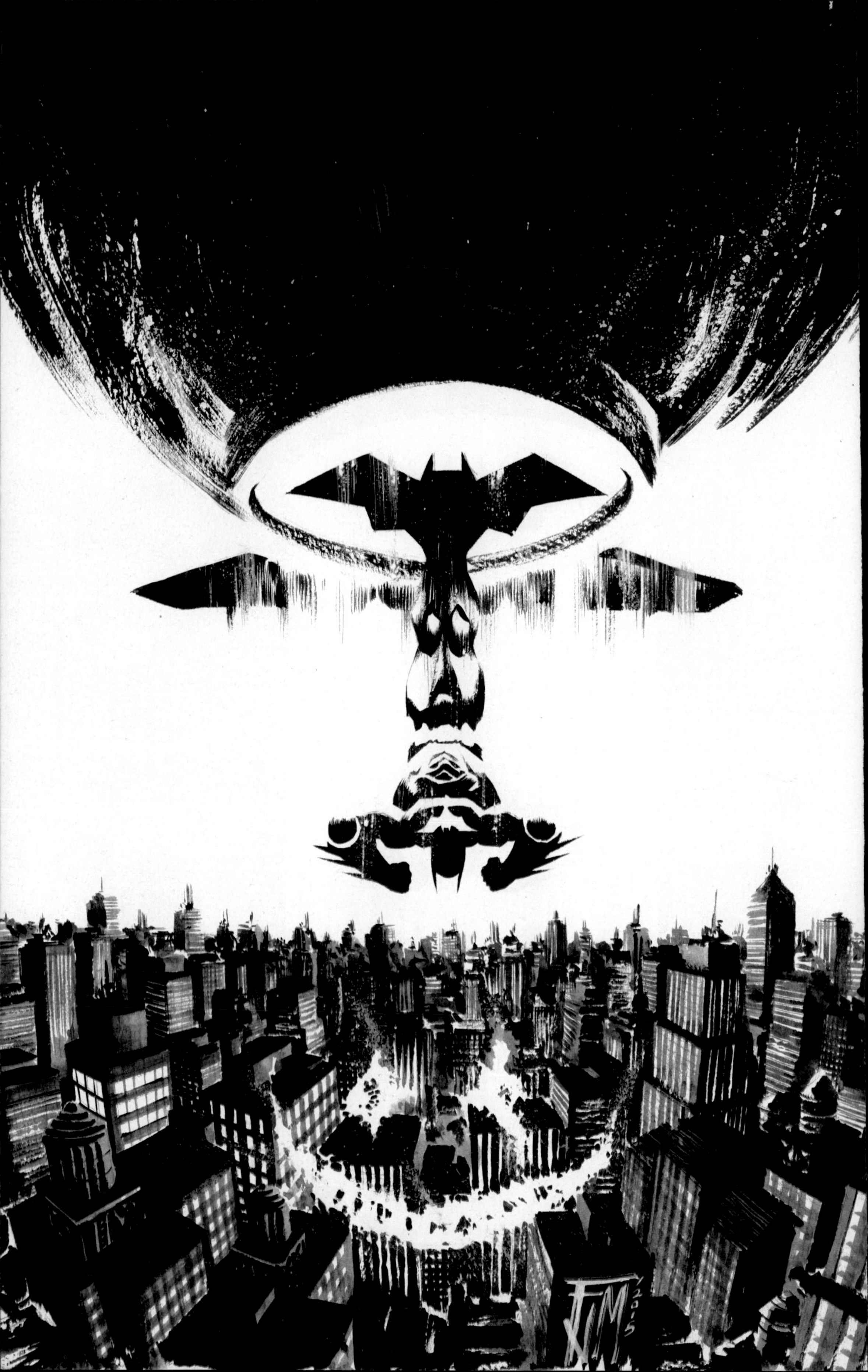

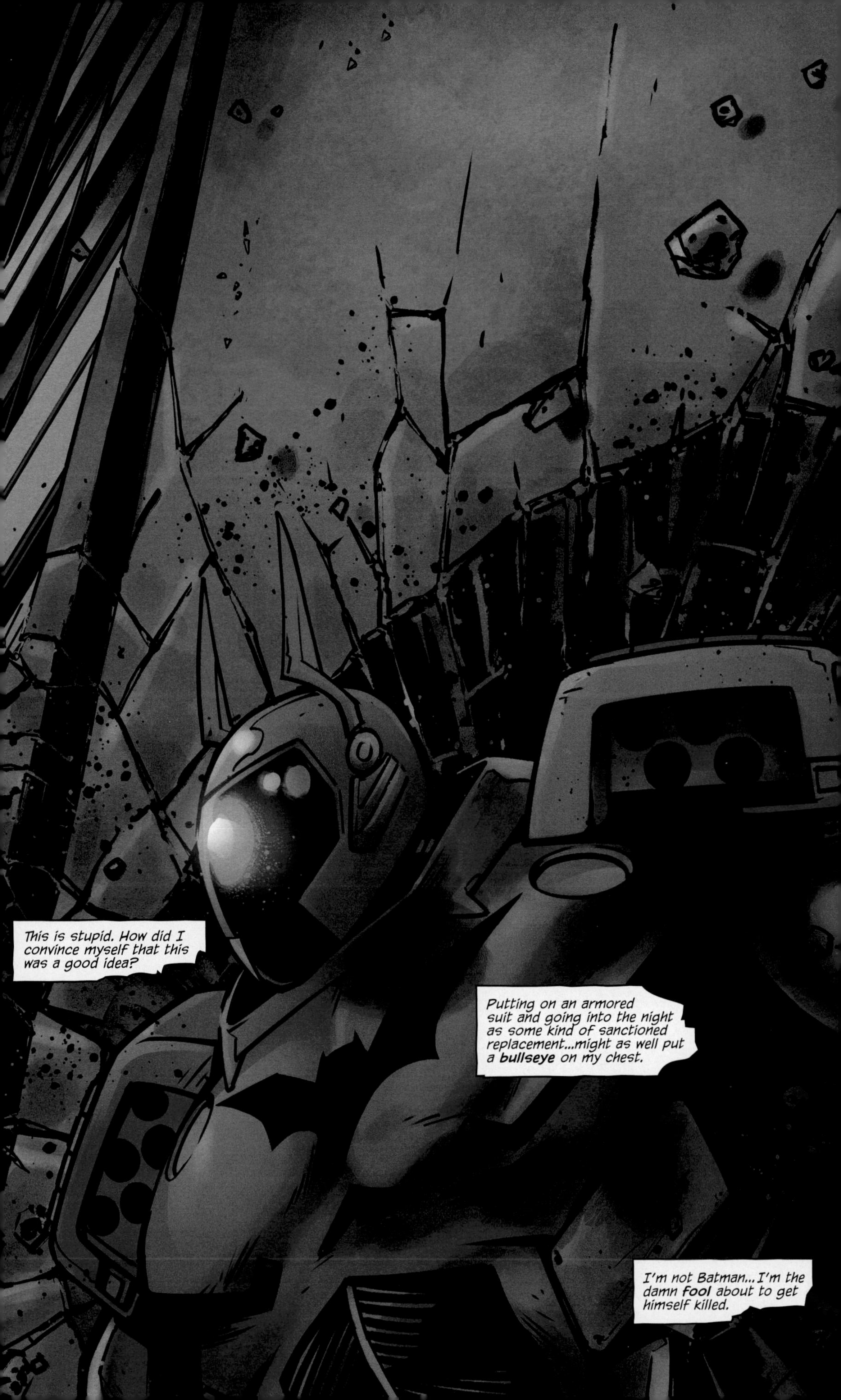
This is stupid. How did I convince myself that this was a good idea?
Putting on an armored suit and going into the night as some kind of sanctioned replacement...might as well put a **bullseye** on my chest.
I'm not Batman...I'm the damn **fool** about to get himself killed.

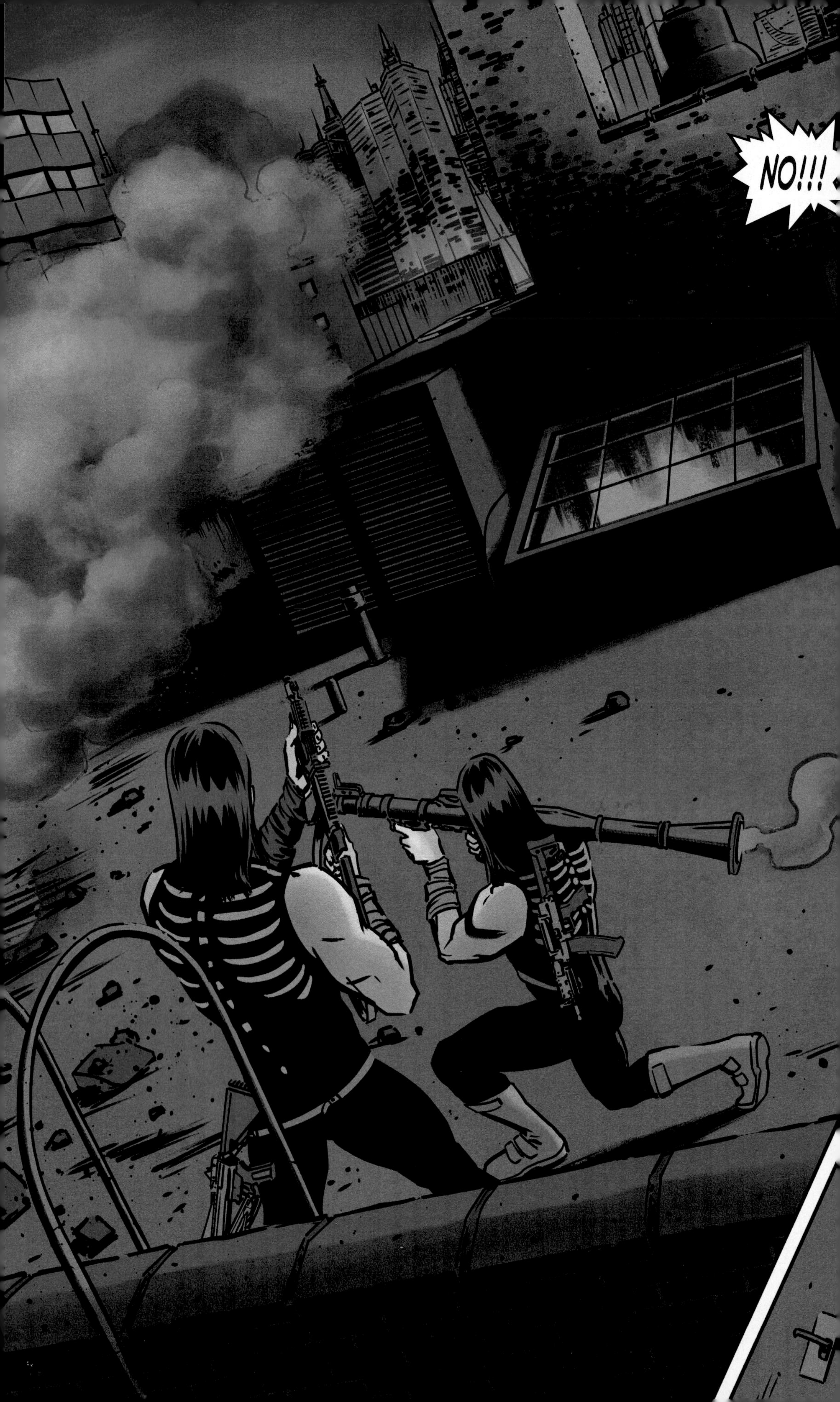
NO!!!

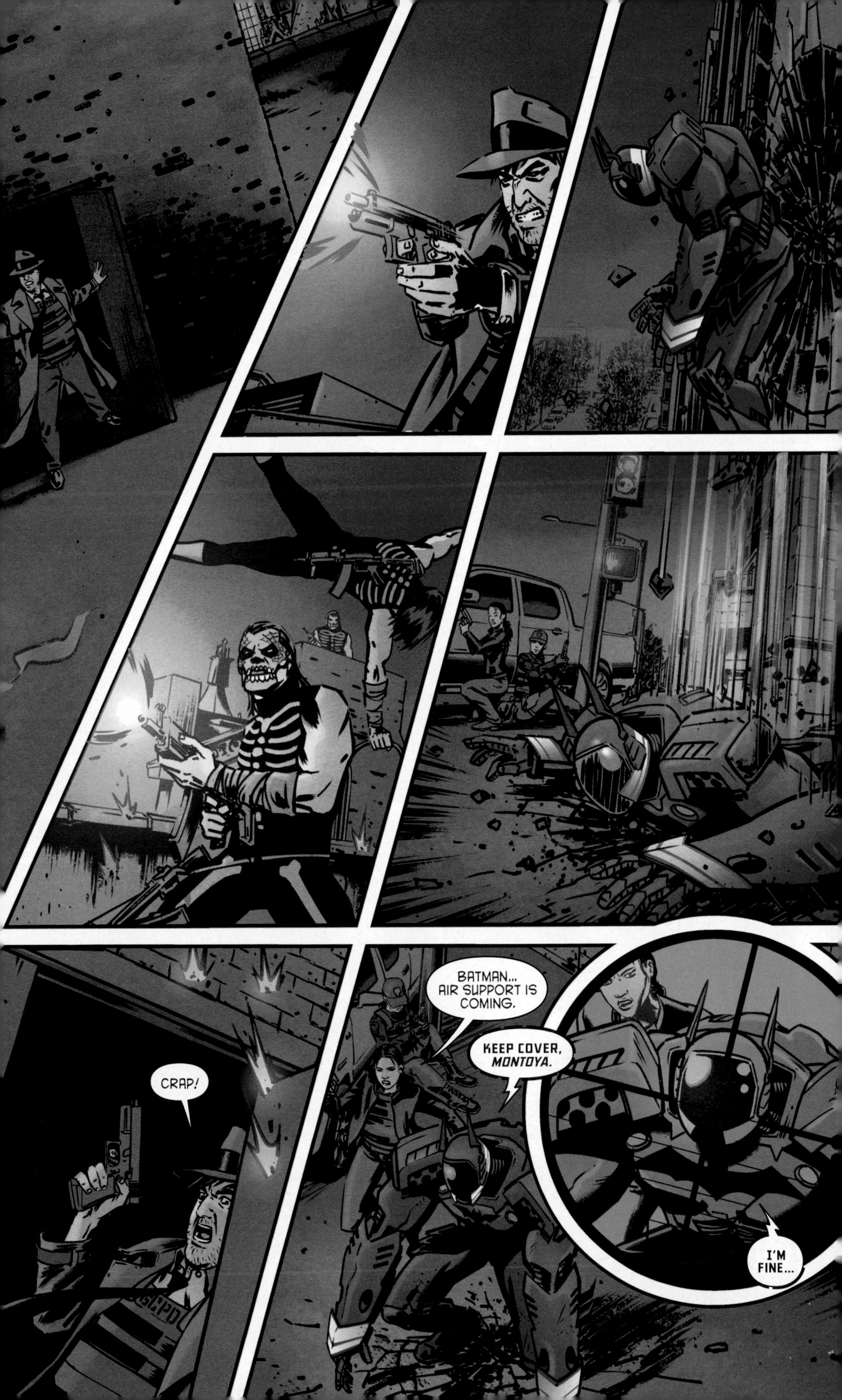
CRAP!
BATMAN... AIR SUPPORT IS COMING.
KEEP COVER, *MONTOYA.*
I'M FINE...

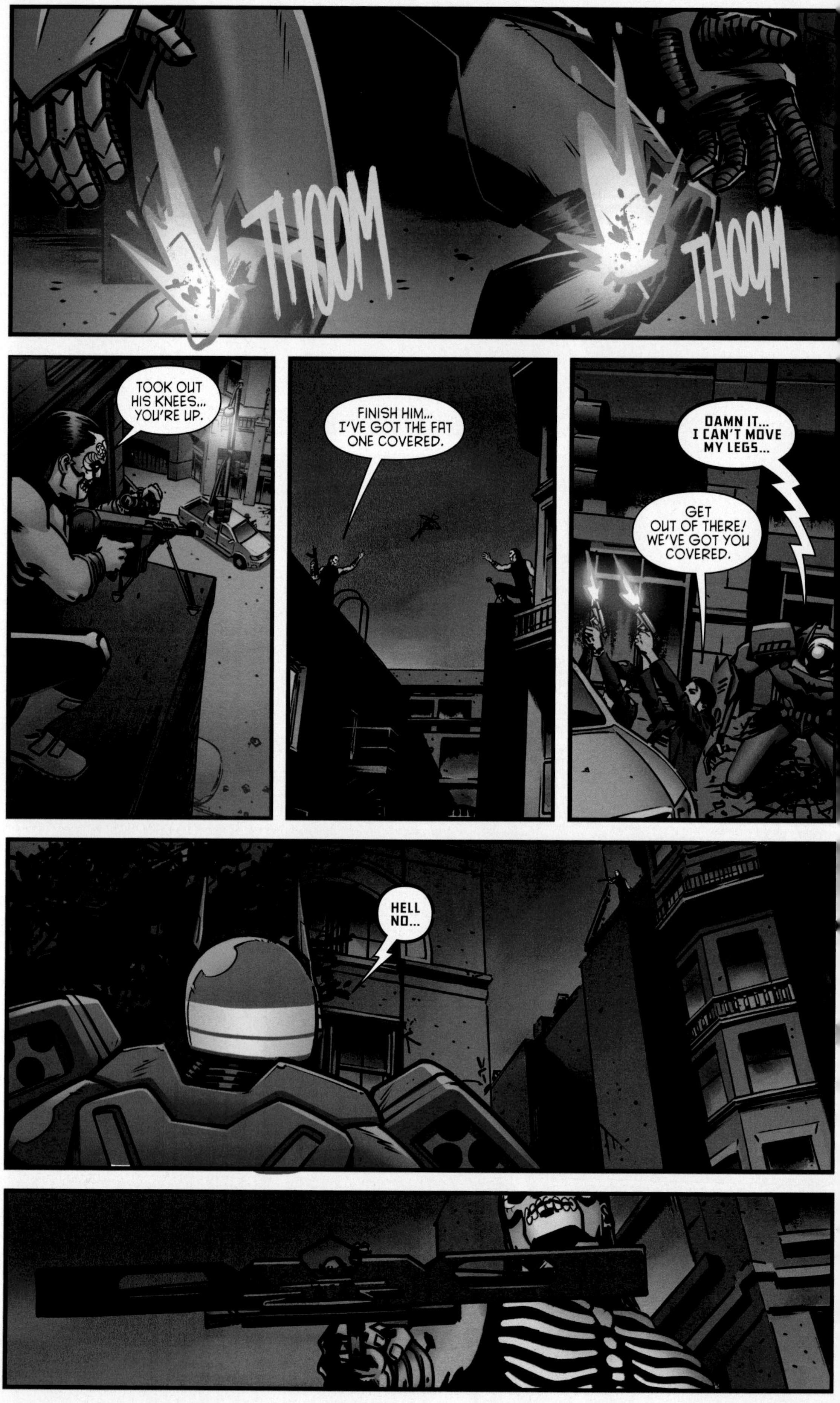
THOOM
THOOM
TOOK OUT HIS KNEES... YOU'RE UP.
FINISH HIM... I'VE GOT THE FAT ONE COVERED.
DAMN IT... I CAN'T MOVE MY LEGS...
GET OUT OF THERE! WE'VE GOT YOU COVERED.
HELL NO...

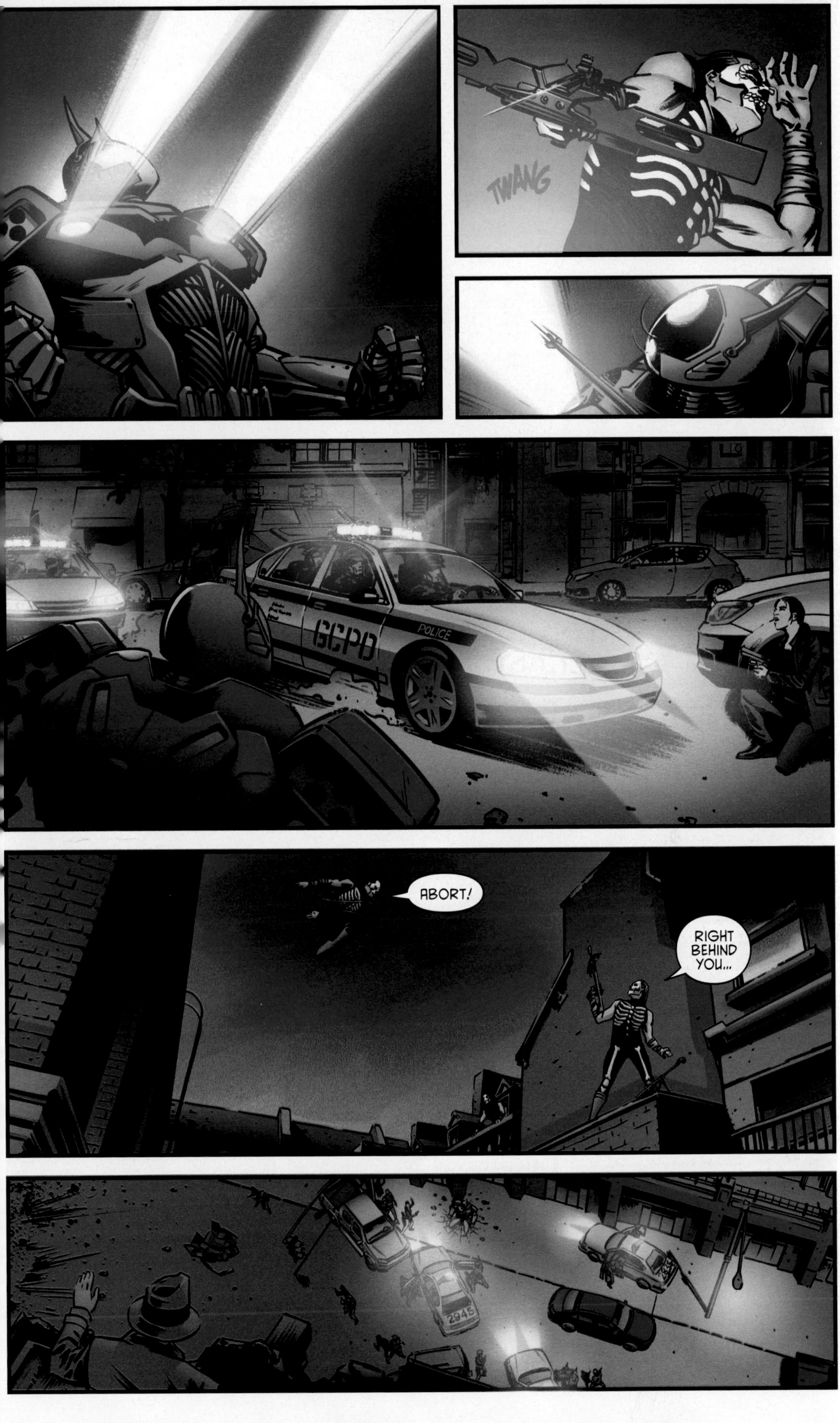
TWANG
GCPD
POLICE
ABORT!
RIGHT BEHIND YOU...
2945

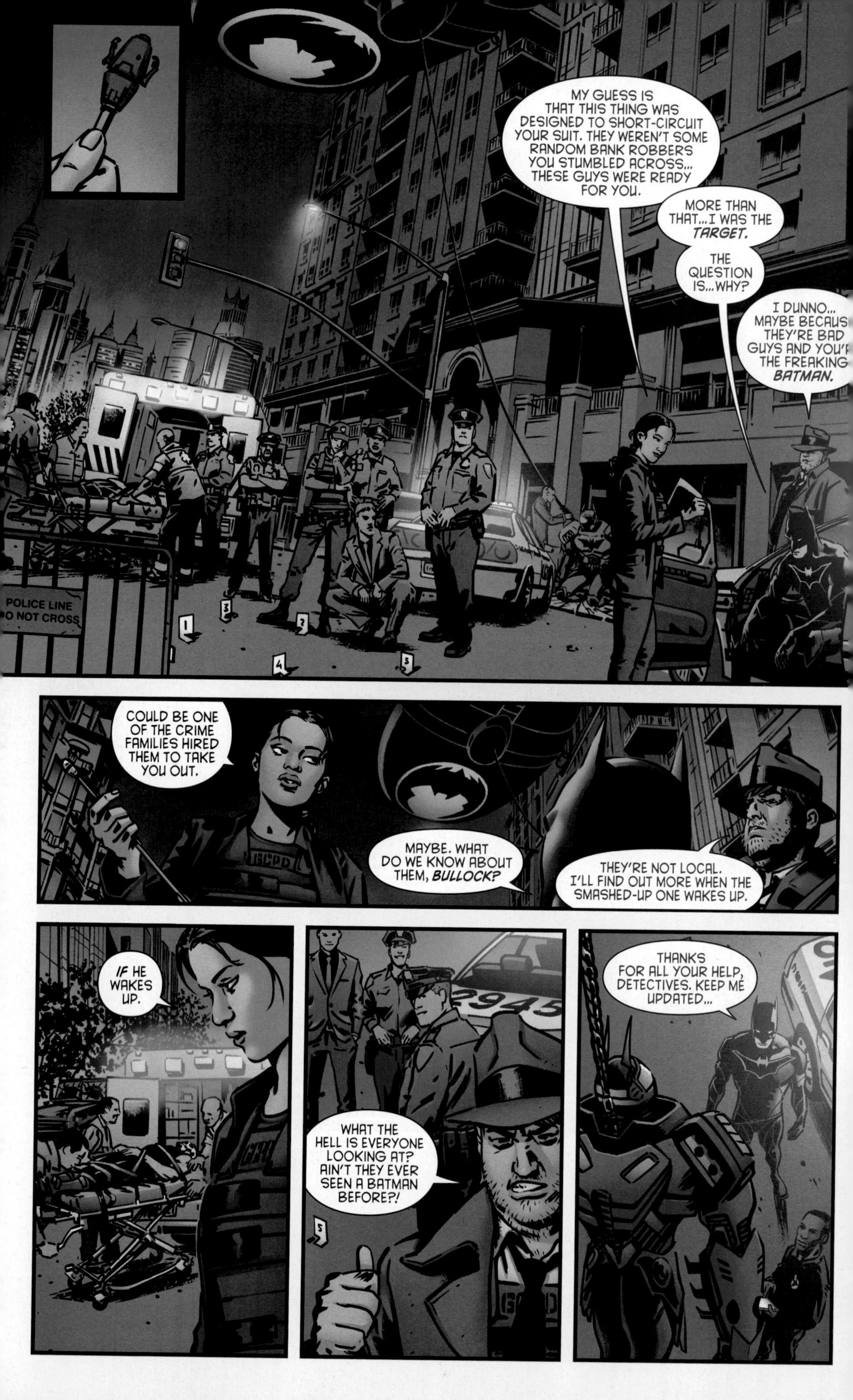
MY GUESS IS THAT THIS THING WAS DESIGNED TO SHORT-CIRCUIT YOUR SUIT. THEY WEREN'T SOME RANDOM BANK ROBBERS YOU STUMBLED ACROSS... THESE GUYS WERE READY FOR YOU.
MORE THAN THAT...I WAS THE *TARGET.*
THE QUESTION IS...WHY?
I DUNNO... MAYBE BECAUS THEY'RE BAD GUYS AND YOU'R THE FREAKING *BATMAN.*
POLICE LINE
O NOT CROSS
COULD BE ONE OF THE CRIME FAMILIES HIRED THEM TO TAKE YOU OUT.
MAYBE. WHAT DO WE KNOW ABOUT THEM, *BULLOCK?*
THEY'RE NOT LOCAL. I'LL FIND OUT MORE WHEN THE SMASHED-UP ONE WAKES UP.
IF HE WAKES UP.
WHAT THE HELL IS EVERYONE LOOKING AT? AIN'T THEY EVER SEEN A BATMAN BEFORE?!
THANKS FOR ALL YOUR HELP, DETECTIVES. KEEP ME UPDATED...

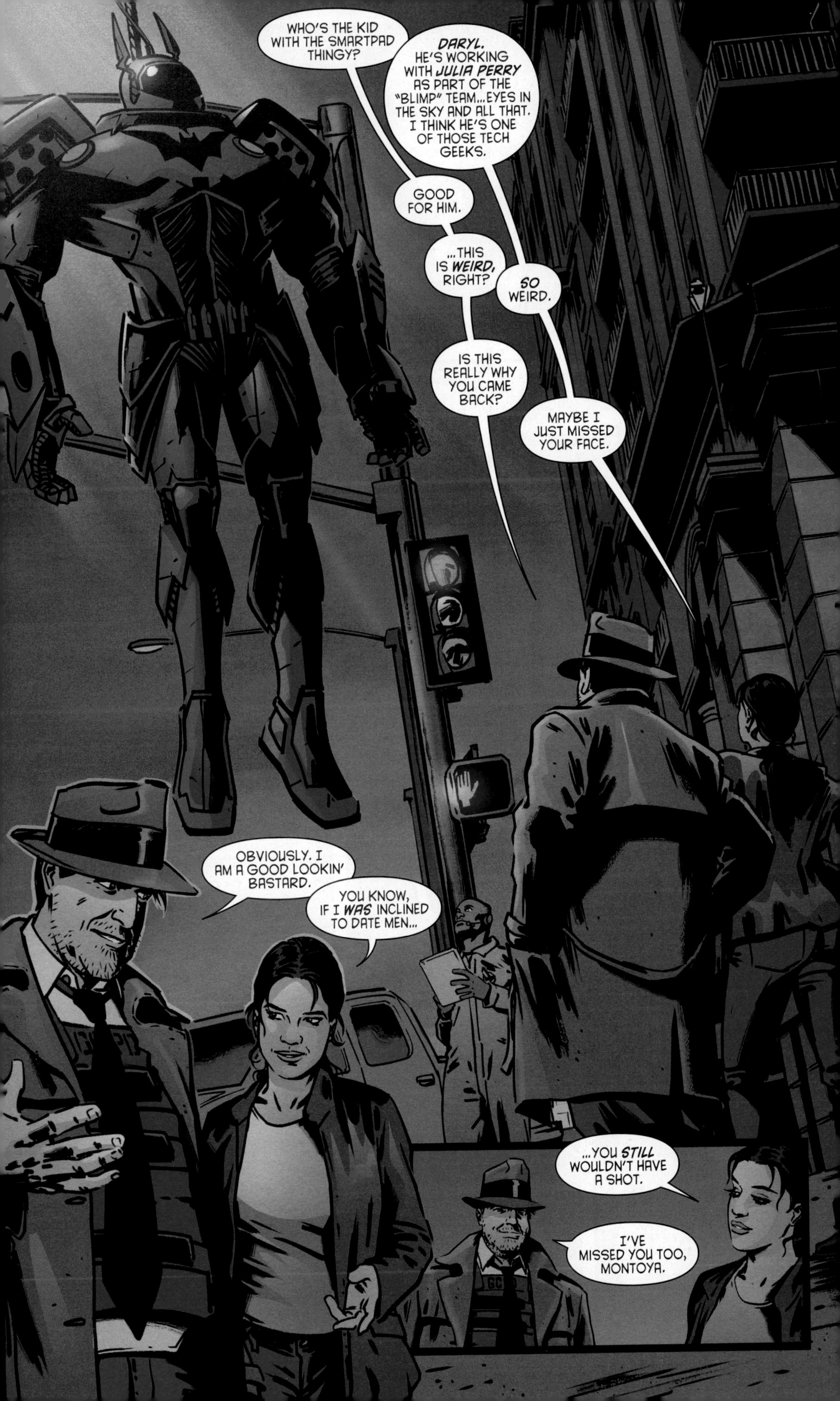
WHO'S THE KID WITH THE SMARTPAD THINGY?
DARYL. HE'S WORKING WITH JULIA PERRY AS PART OF THE "BLIMP" TEAM...EYES IN THE SKY AND ALL THAT. I THINK HE'S ONE OF THOSE TECH GEEKS.
GOOD FOR HIM.
...THIS IS WEIRD, RIGHT?
SO WEIRD.
IS THIS REALLY WHY YOU CAME BACK?
MAYBE I JUST MISSED YOUR FACE.
OBVIOUSLY. I AM A GOOD LOOKIN' BASTARD.
YOU KNOW, IF I WAS INCLINED TO DATE MEN...
...YOU STILL WOULDN'T HAVE A SHOT.
I'VE MISSED YOU TOO, MONTOYA.

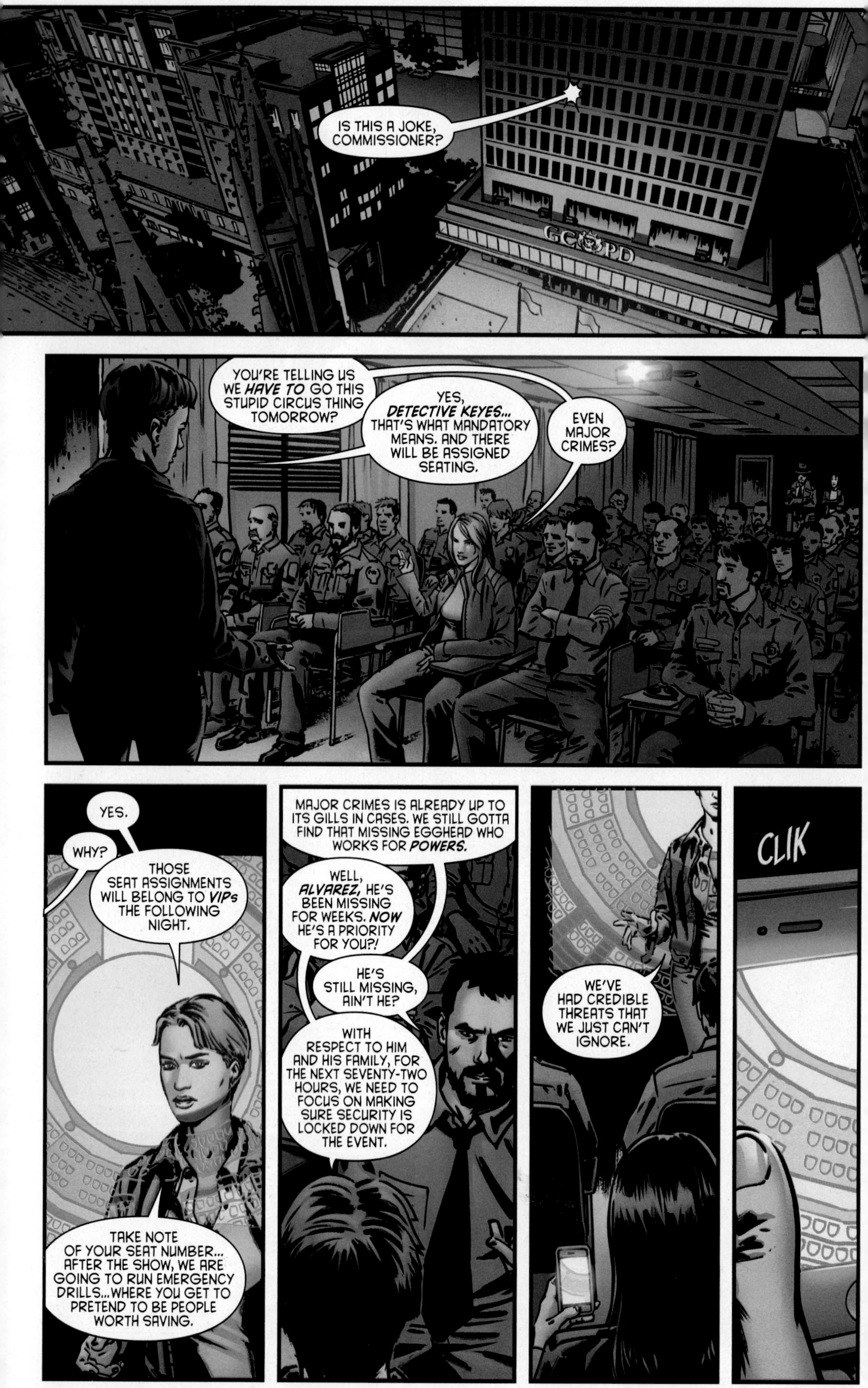
IS THIS A JOKE, COMMISSIONER?
GCPD
YOU'RE TELLING US WE *HAVE TO* GO THIS STUPID CIRCUS THING TOMORROW?
YES, *DETECTIVE KEYES...* THAT'S WHAT MANDATORY MEANS. AND THERE WILL BE ASSIGNED SEATING.
EVEN MAJOR CRIMES?
YES.
WHY?
THOSE SEAT ASSIGNMENTS WILL BELONG TO *VIPs* THE FOLLOWING NIGHT.
TAKE NOTE OF YOUR SEAT NUMBER... AFTER THE SHOW, WE ARE GOING TO RUN EMERGENCY DRILLS...WHERE YOU GET TO PRETEND TO BE PEOPLE WORTH SAVING.
MAJOR CRIMES IS ALREADY UP TO ITS GILLS IN CASES. WE STILL GOTTA FIND THAT MISSING EGGHEAD WHO WORKS FOR *POWERS.*
WELL, *ALVAREZ,* HE'S BEEN MISSING FOR WEEKS. *NOW* HE'S A PRIORITY FOR YOU?!
HE'S STILL MISSING, AIN'T HE?
WITH RESPECT TO HIM AND HIS FAMILY, FOR THE NEXT SEVENTY-TWO HOURS, WE NEED TO FOCUS ON MAKING SURE SECURITY IS LOCKED DOWN FOR THE EVENT.
WE'VE HAD CREDIBLE THREATS THAT WE JUST CAN'T IGNORE.
CLIK

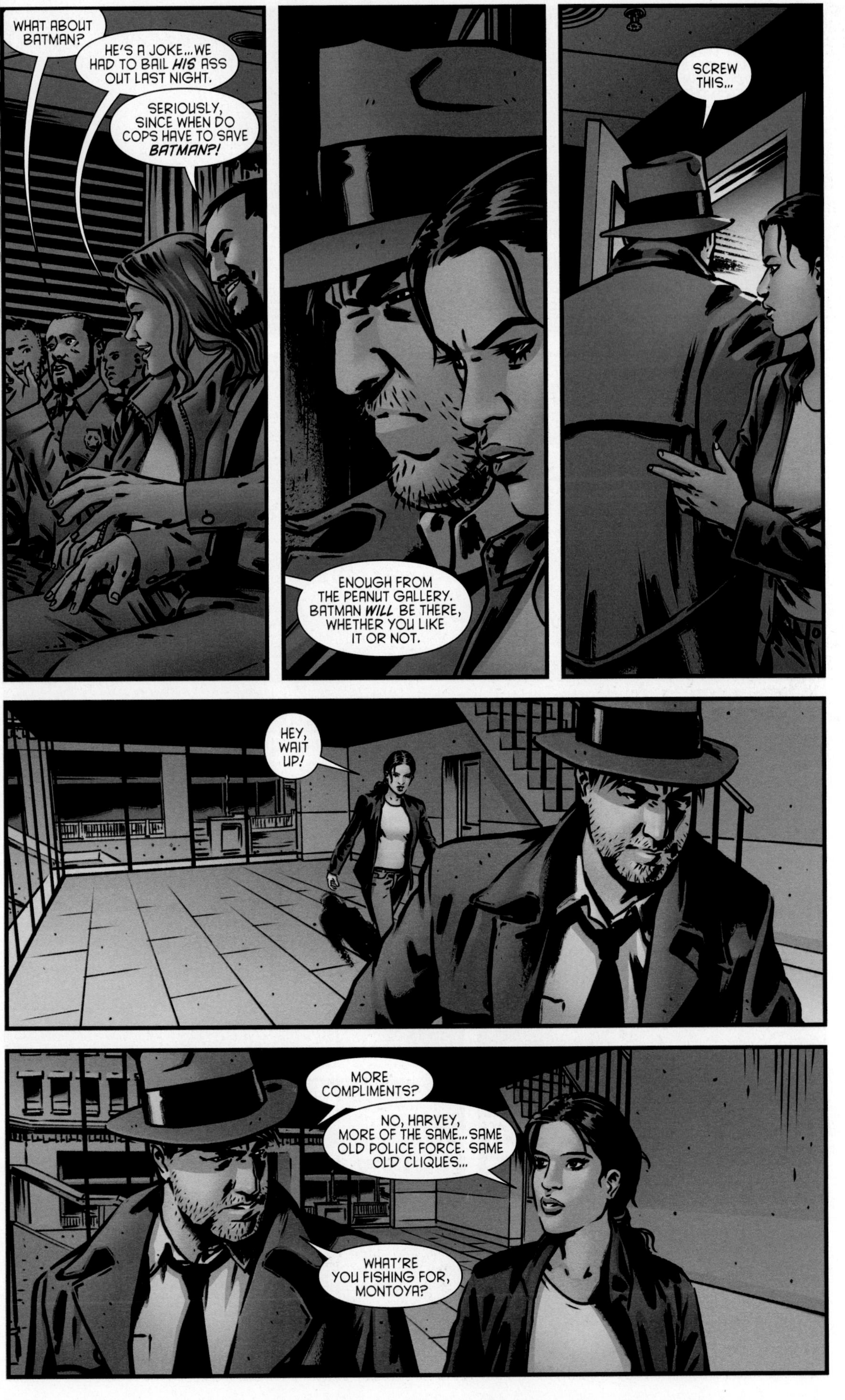
WHAT ABOUT BATMAN?
HE'S A JOKE...WE HAD TO BAIL *HIS* ASS OUT LAST NIGHT.
SERIOUSLY, SINCE WHEN DO COPS HAVE TO SAVE *BATMAN?!*
ENOUGH FROM THE PEANUT GALLERY. BATMAN *WILL* BE THERE, WHETHER YOU LIKE IT OR NOT.
SCREW THIS...
HEY, WAIT UP!
MORE COMPLIMENTS?
NO, HARVEY, MORE OF THE SAME... SAME OLD POLICE FORCE. SAME OLD CLIQUES...
WHAT'RE YOU FISHING FOR, MONTOYA?

I SWEAR, *YIP*... SOMETIMES I FEEL LIKE THE WORLD GOT TURNED INSIDE OUT...

WHAT DO YOU MEAN?

I DUNNO. IT'S LIKE UP IS DOWN AND BLACK IS WHITE...AND EVERYTHING IS ALL MESSED UP. YOU THINK YOU KNOW SOMEONE...

YOU TALKING ABOUT BATMAN?

HE'S JUST THE CHERRY ON THIS *CRAP SUNDAE.*

IT'S MONTOYA...SHE'S BEEN DIGGING AROUND, TRYING TO GET ME TO SPILL SOMETHING. MY GUT SAYS SHE MIGHT BE *INTERNAL AFFAIRS.*

WHAT DOES SHE WANT WITH YOU?

MAYBE YOU'VE GOT IT ALL WRONG--

THAT'S JUST IT...SHE KNOWS BETTER THAN THAT.

GIMME A MINUTE, HONEY...

MAYBE SHE'S NOT INTERESTED IN YOU AT ALL.

SLAM.

YEAH, MAYBE NOT...

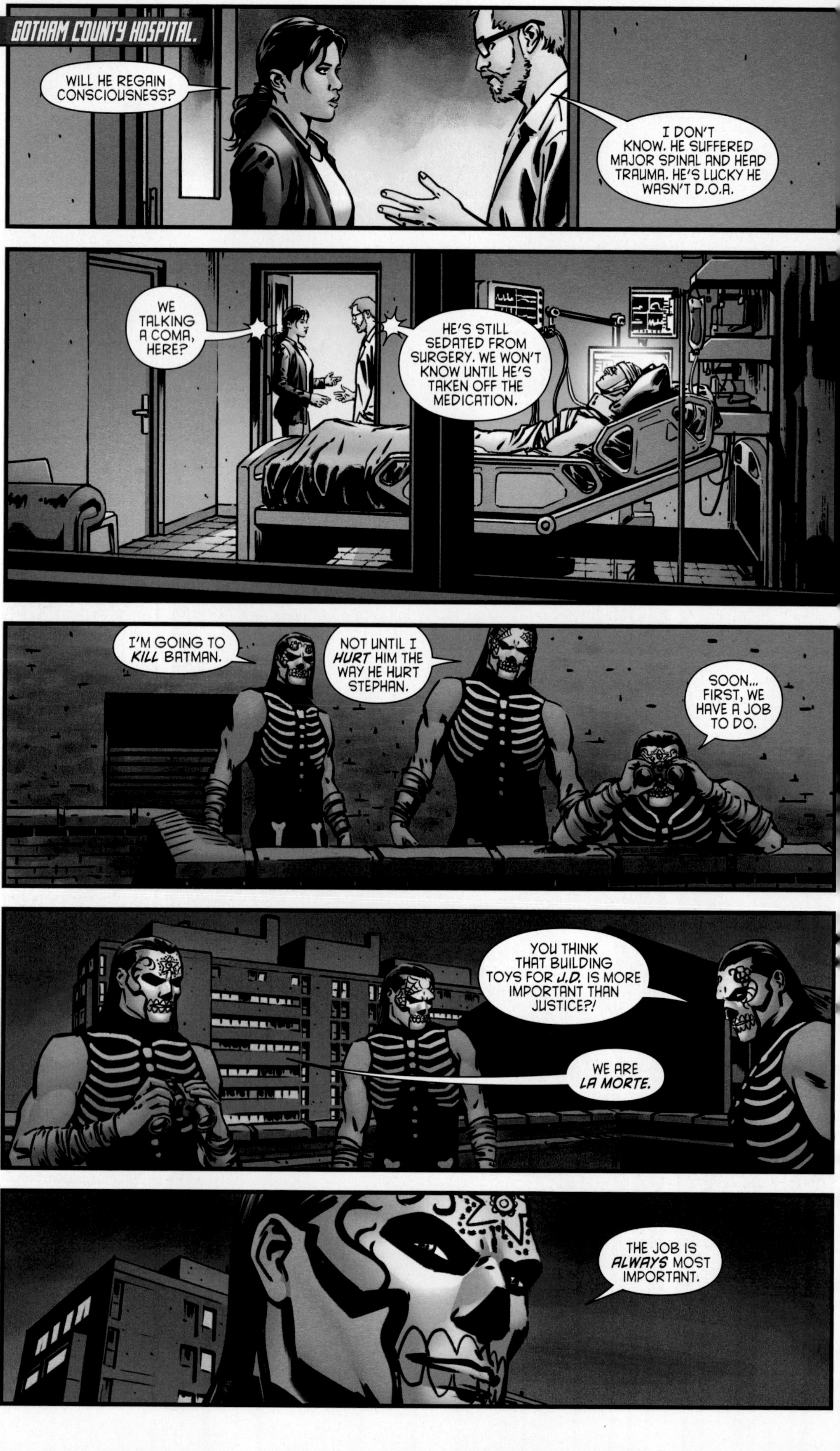
GOTHAM COUNTY HOSPITAL.
WILL HE REGAIN CONSCIOUSNESS?
I DON'T KNOW. HE SUFFERED MAJOR SPINAL AND HEAD TRAUMA. HE'S LUCKY HE WASN'T D.O.A.
WE TALKING A COMA, HERE?
HE'S STILL SEDATED FROM SURGERY. WE WON'T KNOW UNTIL HE'S TAKEN OFF THE MEDICATION.
I'M GOING TO KILL BATMAN.
NOT UNTIL I HURT HIM THE WAY HE HURT STEPHAN.
SOON... FIRST, WE HAVE A JOB TO DO.
YOU THINK THAT BUILDING TOYS FOR J.D. IS MORE IMPORTANT THAN JUSTICE?!
WE ARE LA MORTE.
THE JOB IS ALWAYS MOST IMPORTANT.

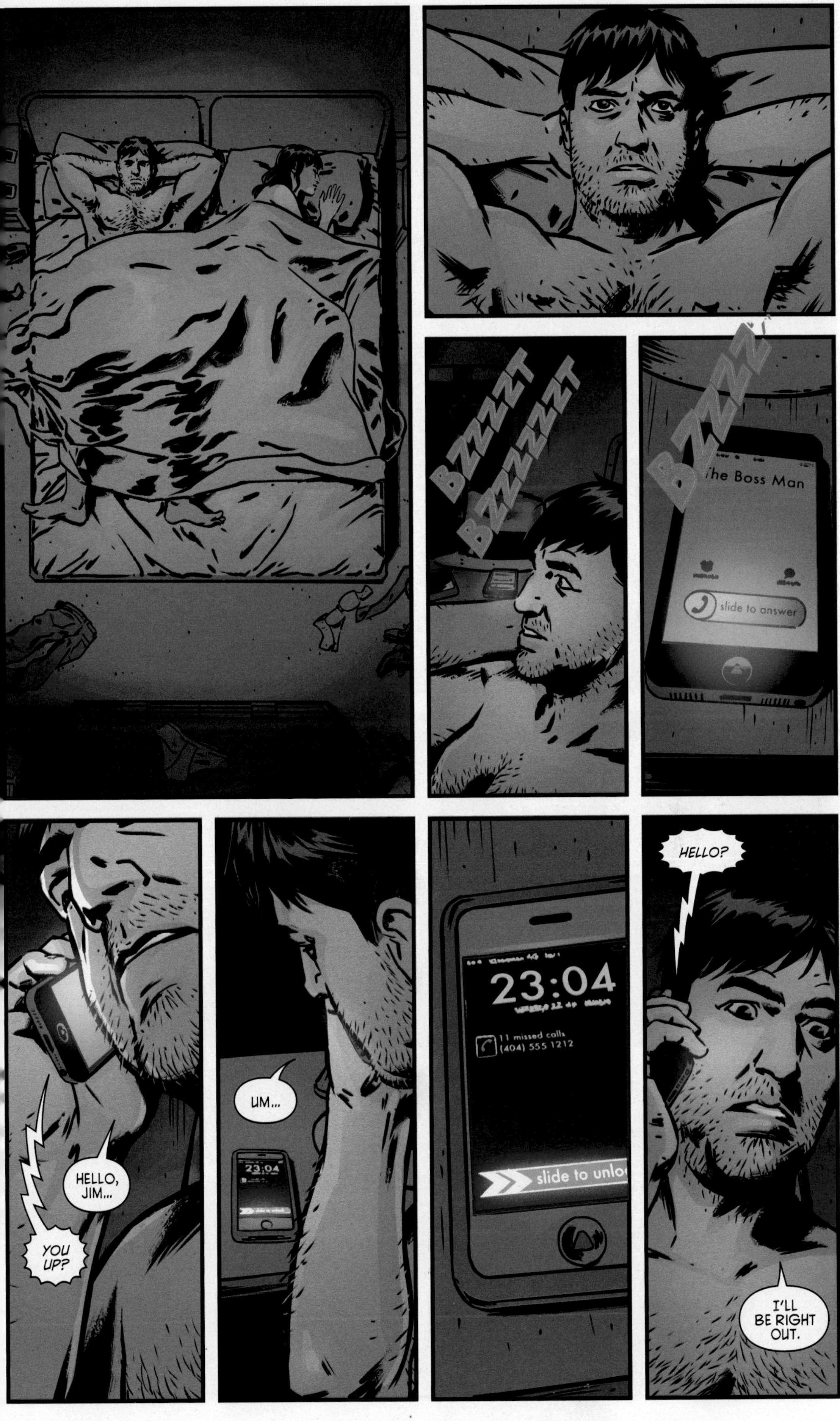
BZZZZZT
BZZZZZZZT
BZZZZ
The Boss Man
slide to answer
HELLO, JIM...
YOU UP?
UM...
23:04
11 missed calls
(404) 555 1212
slide to unlo
HELLO?
I'LL BE RIGHT OUT.

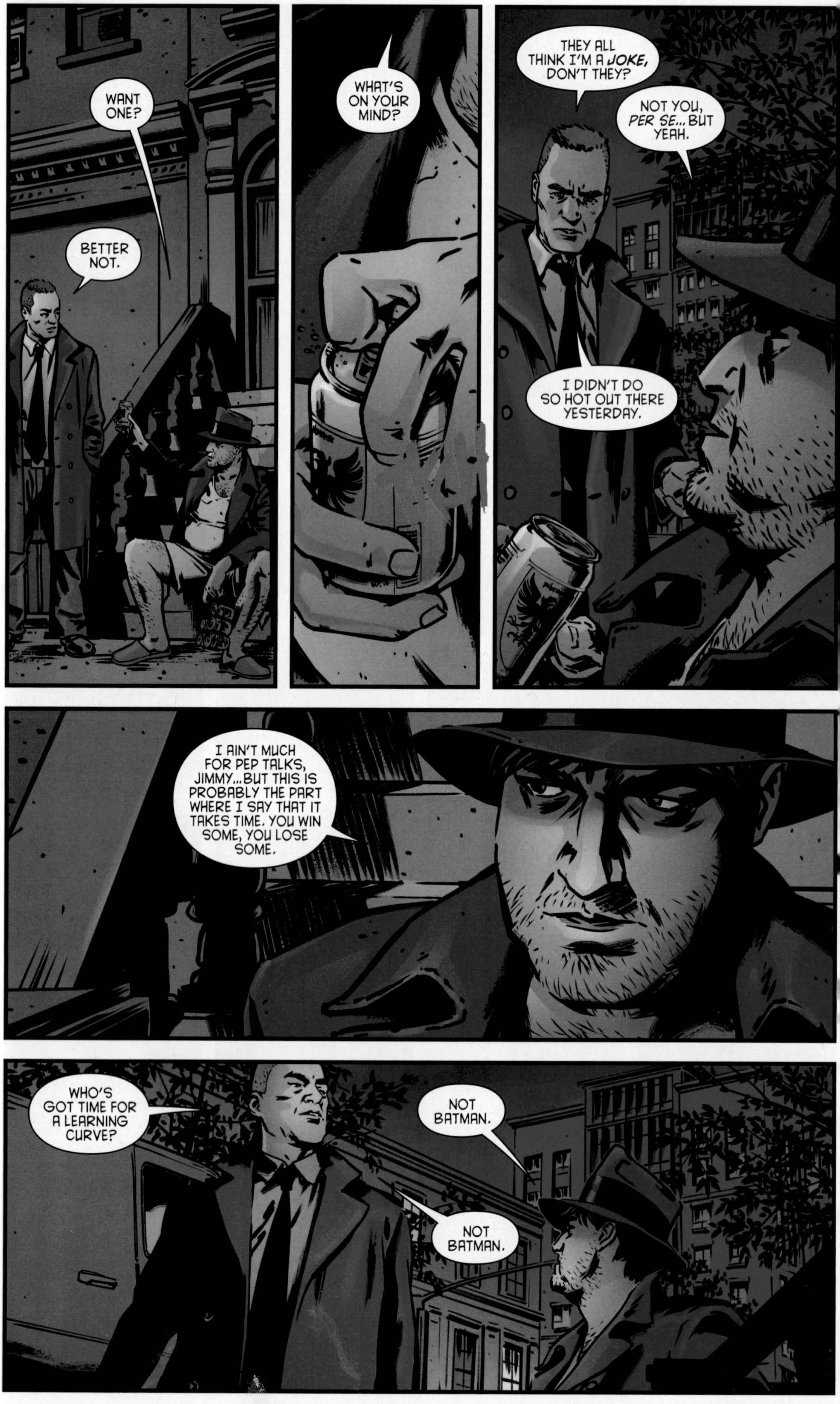
WANT ONE?
BETTER NOT.
WHAT'S ON YOUR MIND?
THEY ALL THINK I'M A *JOKE,* DON'T THEY?
NOT YOU, *PER SE*... BUT YEAH.
I DIDN'T DO SO HOT OUT THERE YESTERDAY.
I AIN'T MUCH FOR PEP TALKS, JIMMY... BUT THIS IS PROBABLY THE PART WHERE I SAY THAT IT TAKES TIME. YOU WIN SOME, YOU LOSE SOME.
WHO'S GOT TIME FOR A LEARNING CURVE?
NOT BATMAN.
NOT BATMAN.

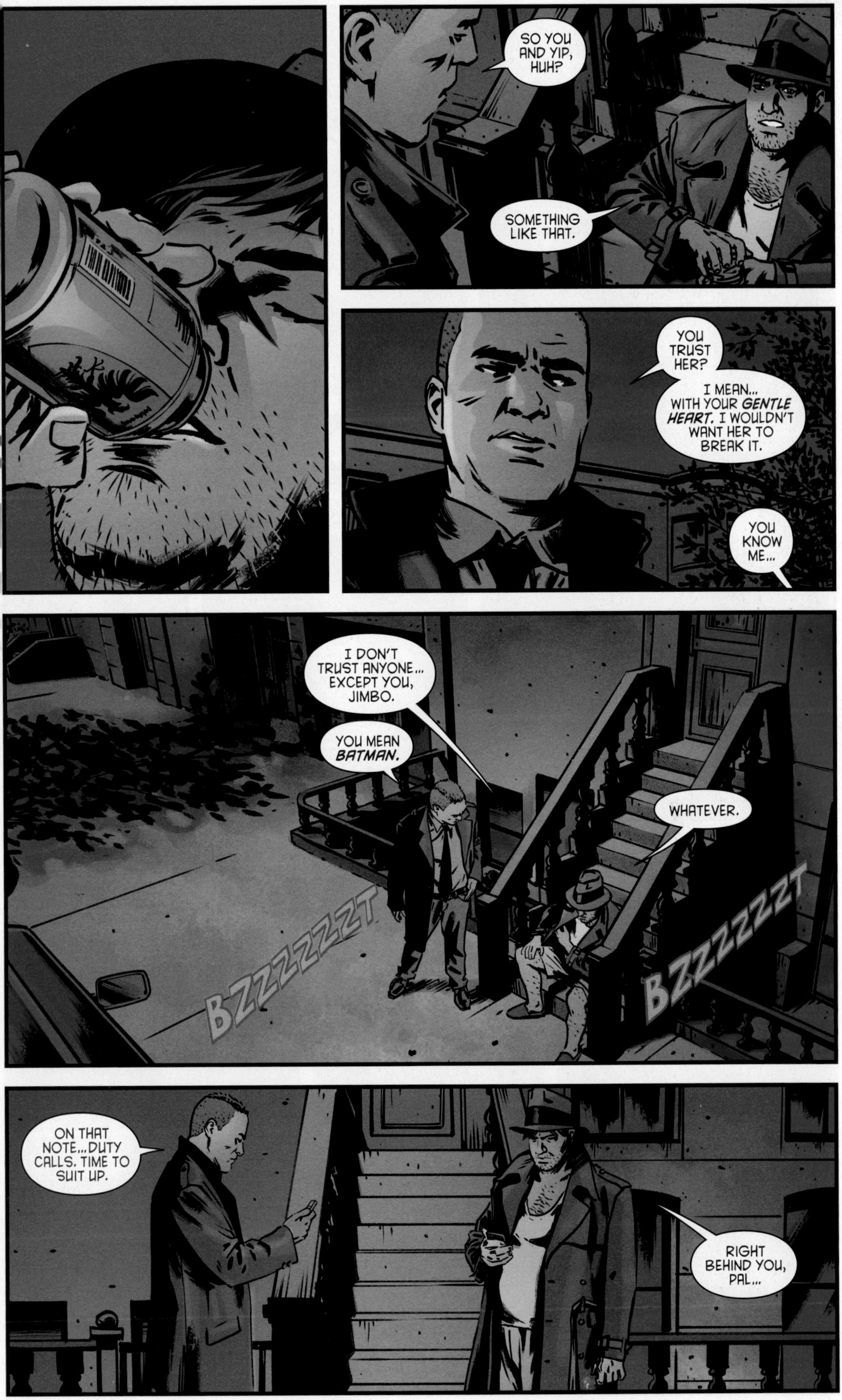
SO YOU AND YIP, HUH?
SOMETHING LIKE THAT.
YOU TRUST HER?
I MEAN... WITH YOUR GENTLE HEART. I WOULDN'T WANT HER TO BREAK IT.
YOU KNOW ME...
I DON'T TRUST ANYONE... EXCEPT YOU, JIMBO.
YOU MEAN BATMAN.
WHATEVER.
BZZZZZZT
BZZZZZZT
ON THAT NOTE...DUTY CALLS. TIME TO SUIT UP.
RIGHT BEHIND YOU, PAL...

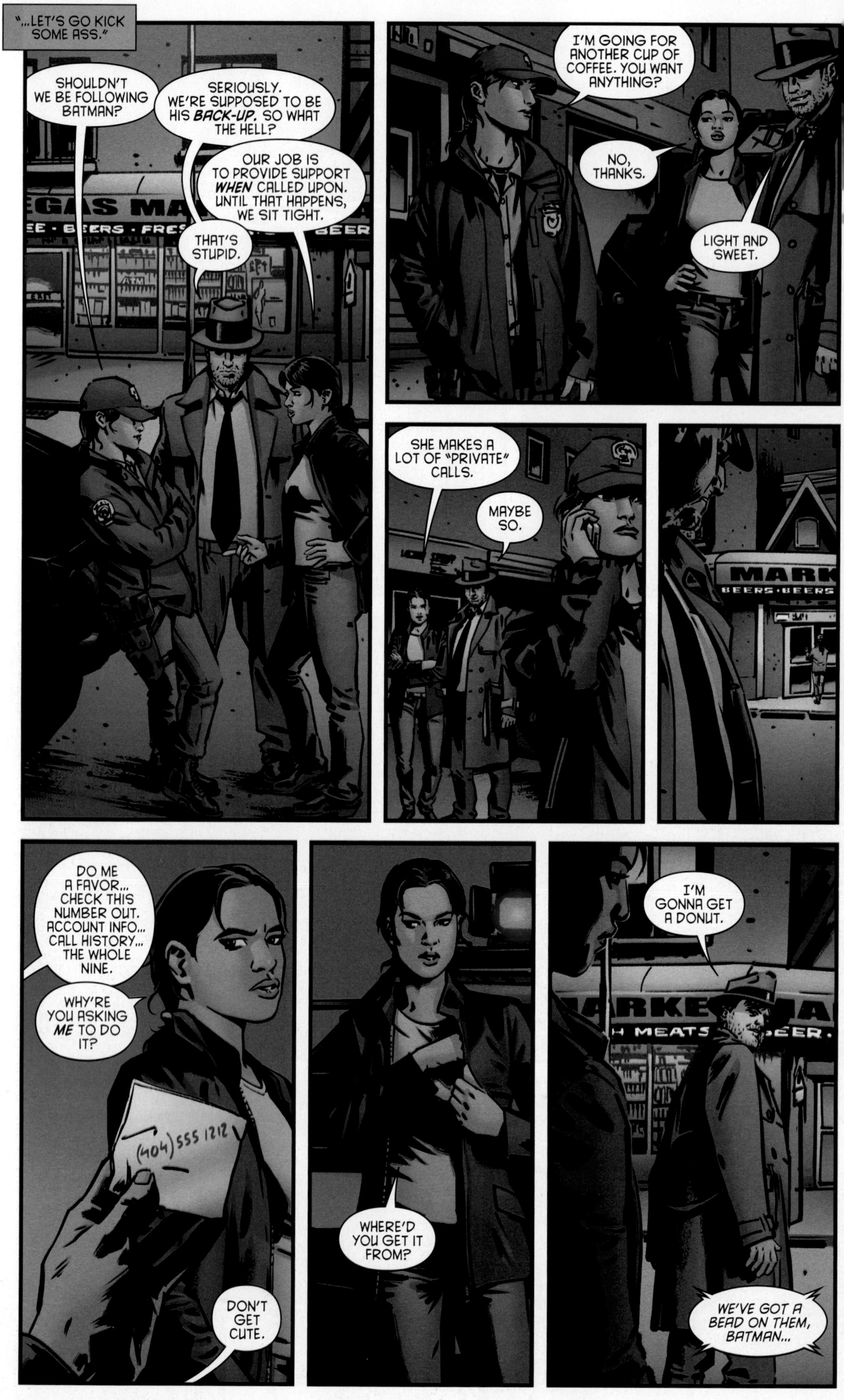
"...LET'S GO KICK SOME ASS."
SHOULDN'T WE BE FOLLOWING BATMAN?
SERIOUSLY. WE'RE SUPPOSED TO BE HIS *BACK-UP.* SO WHAT THE HELL?
OUR JOB IS TO PROVIDE SUPPORT *WHEN* CALLED UPON. UNTIL THAT HAPPENS, WE SIT TIGHT.
THAT'S STUPID.
I'M GOING FOR ANOTHER CUP OF COFFEE. YOU WANT ANYTHING?
NO, THANKS.
LIGHT AND SWEET.
SHE MAKES A LOT OF "PRIVATE" CALLS.
MAYBE SO.
DO ME A FAVOR... CHECK THIS NUMBER OUT. ACCOUNT INFO... CALL HISTORY... THE WHOLE NINE.
WHY'RE YOU ASKING *ME* TO DO IT?
(404) 555 1212
DON'T GET CUTE.
WHERE'D YOU GET IT FROM?
I'M GONNA GET A DONUT.
WE'VE GOT A BEAD ON THEM, BATMAN...

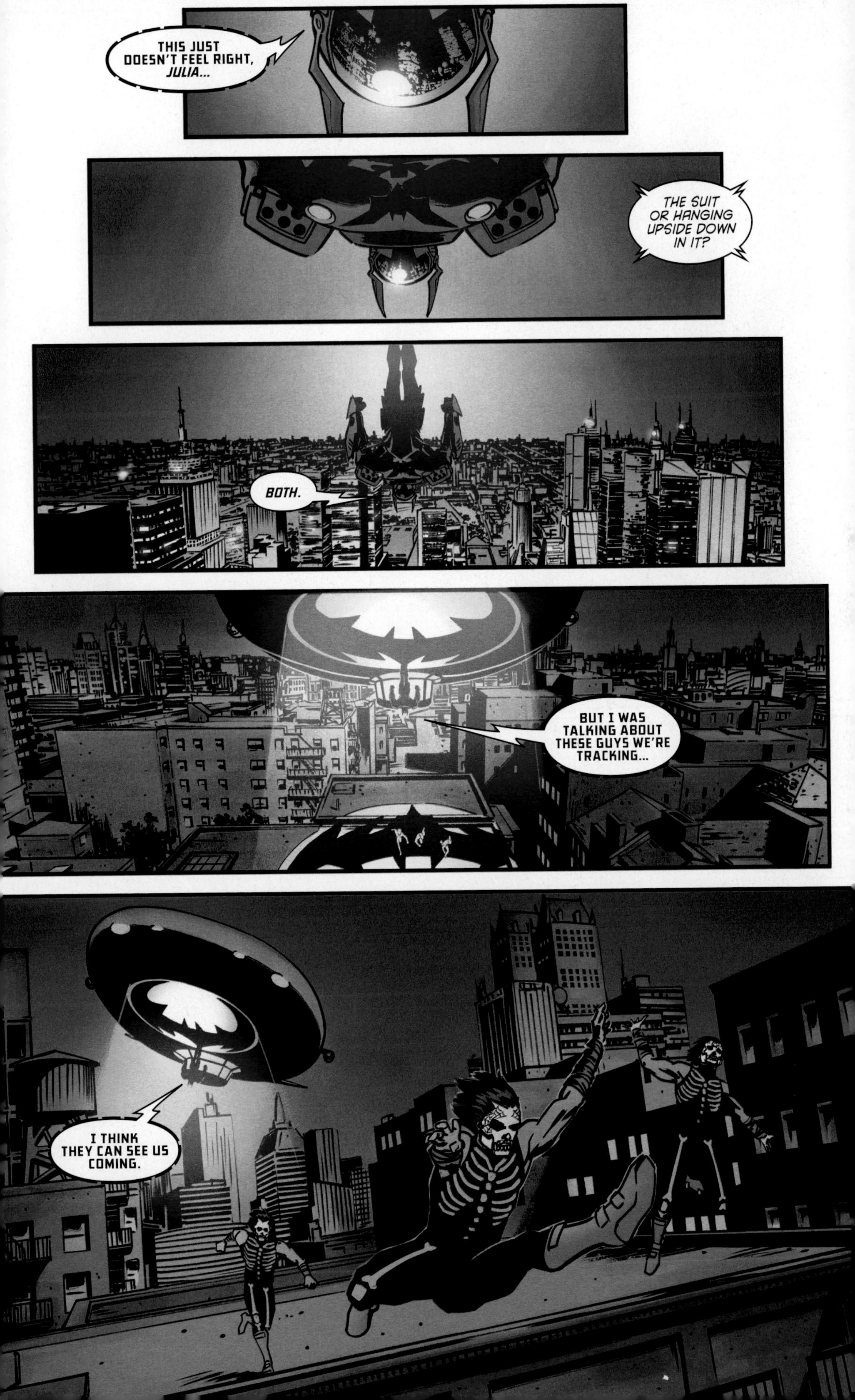
THIS JUST DOESN'T FEEL RIGHT, JULIA...
THE SUIT OR HANGING UPSIDE DOWN IN IT?
BOTH.
BUT I WAS TALKING ABOUT THESE GUYS WE'RE TRACKING...
I THINK THEY CAN SEE US COMING.

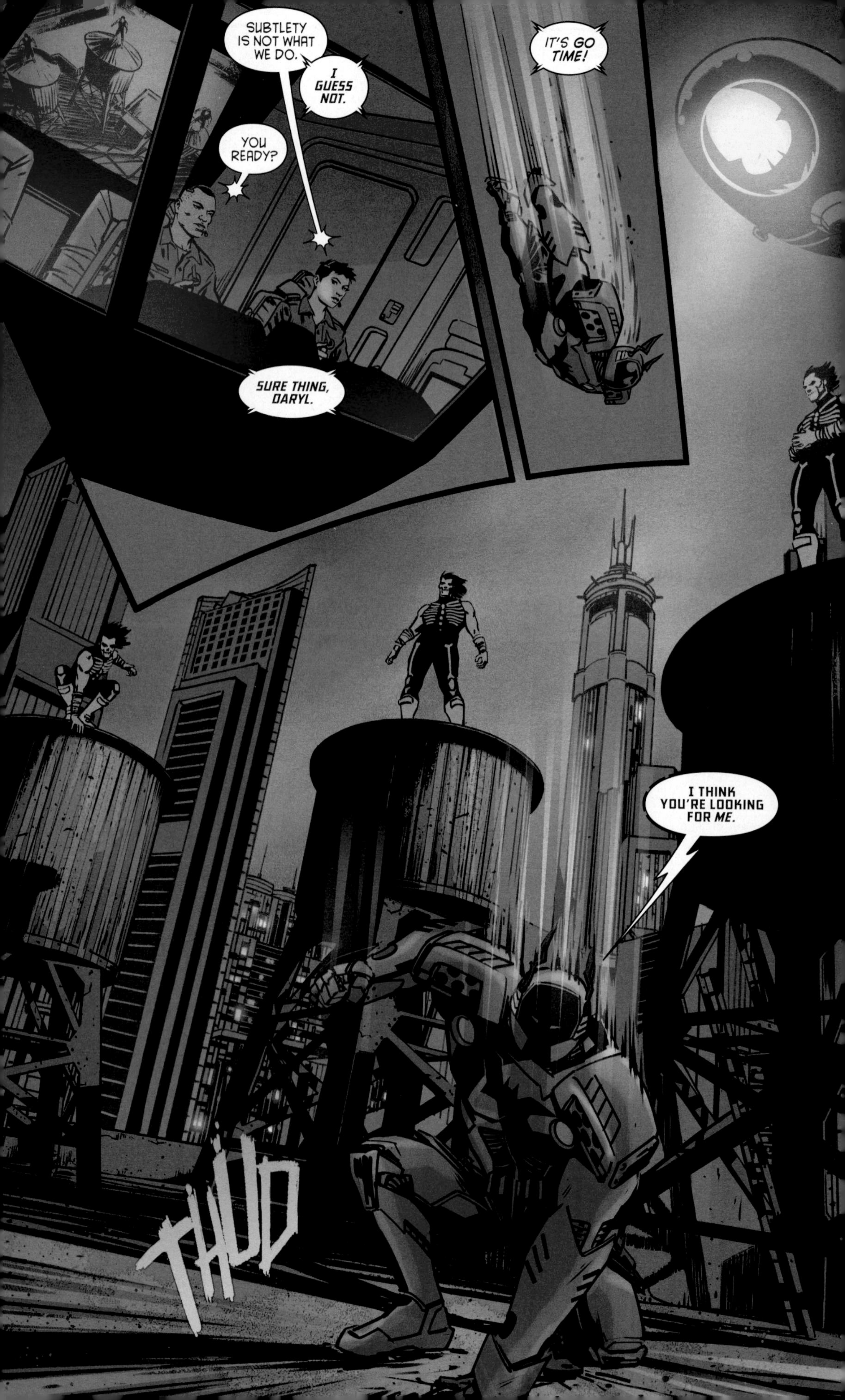
SUBTLETY IS NOT WHAT WE DO.
I GUESS NOT.
YOU READY?
SURE THING, DARYL.
IT'S GO TIME!
I THINK YOU'RE LOOKING FOR ME.
THUD

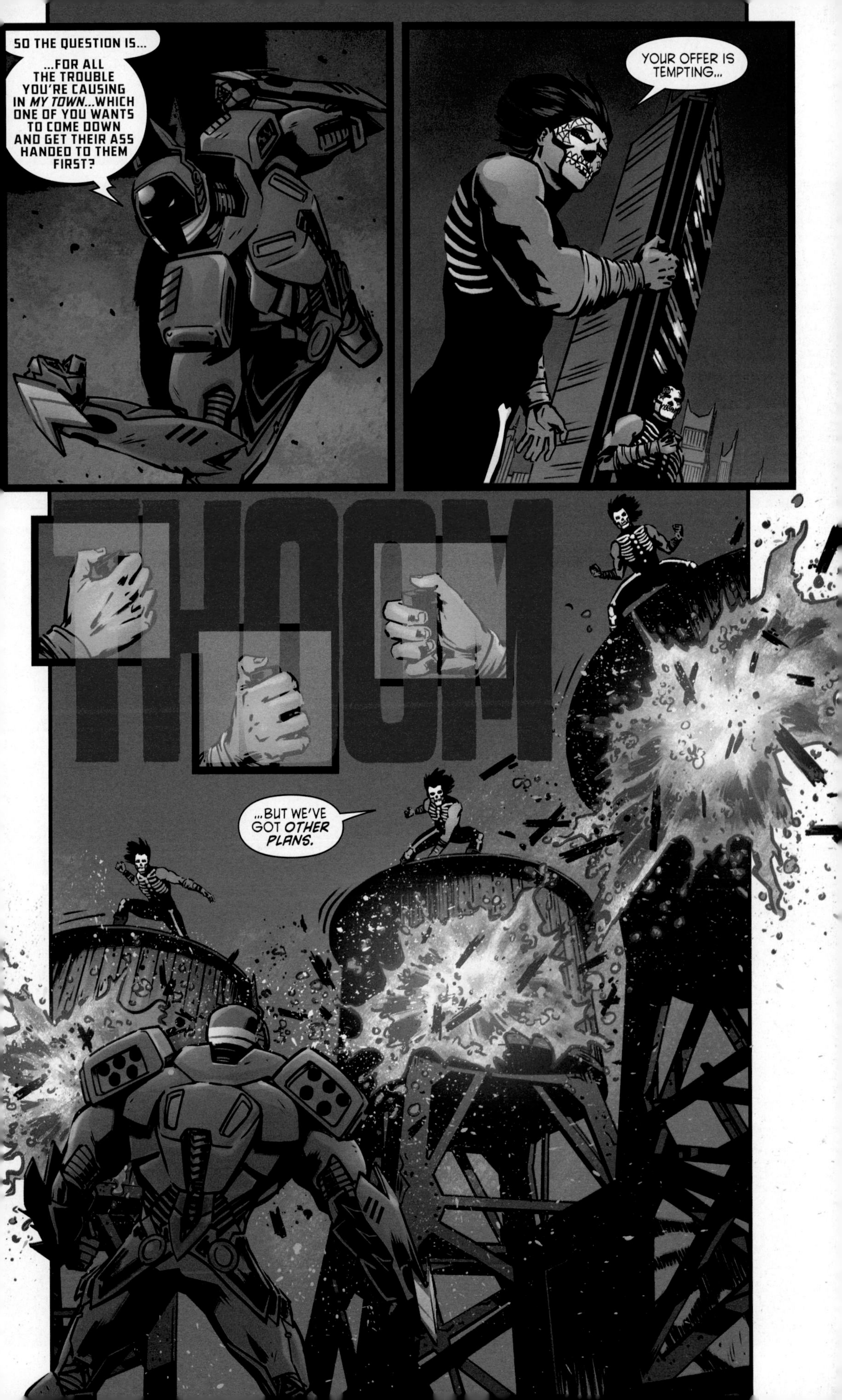
SO THE QUESTION IS...
...FOR ALL THE TROUBLE YOU'RE CAUSING IN *MY TOWN*...WHICH ONE OF YOU WANTS TO COME DOWN AND GET THEIR ASS HANDED TO THEM FIRST?
YOUR OFFER IS TEMPTING...
THOOM
...BUT WE'VE GOT *OTHER PLANS.*

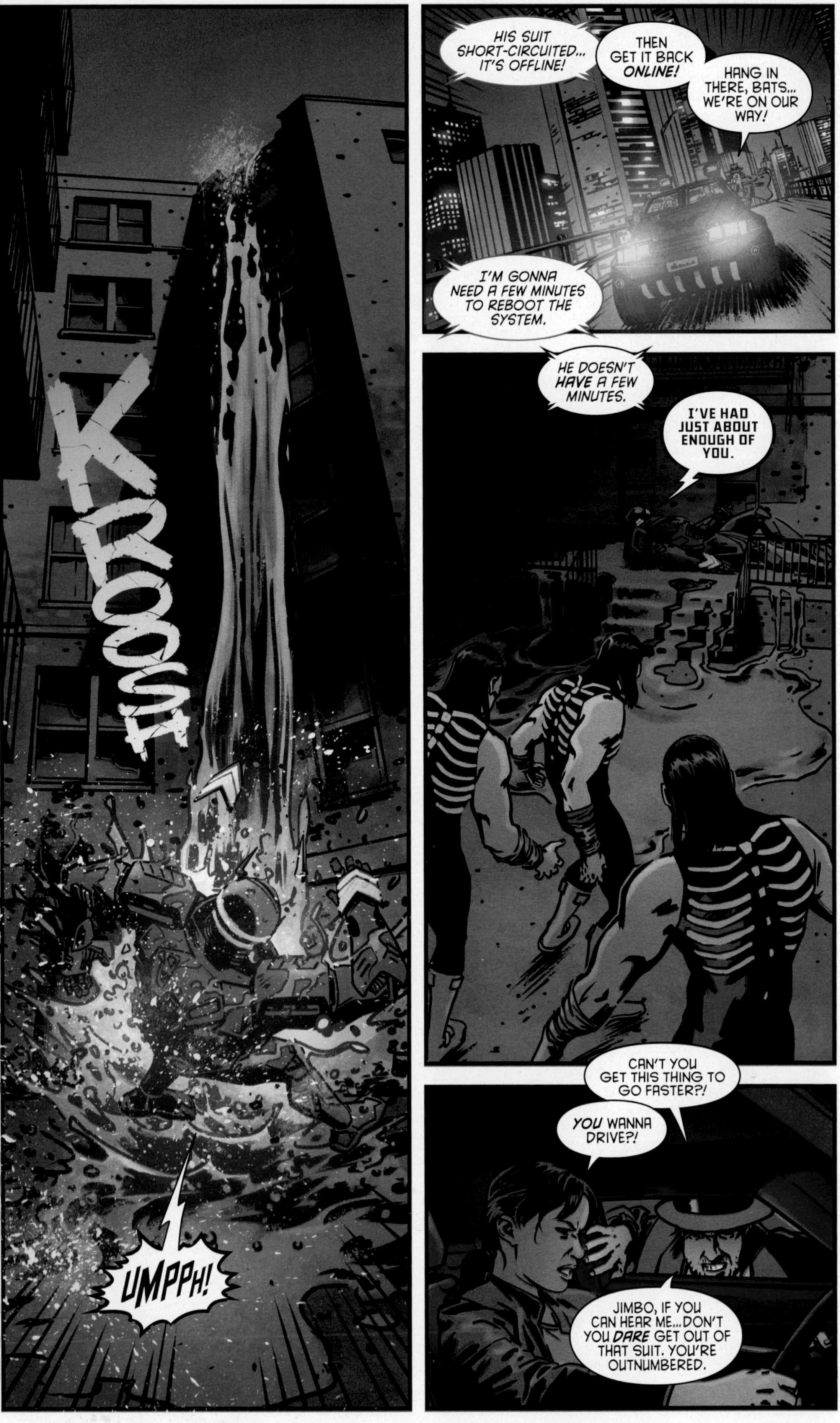
KROOSH
UMPPH!
HIS SUIT SHORT-CIRCUITED... IT'S OFFLINE!
THEN GET IT BACK ONLINE!
HANG IN THERE, BATS... WE'RE ON OUR WAY!
I'M GONNA NEED A FEW MINUTES TO REBOOT THE SYSTEM.
HE DOESN'T HAVE A FEW MINUTES.
I'VE HAD JUST ABOUT ENOUGH OF YOU.
CAN'T YOU GET THIS THING TO GO FASTER?!
YOU WANNA DRIVE?!
JIMBO, IF YOU CAN HEAR ME... DON'T YOU DARE GET OUT OF THAT SUIT. YOU'RE OUTNUMBERED.

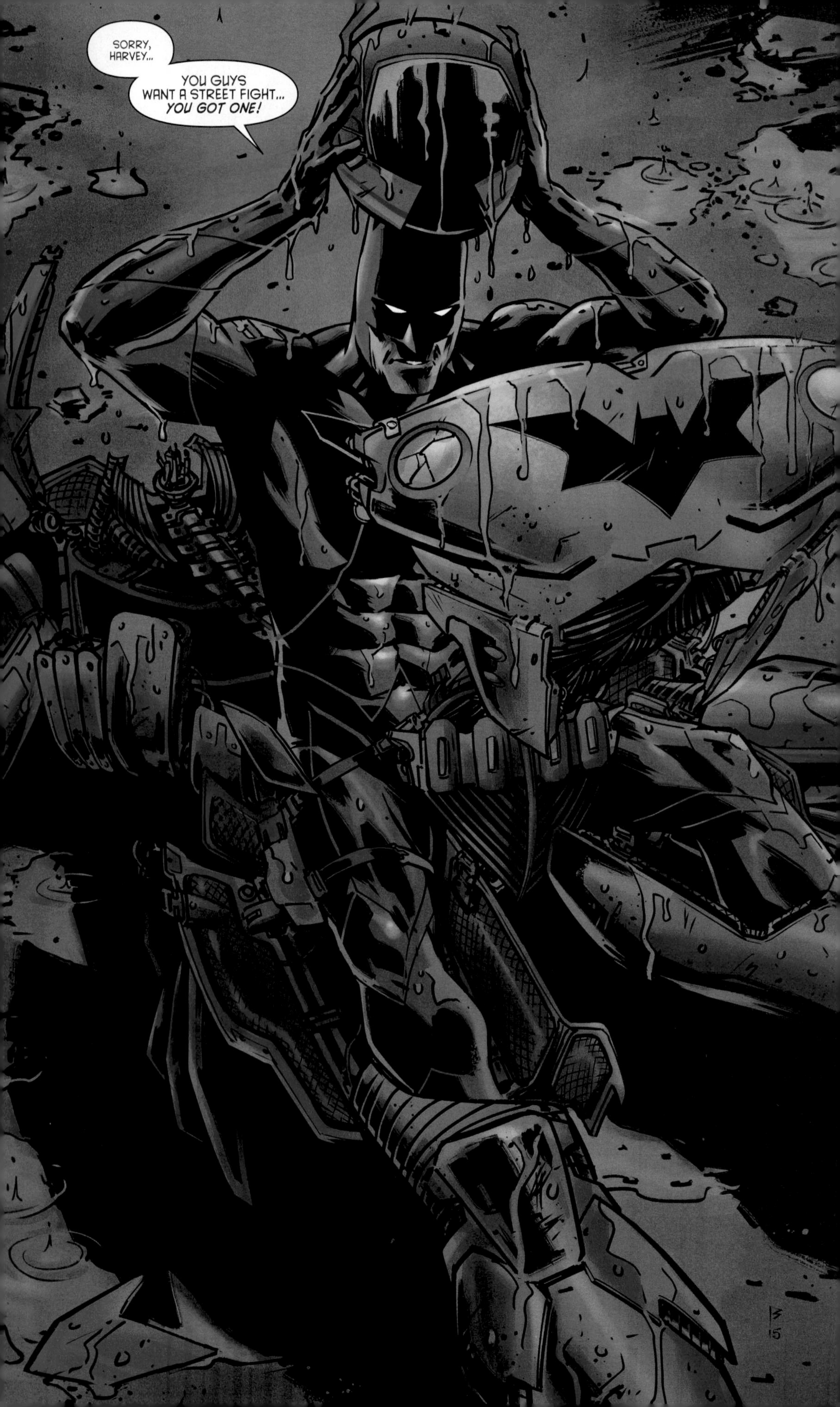
SORRY, HARVEY...
YOU GUYS WANT A STREET FIGHT... YOU GOT ONE!

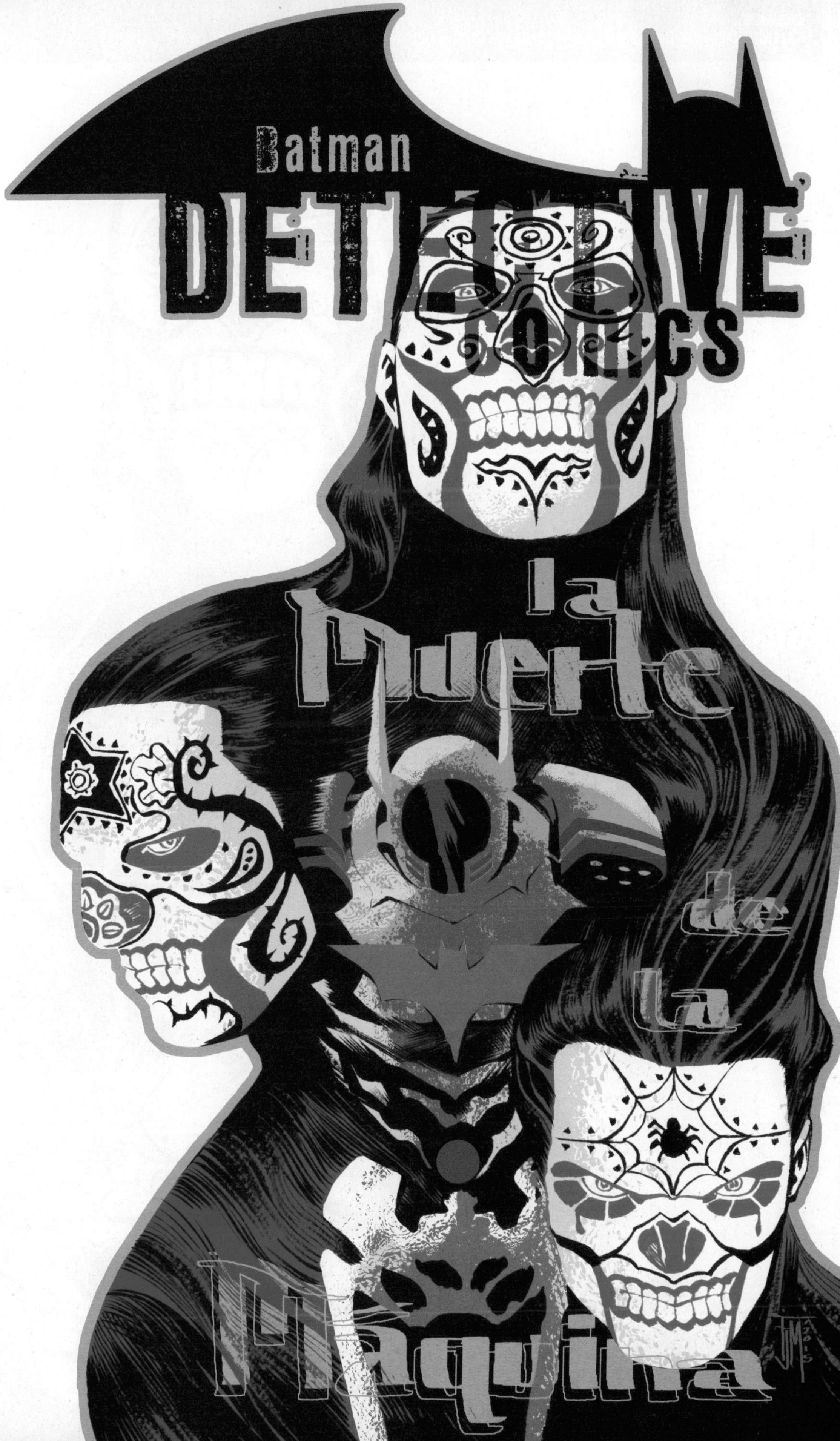
Batman
DETECTIVE
COMICS
la
Muerte
de
la
Maquina

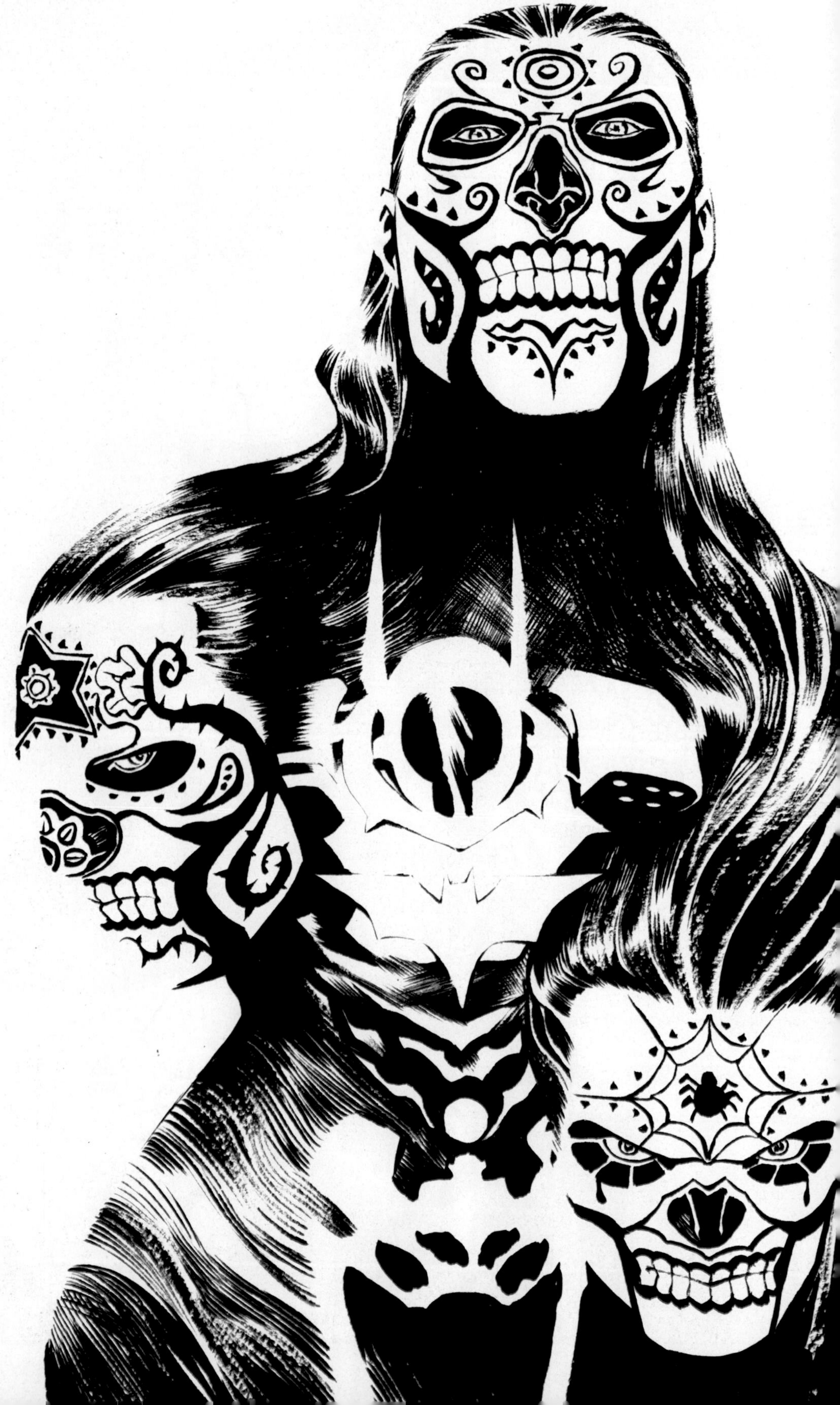

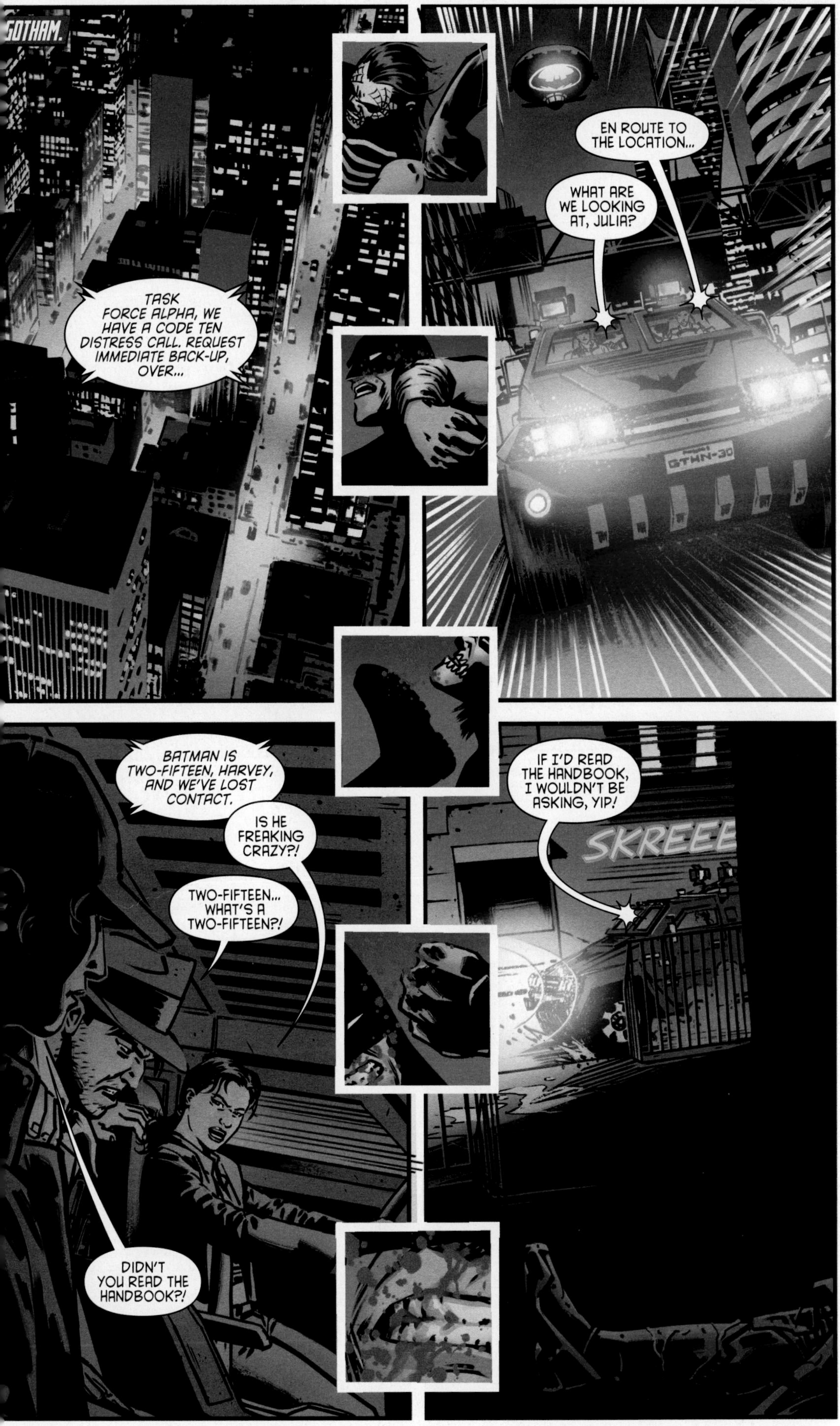
GOTHAM.
TASK FORCE ALPHA, WE HAVE A CODE TEN DISTRESS CALL. REQUEST IMMEDIATE BACK-UP, OVER...
EN ROUTE TO THE LOCATION...
WHAT ARE WE LOOKING AT, JULIA?
GTHN-30
BATMAN IS TWO-FIFTEEN, HARVEY, AND WE'VE LOST CONTACT.
IS HE FREAKING CRAZY?!
TWO-FIFTEEN... WHAT'S A TWO-FIFTEEN?!
DIDN'T YOU READ THE HANDBOOK?!
IF I'D READ THE HANDBOOK, I WOULDN'T BE ASKING, YIP!
SKREEE

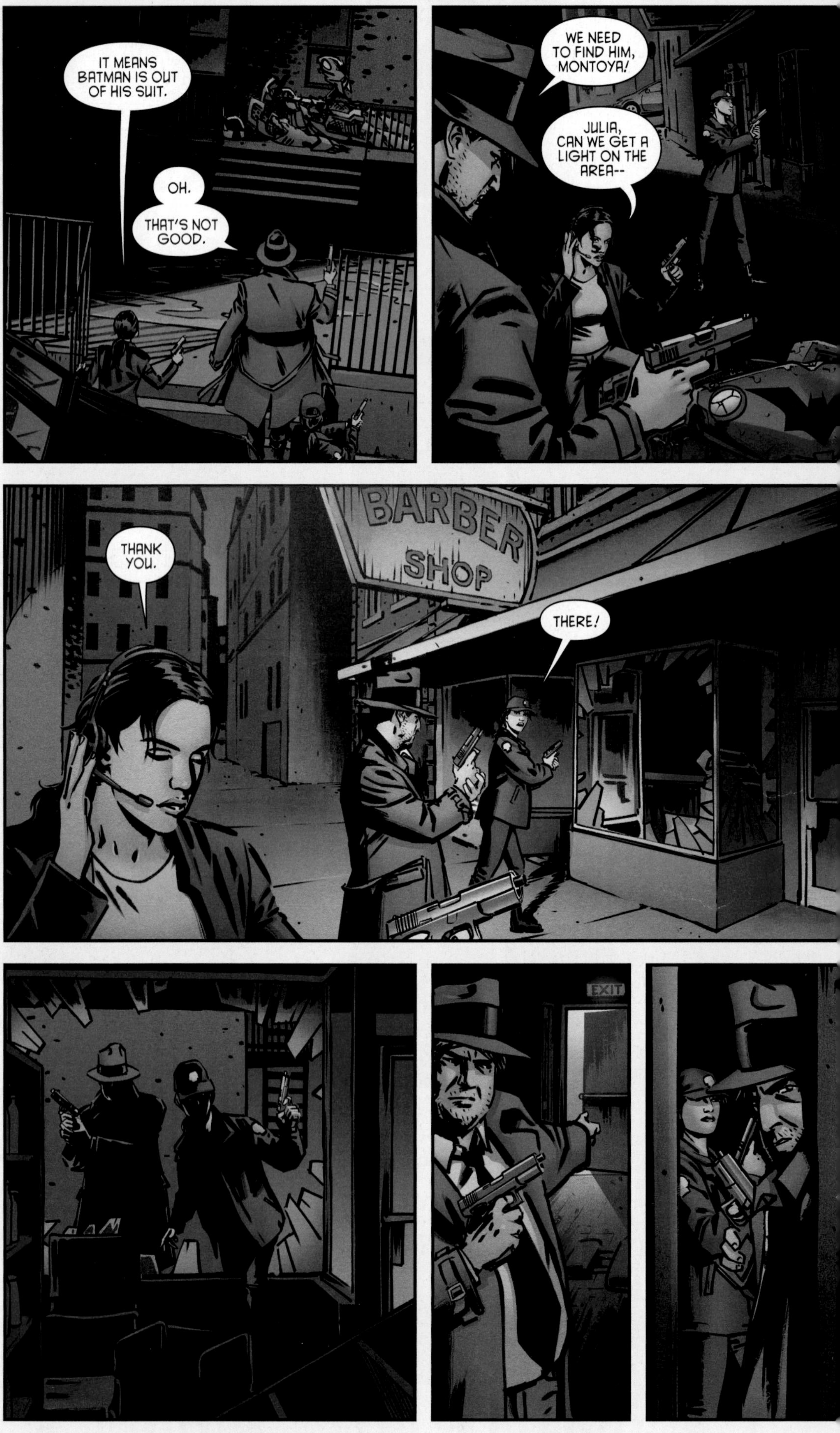
IT MEANS BATMAN IS OUT OF HIS SUIT.
OH.
THAT'S NOT GOOD.
WE NEED TO FIND HIM, MONTOYA!
JULIA, CAN WE GET A LIGHT ON THE AREA--
BARBER SHOP
THANK YOU.
THERE!
EXIT

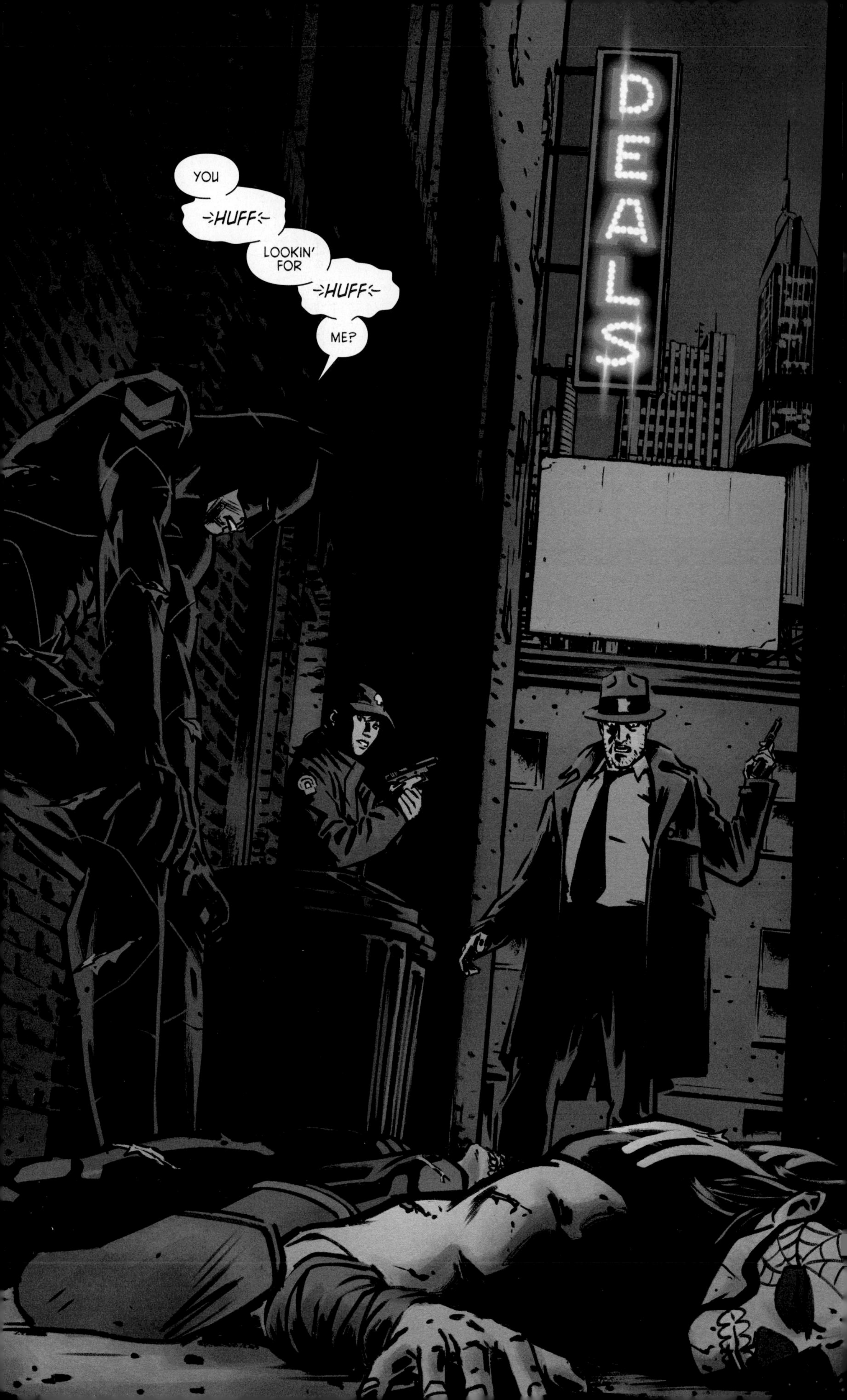
YOU
-HUFF-
LOOKIN' FOR
-HUFF-
ME?
DEALS

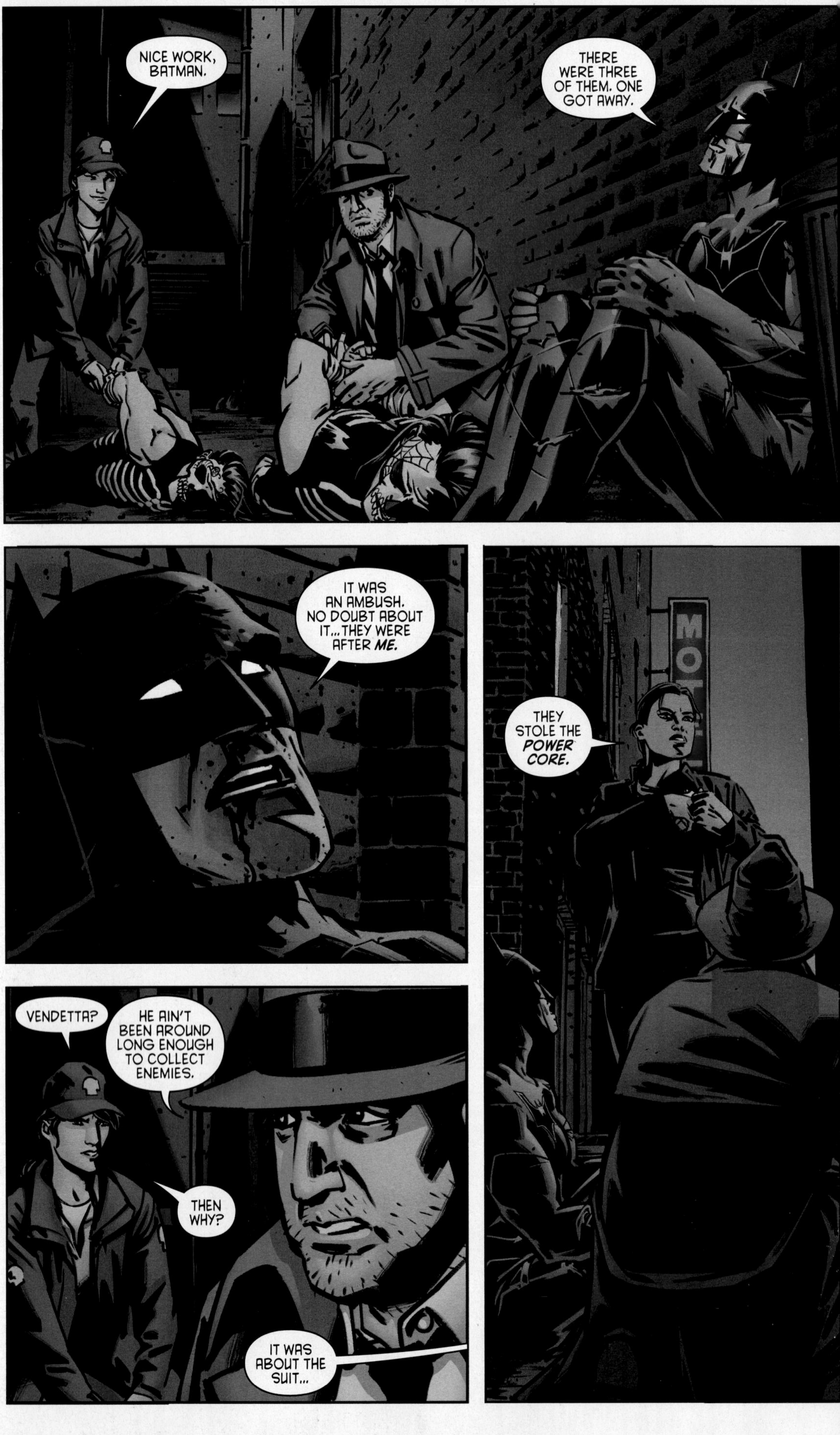
NICE WORK, BATMAN.
THERE WERE THREE OF THEM. ONE GOT AWAY.
IT WAS AN AMBUSH. NO DOUBT ABOUT IT... THEY WERE AFTER *ME*.
VENDETTA?
HE AIN'T BEEN AROUND LONG ENOUGH TO COLLECT ENEMIES.
THEN WHY?
IT WAS ABOUT THE SUIT...
THEY STOLE THE *POWER CORE*.
MOT

IT'S BASICALLY A FUSION REACTOR. THERE ARE ANY NUMBER OF HORRIFYING WAYS YOU COULD MANIPULATE ITS POWER.

WE NEED TO GET THE CORE BACK. IS THERE ANY WAY TO *TRACE* IT?

REALLY.

THERE'S A TRACKING DEVICE IN THE SUIT...BUT NOT IN THE CORE ITSELF.

ACTUALLY... THERE IS A WAY.

WE HAVE ADVANCED THERMAL IMAGING CAPABILITY THAT CAN LOCATE THAT TYPE OF *CONCENTRATED ENERGY*. I CAN REFERENCE IT AGAINST THE DATA WE ALREADY HAVE ON THE ENERGY THAT THE CORE PRODUCED WHILE YOU USED THE SUIT...KIND OF LIKE A *FINGERPRINT*.

OF COURSE, THERE IS A COMPLICATION...BECAUSE THE CORE WOULD NEED TO BE IN USE FOR US TO TRACK IT.

IT'S BASICALLY A FUSION REACTOR. THERE ARE ANY NUMBER OF HORRIFYING WAYS YOU COULD MANIPULATE ITS POWER.

THERE WE GO. AT LEAST WE HAVE SOMEPLACE WE CAN START.

LET'S SEE IF WE CAN MAKE SOME HEADWAY ASAP. TOMORROW THERE WILL BE A *LOT* OF VERY IMPORTANT PEOPLE AT THE CIRCUS, AND WE NEED TO MAKE SURE THEY ARE SAFE.

SPEAKING OF WHICH...

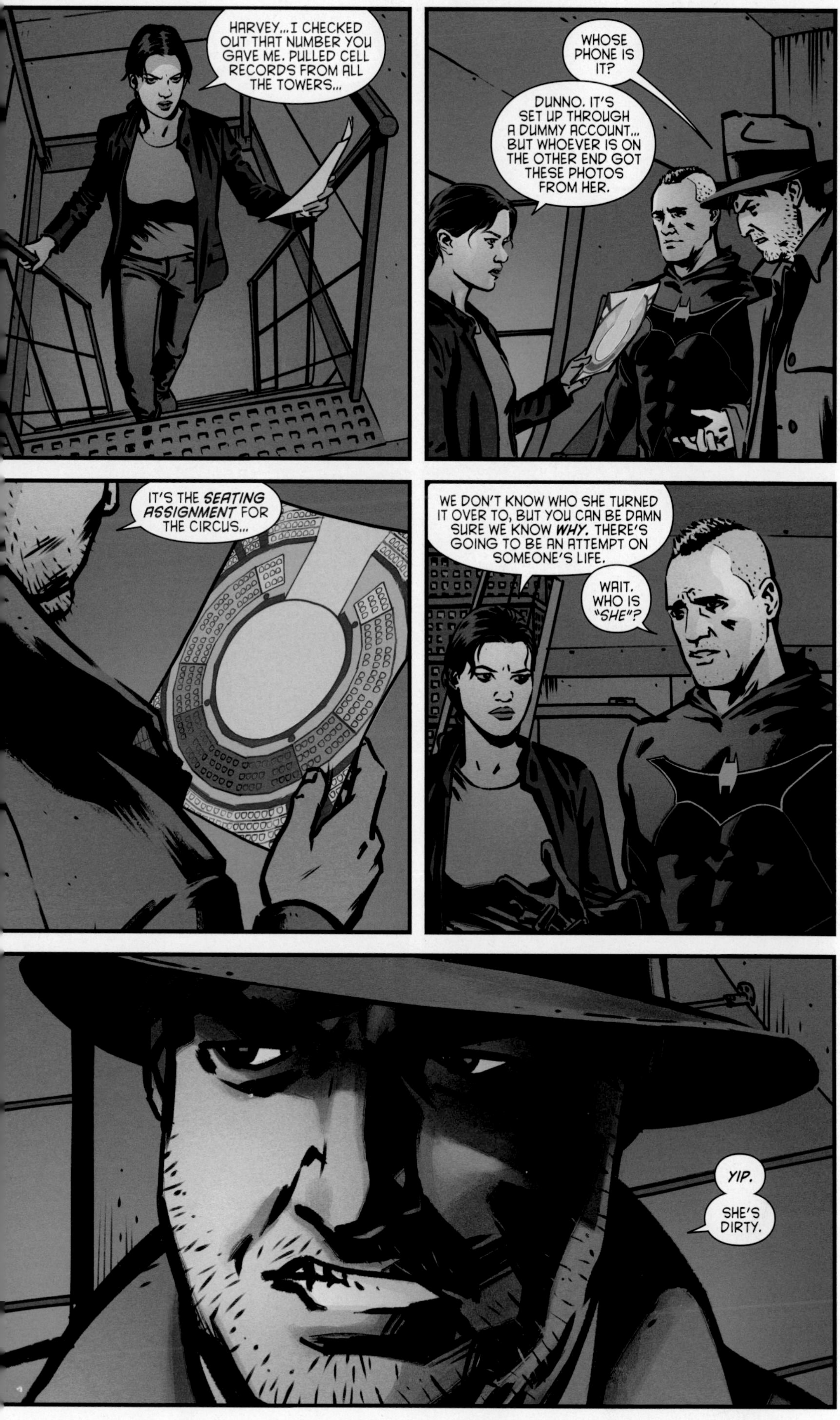
HARVEY... I CHECKED OUT THAT NUMBER YOU GAVE ME. PULLED CELL RECORDS FROM ALL THE TOWERS...
WHOSE PHONE IS IT?
DUNNO. IT'S SET UP THROUGH A DUMMY ACCOUNT... BUT WHOEVER IS ON THE OTHER END GOT THESE PHOTOS FROM HER.
IT'S THE SEATING ASSIGNMENT FOR THE CIRCUS...
WE DON'T KNOW WHO SHE TURNED IT OVER TO, BUT YOU CAN BE DAMN SURE WE KNOW WHY. THERE'S GOING TO BE AN ATTEMPT ON SOMEONE'S LIFE.
WAIT. WHO IS "SHE"?
YIP.
SHE'S DIRTY.

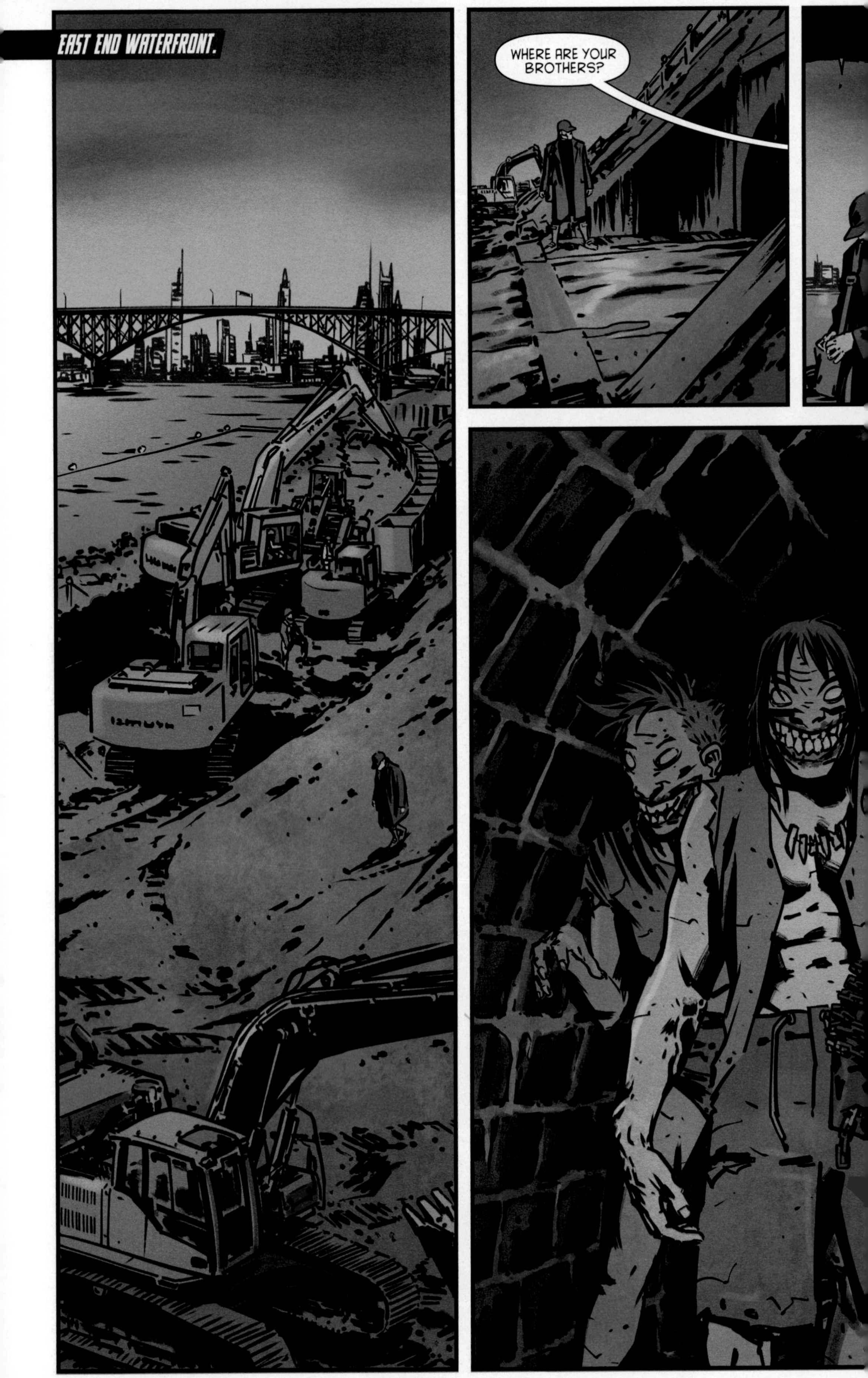
EAST END WATERFRONT.
WHERE ARE YOUR BROTHERS?

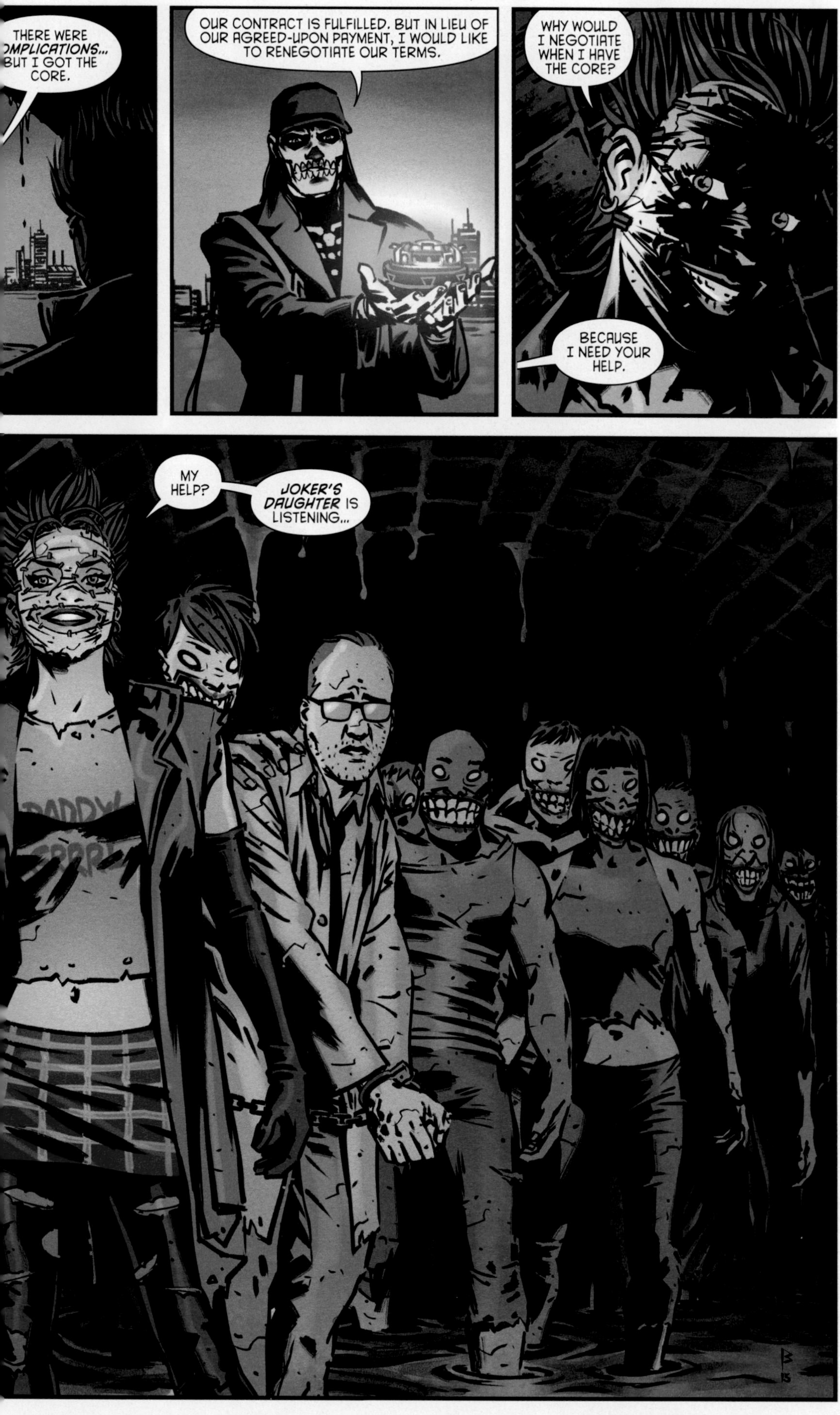
THERE WERE
OMPLICATIONS...
BUT I GOT THE
CORE.
OUR CONTRACT IS FULFILLED. BUT IN LIEU OF OUR AGREED-UPON PAYMENT, I WOULD LIKE TO RENEGOTIATE OUR TERMS.
WHY WOULD I NEGOTIATE WHEN I HAVE THE CORE?
BECAUSE I NEED YOUR HELP.
MY HELP?
JOKER'S DAUGHTER IS LISTENING...

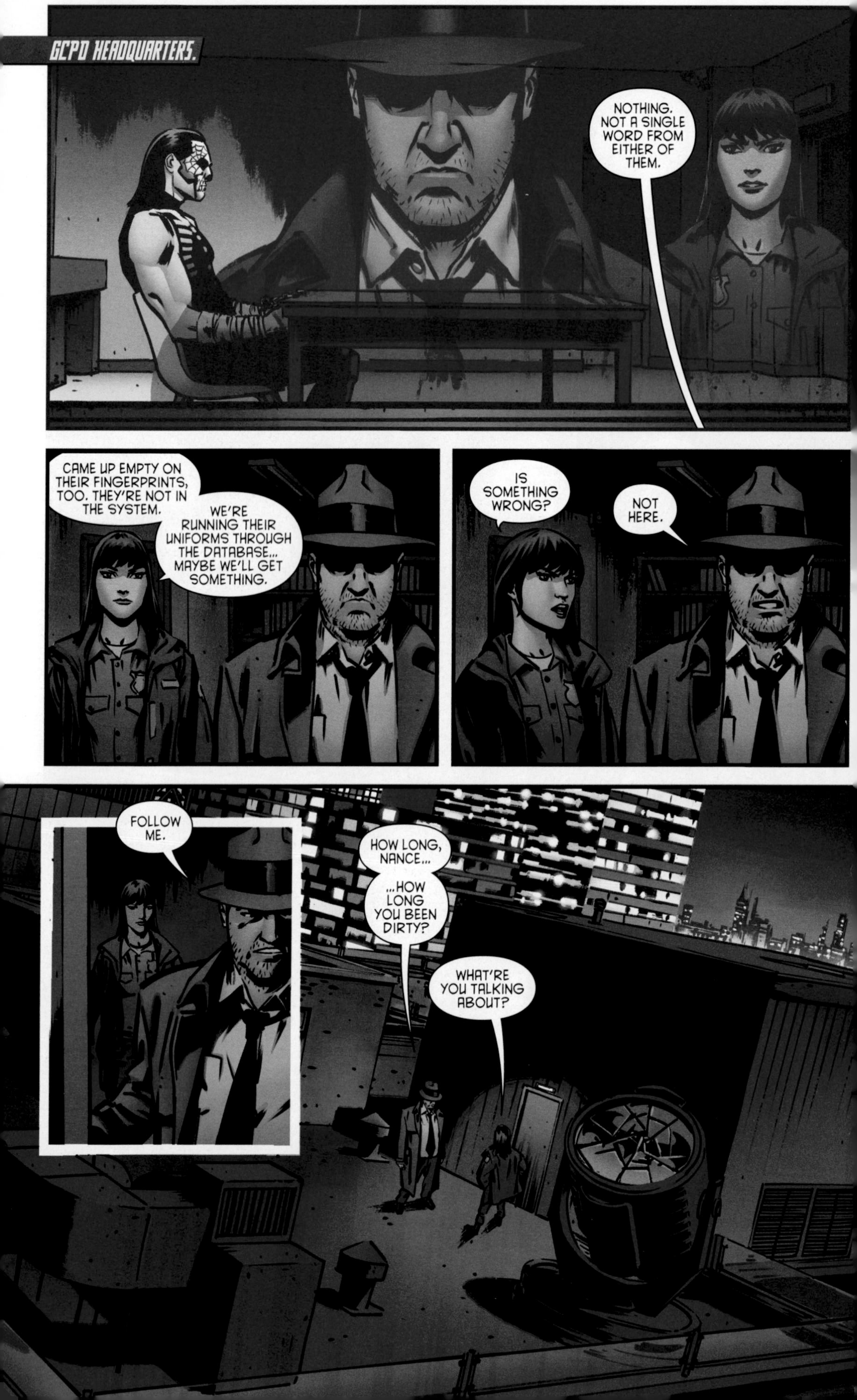
GCPD HEADQUARTERS.
NOTHING. NOT A SINGLE WORD FROM EITHER OF THEM.
CAME UP EMPTY ON THEIR FINGERPRINTS, TOO. THEY'RE NOT IN THE SYSTEM.
WE'RE RUNNING THEIR UNIFORMS THROUGH THE DATABASE... MAYBE WE'LL GET SOMETHING.
IS SOMETHING WRONG?
NOT HERE.
FOLLOW ME.
HOW LONG, NANCE...
...HOW LONG YOU BEEN DIRTY?
WHAT'RE YOU TALKING ABOUT?

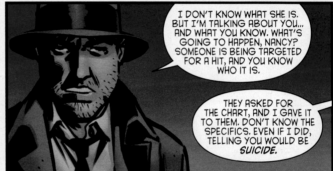

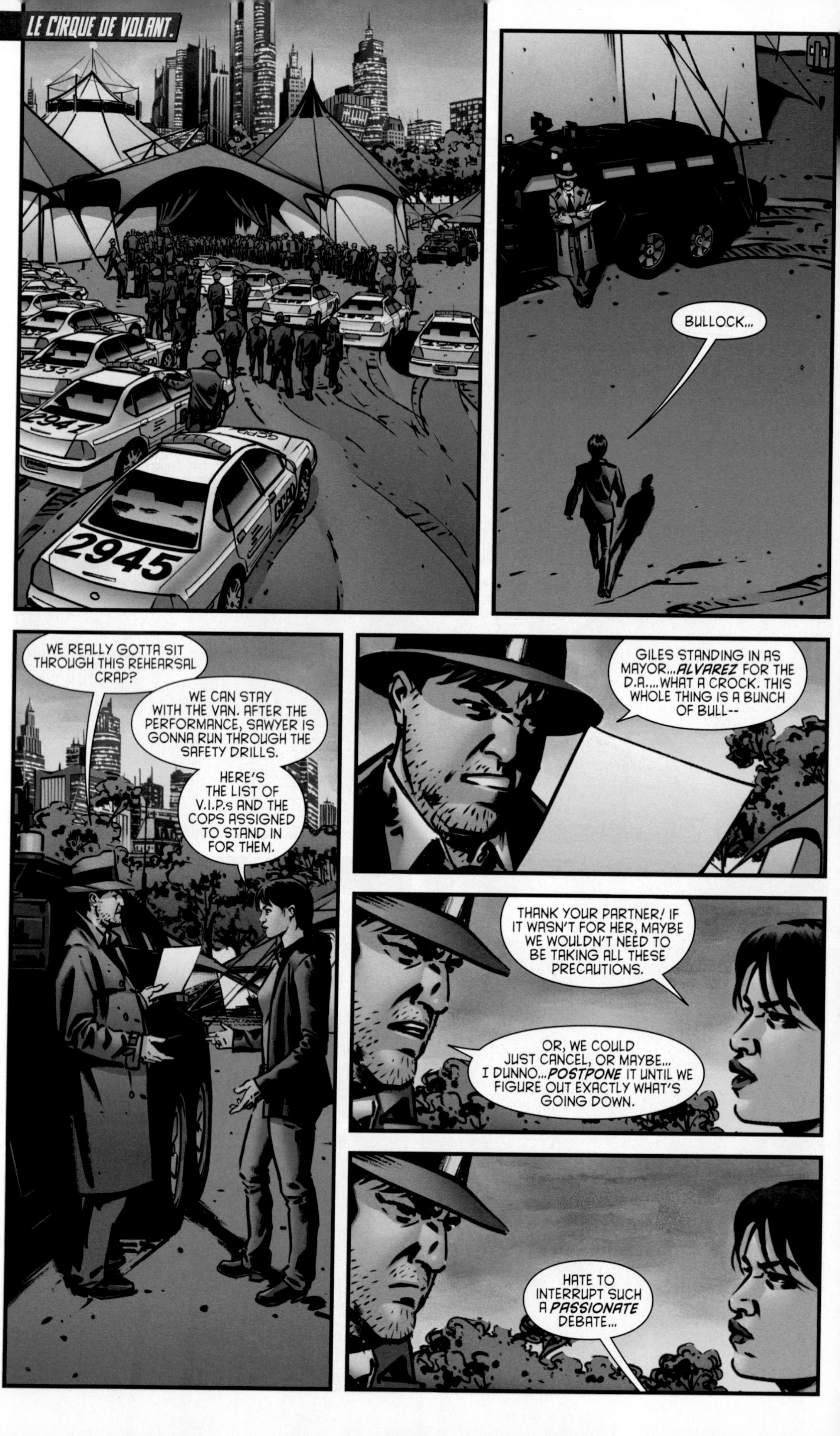
LE CIRQUE DE VOLANT.
BULLOCK...
WE REALLY GOTTA SIT THROUGH THIS REHEARSAL CRAP?
WE CAN STAY WITH THE VAN. AFTER THE PERFORMANCE, SAWYER IS GONNA RUN THROUGH THE SAFETY DRILLS.
HERE'S THE LIST OF V.I.P.s AND THE COPS ASSIGNED TO STAND IN FOR THEM.
GILES STANDING IN AS MAYOR...*ALVAREZ* FOR THE D.A....WHAT A CROCK. THIS WHOLE THING IS A BUNCH OF BULL--
THANK YOUR PARTNER! IF IT WASN'T FOR HER, MAYBE WE WOULDN'T NEED TO BE TAKING ALL THESE PRECAUTIONS.
OR, WE COULD JUST CANCEL, OR MAYBE... I DUNNO...*POSTPONE* IT UNTIL WE FIGURE OUT EXACTLY WHAT'S GOING DOWN.
HATE TO INTERRUPT SUCH A *PASSIONATE* DEBATE...

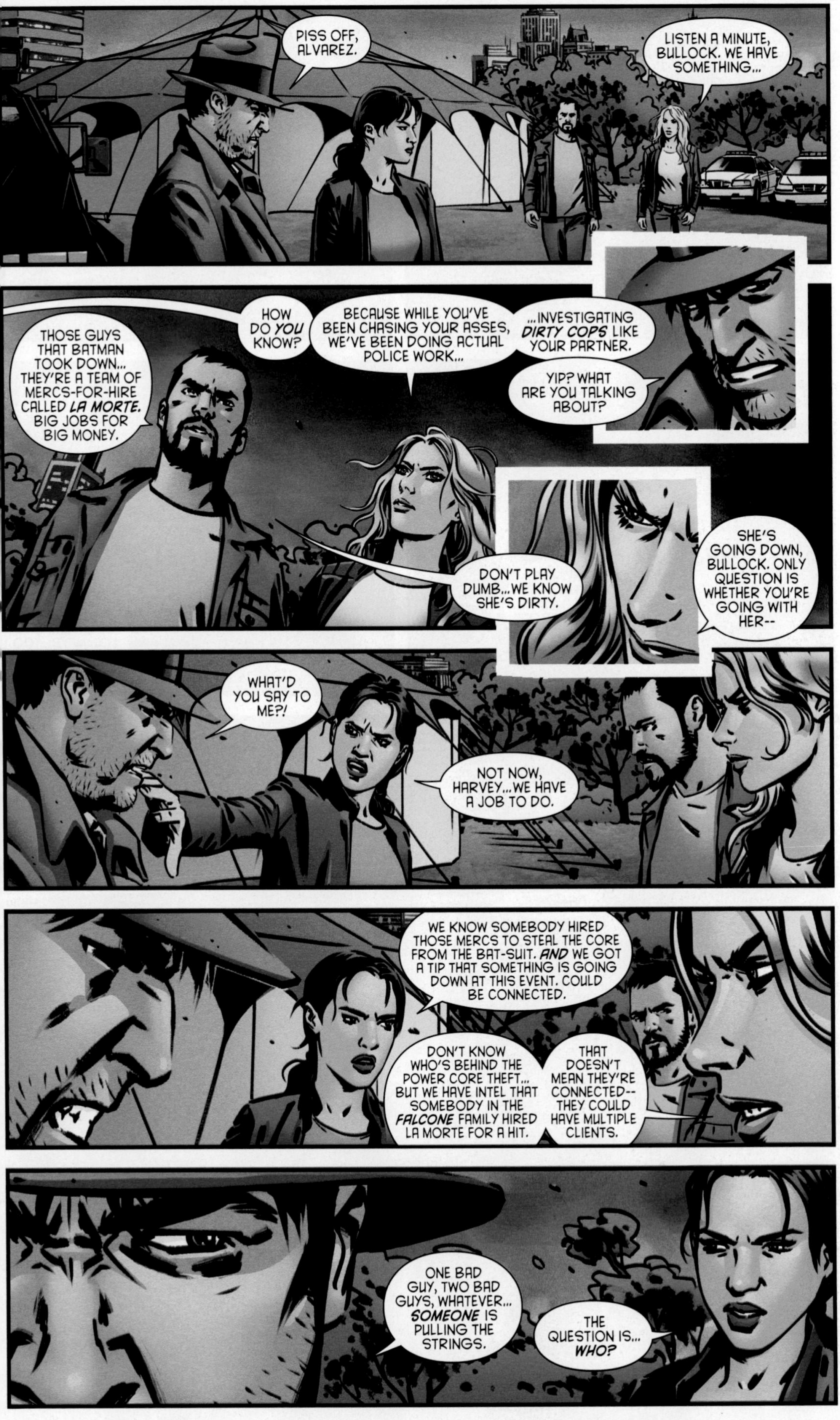
PISS OFF, ALVAREZ.
LISTEN A MINUTE, BULLOCK. WE HAVE SOMETHING...
THOSE GUYS THAT BATMAN TOOK DOWN... THEY'RE A TEAM OF MERCS-FOR-HIRE CALLED *LA MORTE.* BIG JOBS FOR BIG MONEY.
HOW DO *YOU* KNOW?
BECAUSE WHILE YOU'VE BEEN CHASING YOUR ASSES, WE'VE BEEN DOING ACTUAL POLICE WORK...
...INVESTIGATING *DIRTY COPS* LIKE YOUR PARTNER.
YIP? WHAT ARE YOU TALKING ABOUT?
DON'T PLAY DUMB...WE KNOW SHE'S DIRTY.
SHE'S GOING DOWN, BULLOCK. ONLY QUESTION IS WHETHER YOU'RE GOING WITH HER--
WHAT'D YOU SAY TO ME?!
NOT NOW, HARVEY...WE HAVE A JOB TO DO.
WE KNOW SOMEBODY HIRED THOSE MERCS TO STEAL THE CORE FROM THE BAT-SUIT. *AND* WE GOT A TIP THAT SOMETHING IS GOING DOWN AT THIS EVENT. COULD BE CONNECTED.
DON'T KNOW WHO'S BEHIND THE POWER CORE THEFT... BUT WE HAVE INTEL THAT SOMEBODY IN THE *FALCONE* FAMILY HIRED LA MORTE FOR A HIT.
THAT DOESN'T MEAN THEY'RE CONNECTED-- THEY COULD HAVE MULTIPLE CLIENTS.
ONE BAD GUY, TWO BAD GUYS, WHATEVER... *SOMEONE* IS PULLING THE STRINGS.
THE QUESTION IS... *WHO?*

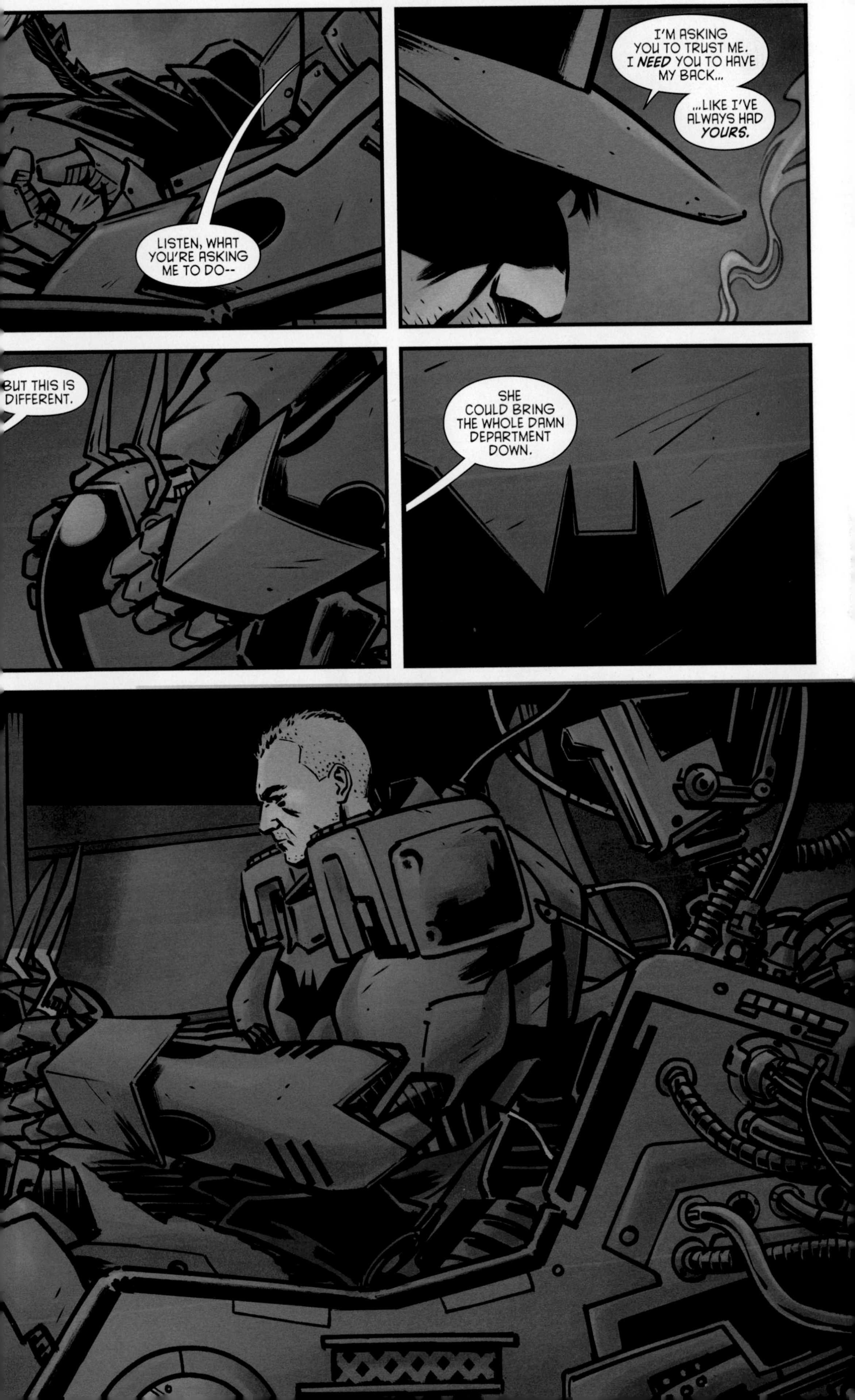

LISTEN, WHAT YOU'RE ASKING ME TO DO--
I'M ASKING YOU TO TRUST ME. I NEED YOU TO HAVE MY BACK...
...LIKE I'VE ALWAYS HAD YOURS.
BUT THIS IS DIFFERENT.
SHE COULD BRING THE WHOLE DAMN DEPARTMENT DOWN.

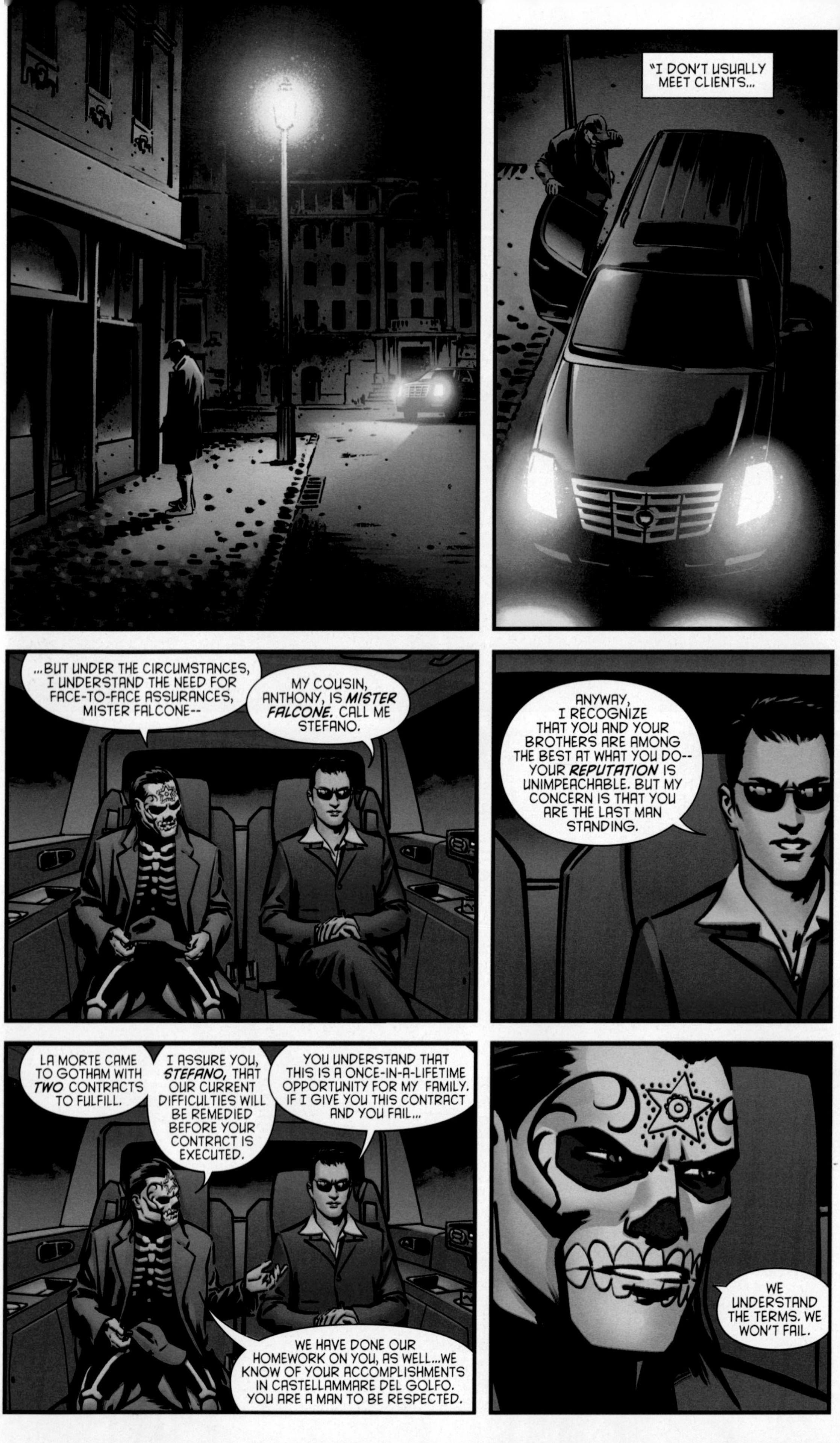

"I DON'T USUALLY MEET CLIENTS...
...BUT UNDER THE CIRCUMSTANCES, I UNDERSTAND THE NEED FOR FACE-TO-FACE ASSURANCES, MISTER FALCONE--
MY COUSIN, ANTHONY, IS MISTER FALCONE. CALL ME STEFANO.
ANYWAY, I RECOGNIZE THAT YOU AND YOUR BROTHERS ARE AMONG THE BEST AT WHAT YOU DO-- YOUR REPUTATION IS UNIMPEACHABLE. BUT MY CONCERN IS THAT YOU ARE THE LAST MAN STANDING.
LA MORTE CAME TO GOTHAM WITH TWO CONTRACTS TO FULFILL.
I ASSURE YOU, STEFANO, THAT OUR CURRENT DIFFICULTIES WILL BE REMEDIED BEFORE YOUR CONTRACT IS EXECUTED.
YOU UNDERSTAND THAT THIS IS A ONCE-IN-A-LIFETIME OPPORTUNITY FOR MY FAMILY. IF I GIVE YOU THIS CONTRACT AND YOU FAIL...
WE HAVE DONE OUR HOMEWORK ON YOU, AS WELL...WE KNOW OF YOUR ACCOMPLISHMENTS IN CASTELLAMMARE DEL GOLFO. YOU ARE A MAN TO BE RESPECTED.
WE UNDERSTAND THE TERMS. WE WON'T FAIL.

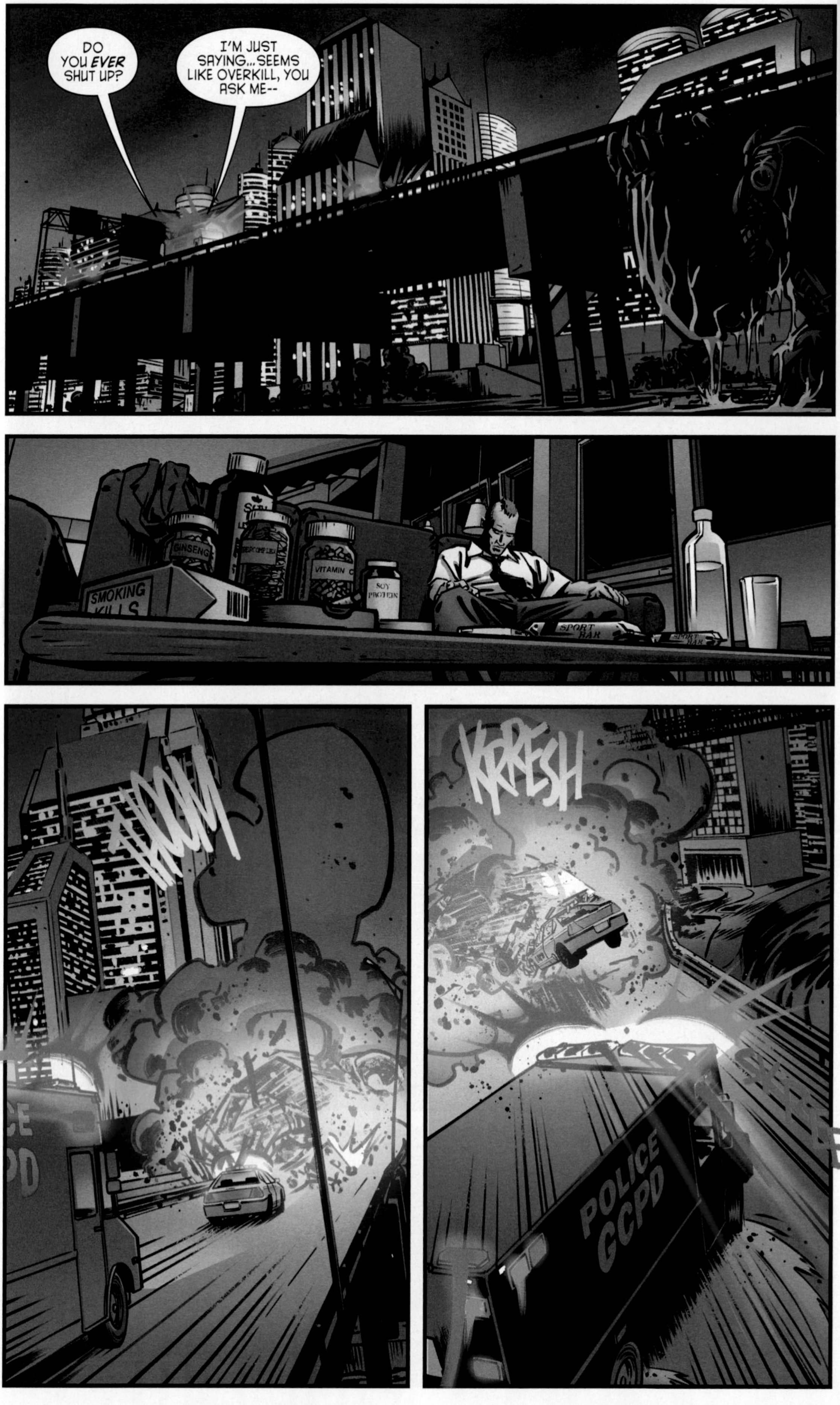
DO YOU *EVER* SHUT UP?
I'M JUST SAYING... SEEMS LIKE OVERKILL, YOU ASK ME--
GINSENG
SMOKING KILLS
VITAMIN C
SOY PROTEIN
SPORT BAR
SPORT BAR
KRRESH
POLICE GCPD

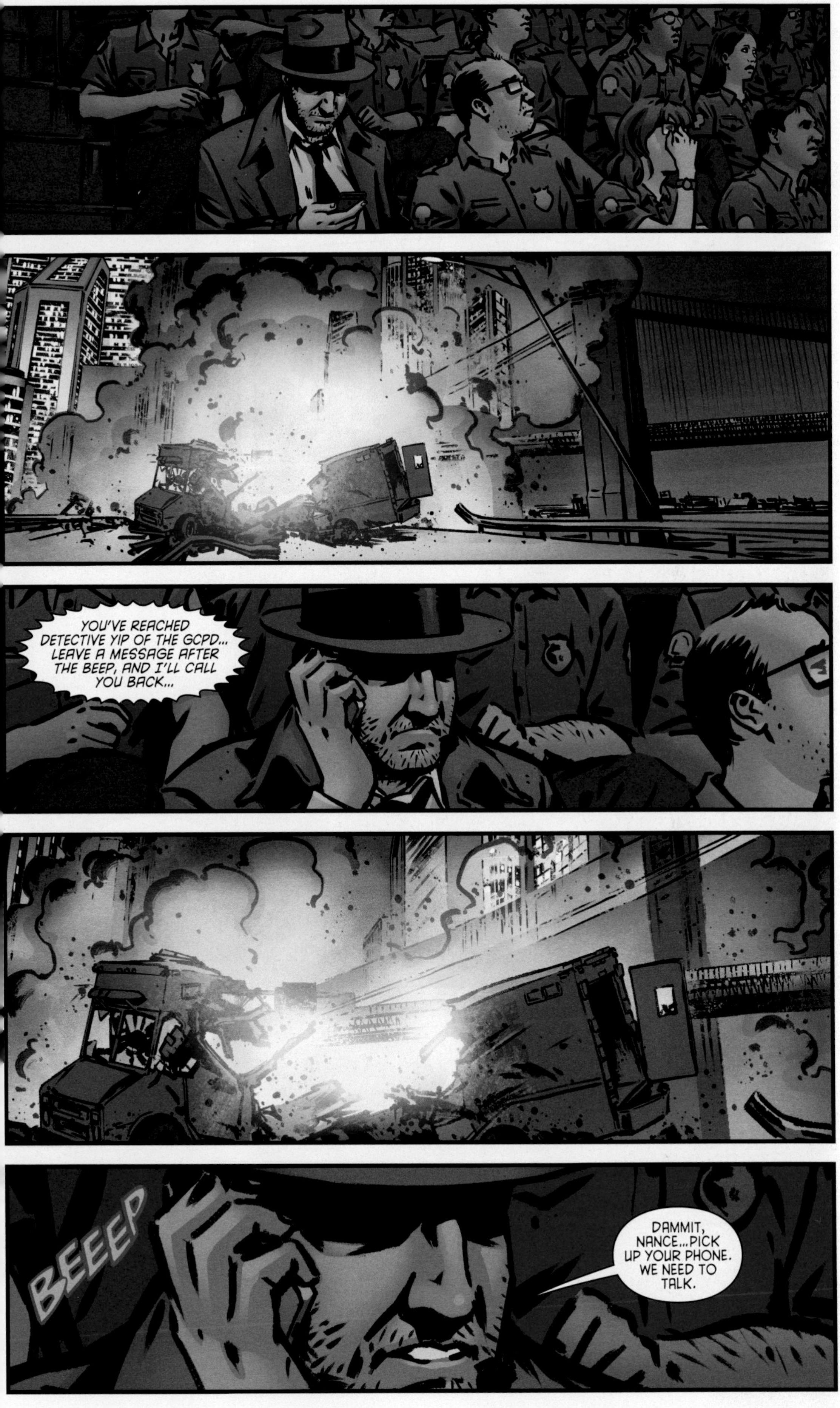
YOU'VE REACHED DETECTIVE YIP OF THE GCPD... LEAVE A MESSAGE AFTER THE BEEP, AND I'LL CALL YOU BACK...
BEEEP
DAMMIT, NANCE...PICK UP YOUR PHONE. WE NEED TO TALK.

YOU READY?

DOES IT MATTER?

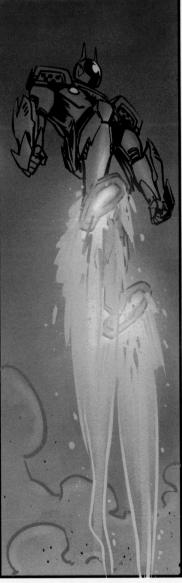

WHEN YOU LAND, THE TARGET SHOULD BE RIGHT THERE AT YOUR TWELVE.

YOU'RE RIGHT ON TOP OF IT.

DO YOU HAVE A VISUAL?

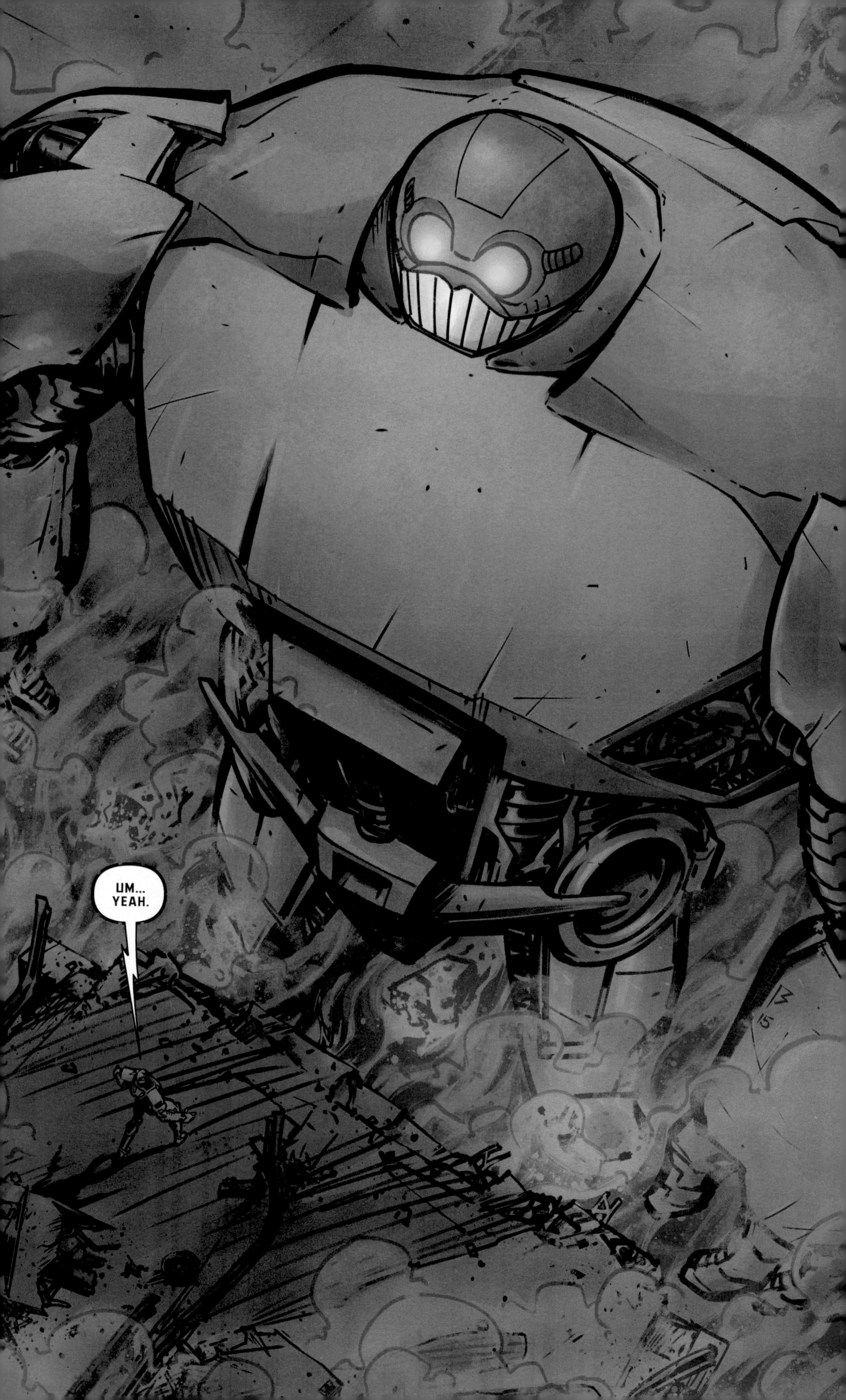
UM... YEAH.

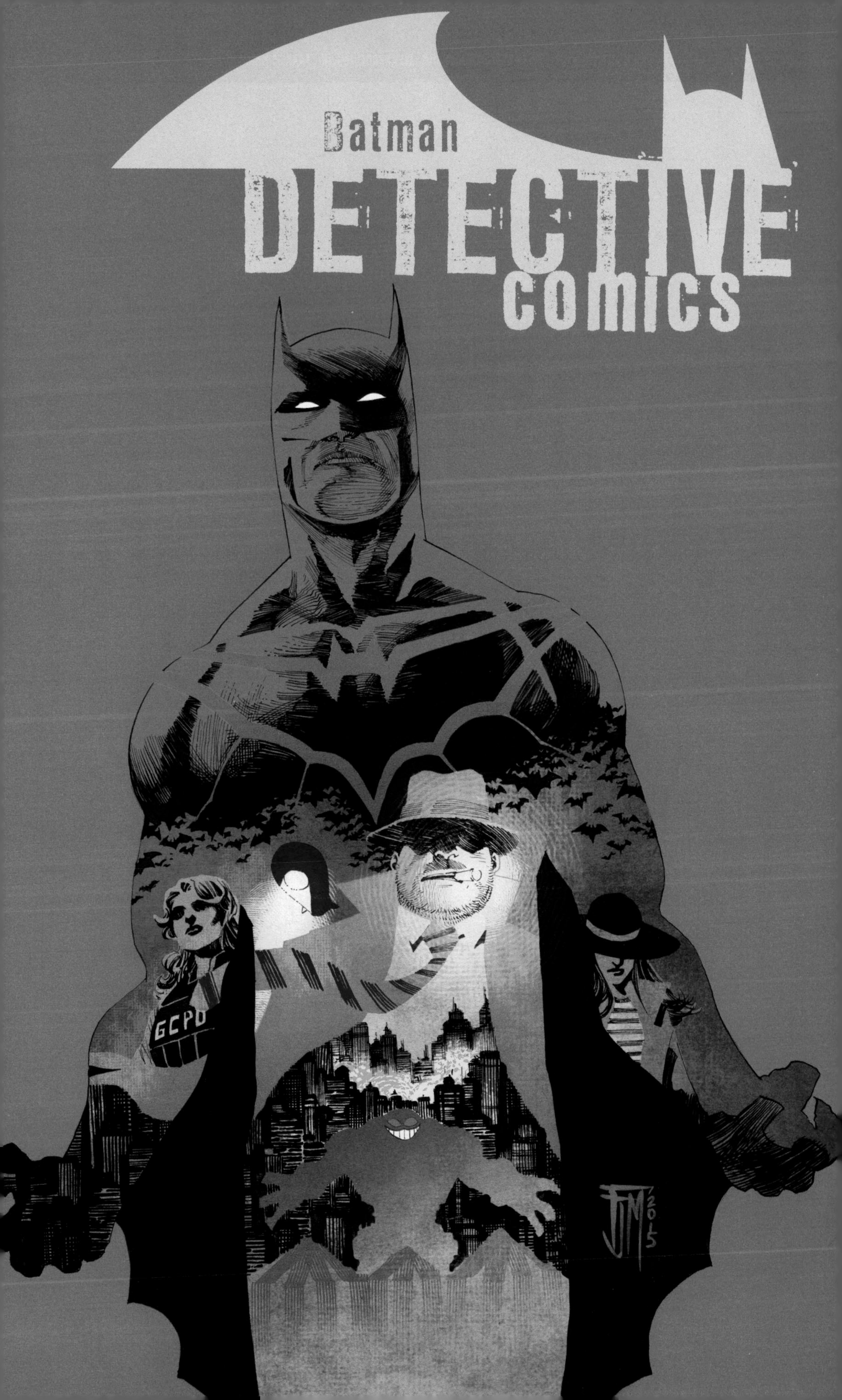

Batman
DETECTIVE
COMICS
GCPD
FJM 2015

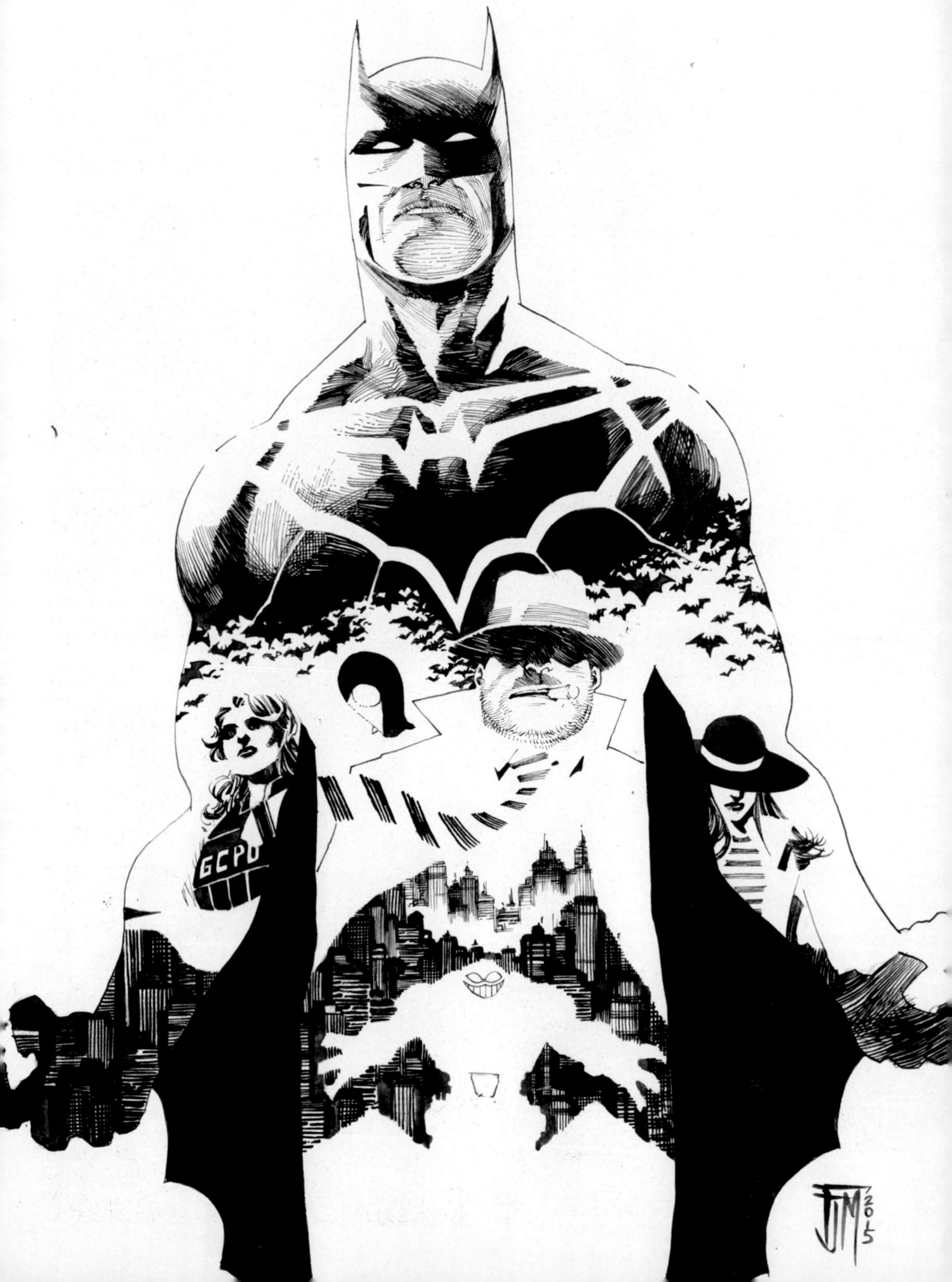
GCPD

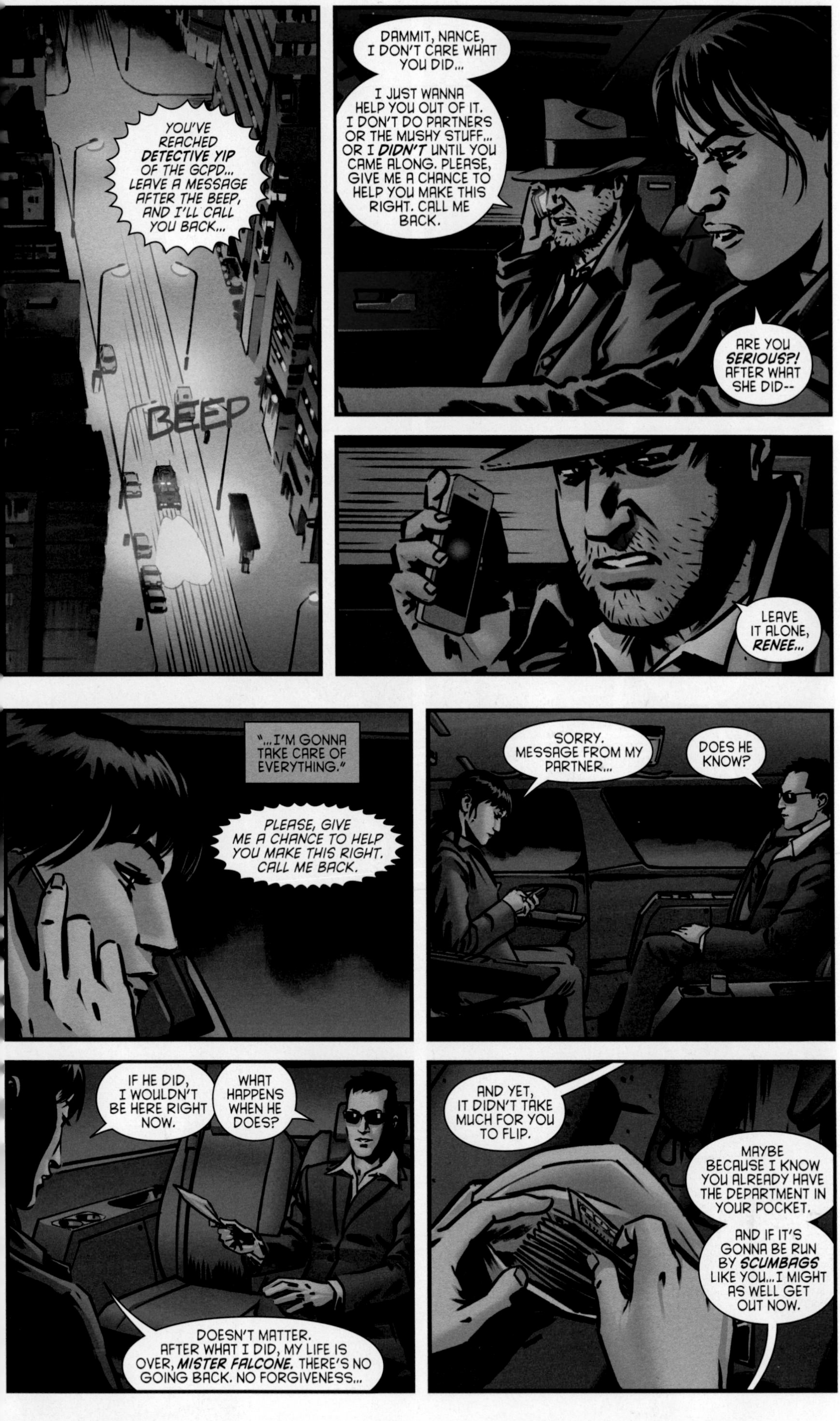
YOU'VE REACHED DETECTIVE YIP OF THE GCPD... LEAVE A MESSAGE AFTER THE BEEP, AND I'LL CALL YOU BACK...
BEEP
DAMMIT, NANCE, I DON'T CARE WHAT YOU DID...
I JUST WANNA HELP YOU OUT OF IT. I DON'T DO PARTNERS OR THE MUSHY STUFF... OR I DIDN'T UNTIL YOU CAME ALONG. PLEASE, GIVE ME A CHANCE TO HELP YOU MAKE THIS RIGHT. CALL ME BACK.
ARE YOU SERIOUS?! AFTER WHAT SHE DID--
LEAVE IT ALONE, RENEE...
"...I'M GONNA TAKE CARE OF EVERYTHING."
PLEASE, GIVE ME A CHANCE TO HELP YOU MAKE THIS RIGHT. CALL ME BACK.
SORRY. MESSAGE FROM MY PARTNER...
DOES HE KNOW?
IF HE DID, I WOULDN'T BE HERE RIGHT NOW.
WHAT HAPPENS WHEN HE DOES?
DOESN'T MATTER. AFTER WHAT I DID, MY LIFE IS OVER, MISTER FALCONE. THERE'S NO GOING BACK. NO FORGIVENESS...
AND YET, IT DIDN'T TAKE MUCH FOR YOU TO FLIP.
MAYBE BECAUSE I KNOW YOU ALREADY HAVE THE DEPARTMENT IN YOUR POCKET.
AND IF IT'S GONNA BE RUN BY SCUMBAGS LIKE YOU...I MIGHT AS WELL GET OUT NOW.

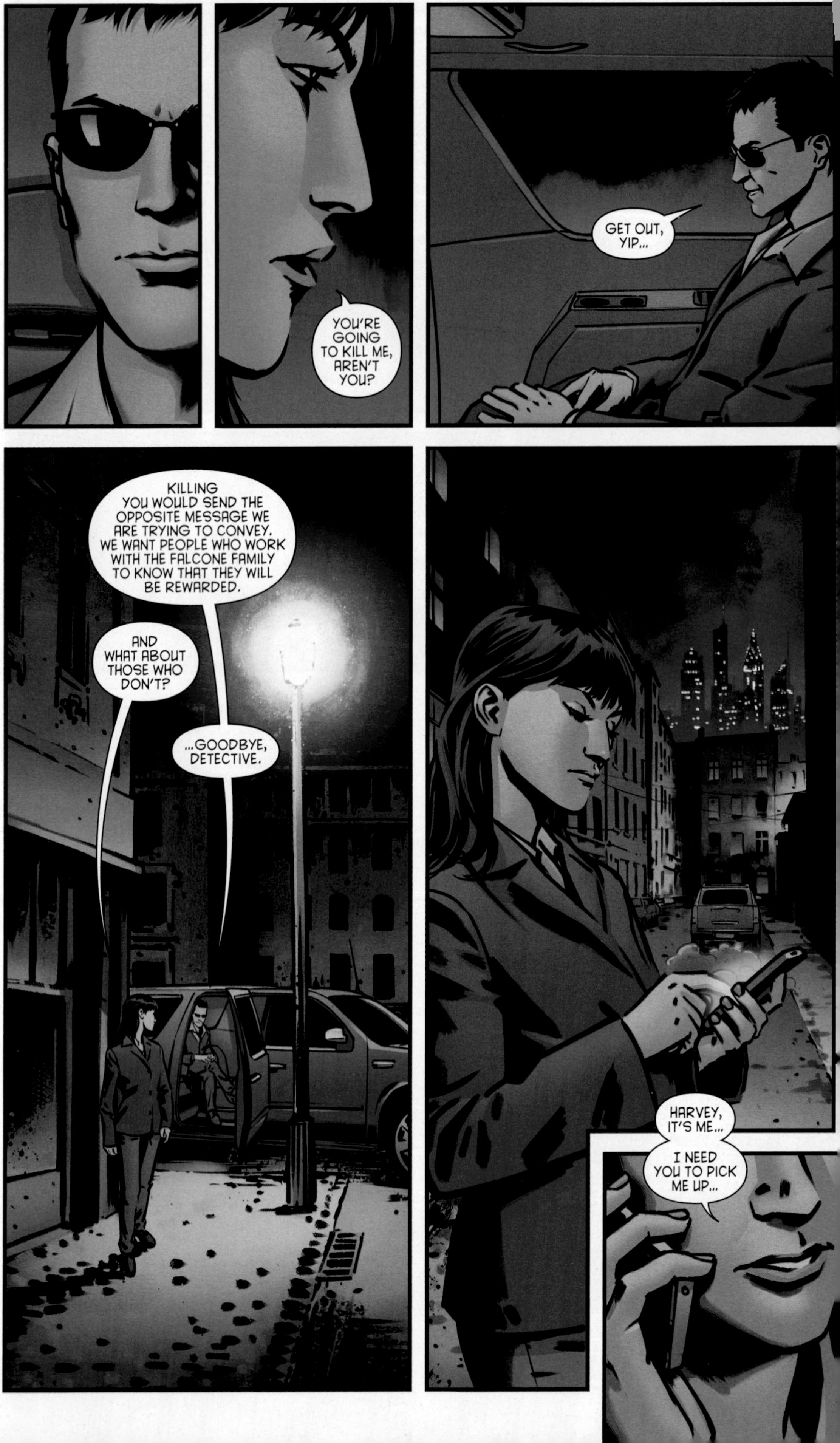
YOU'RE GOING TO KILL ME, AREN'T YOU?
GET OUT, YIP...
KILLING YOU WOULD SEND THE OPPOSITE MESSAGE WE ARE TRYING TO CONVEY. WE WANT PEOPLE WHO WORK WITH THE FALCONE FAMILY TO KNOW THAT THEY WILL BE REWARDED.
AND WHAT ABOUT THOSE WHO DON'T?
...GOODBYE, DETECTIVE.
HARVEY, IT'S ME...
I NEED YOU TO PICK ME UP...

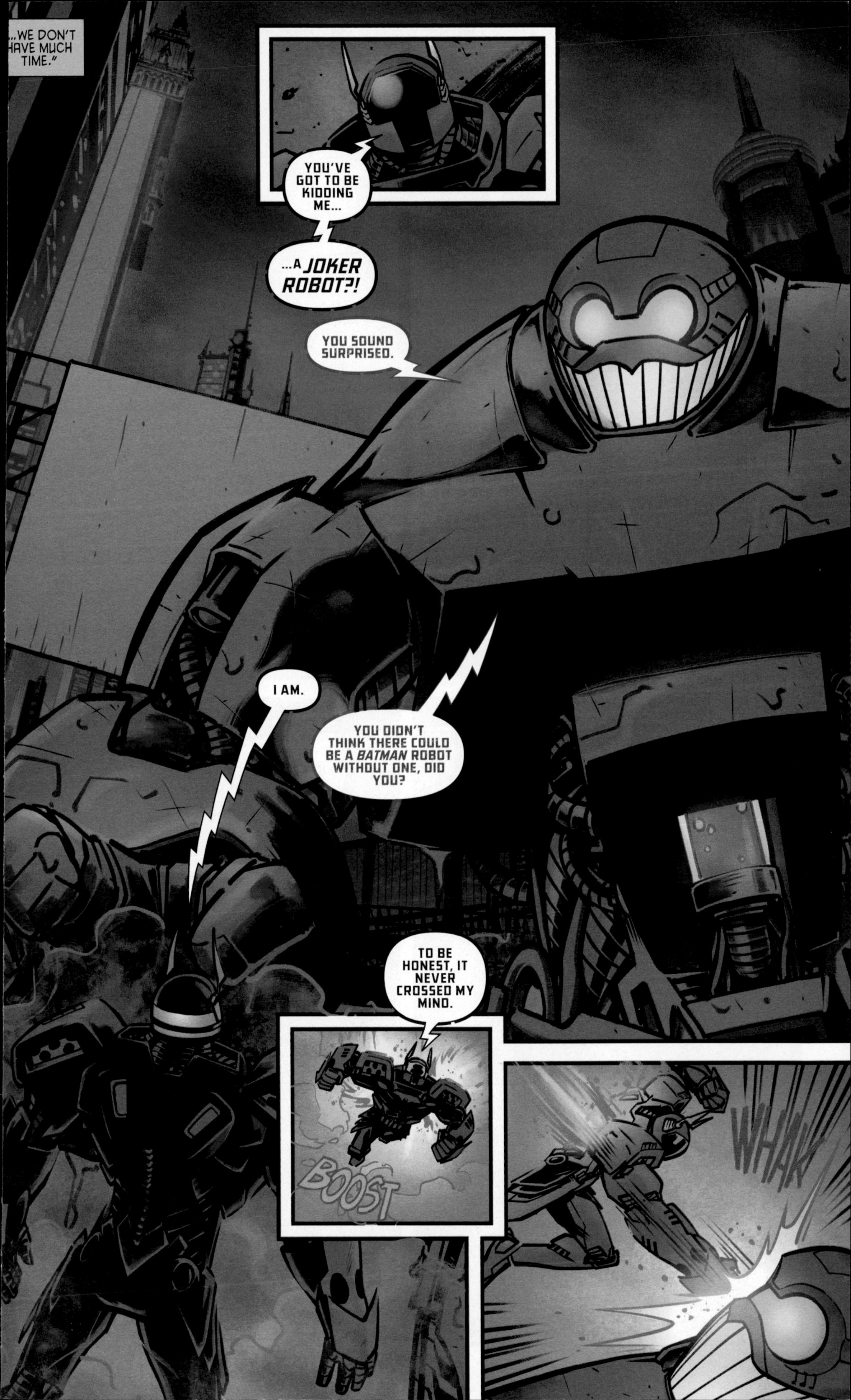

...WE DON'T HAVE MUCH TIME."
YOU'VE GOT TO BE KIDDING ME...
...A JOKER ROBOT?!
YOU SOUND SURPRISED.
I AM.
YOU DIDN'T THINK THERE COULD BE A BATMAN ROBOT WITHOUT ONE, DID YOU?
TO BE HONEST, IT NEVER CROSSED MY MIND.
BOOST
WHAK

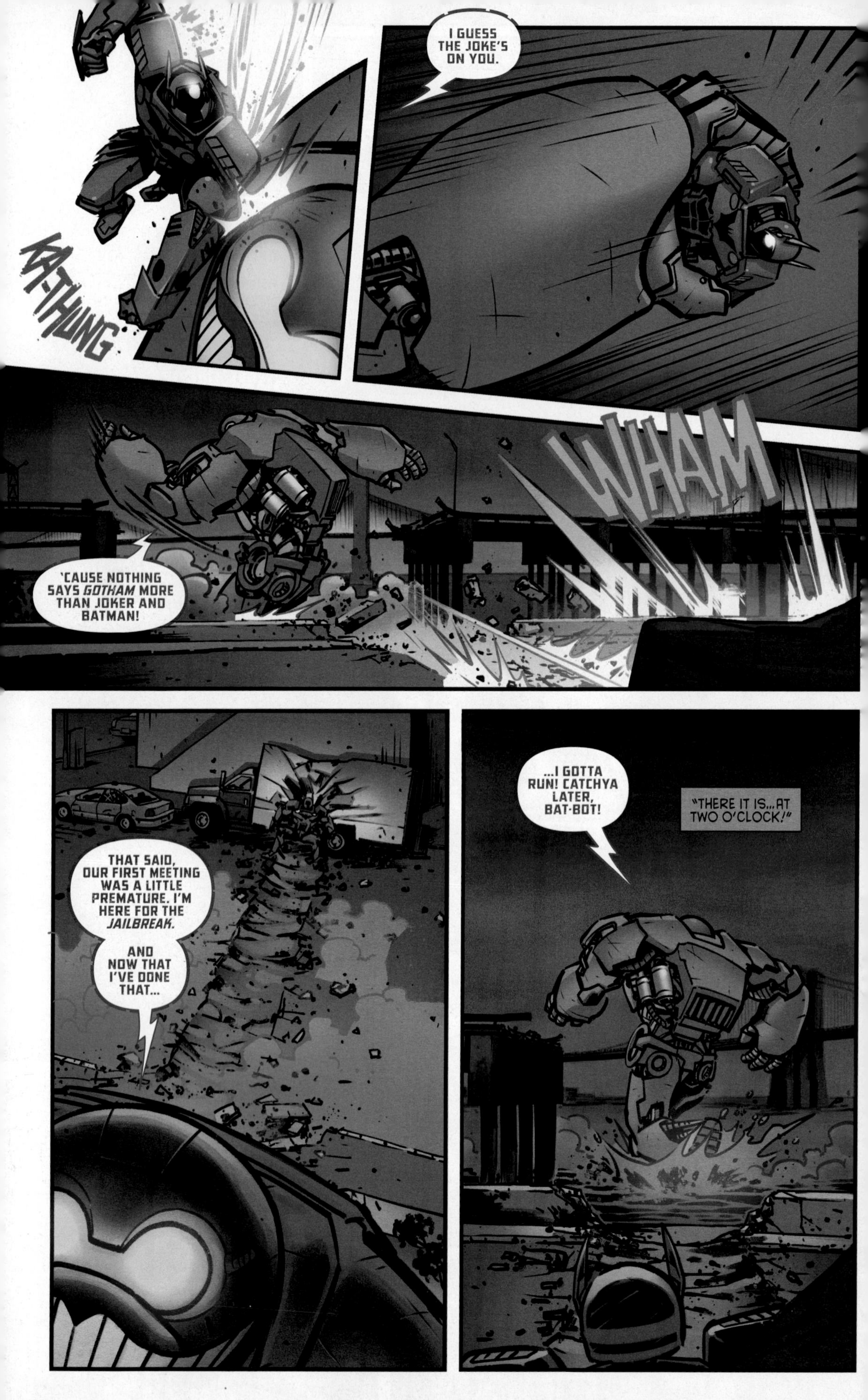
KA-THUNG
I GUESS THE JOKE'S ON YOU.
WHAM
'CAUSE NOTHING SAYS *GOTHAM* MORE THAN JOKER AND BATMAN!
THAT SAID, OUR FIRST MEETING WAS A LITTLE PREMATURE. I'M HERE FOR THE *JAILBREAK.*
AND NOW THAT I'VE DONE THAT...
...I GOTTA RUN! CATCHYA LATER, BAT-BOT!
"THERE IT IS...AT TWO O'CLOCK!"

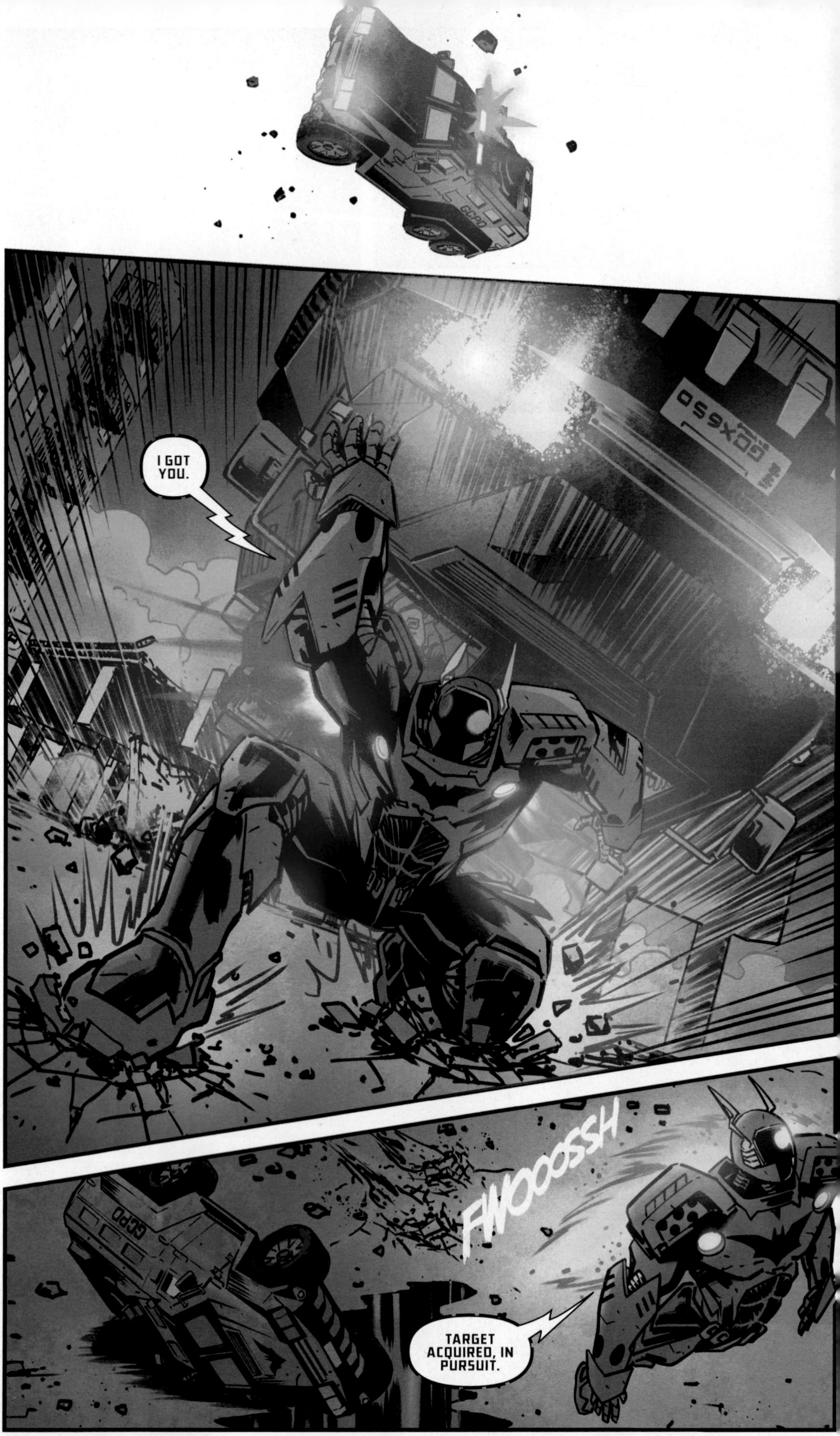
I GOT YOU.
FWOOOSSH
TARGET ACQUIRED, IN PURSUIT.

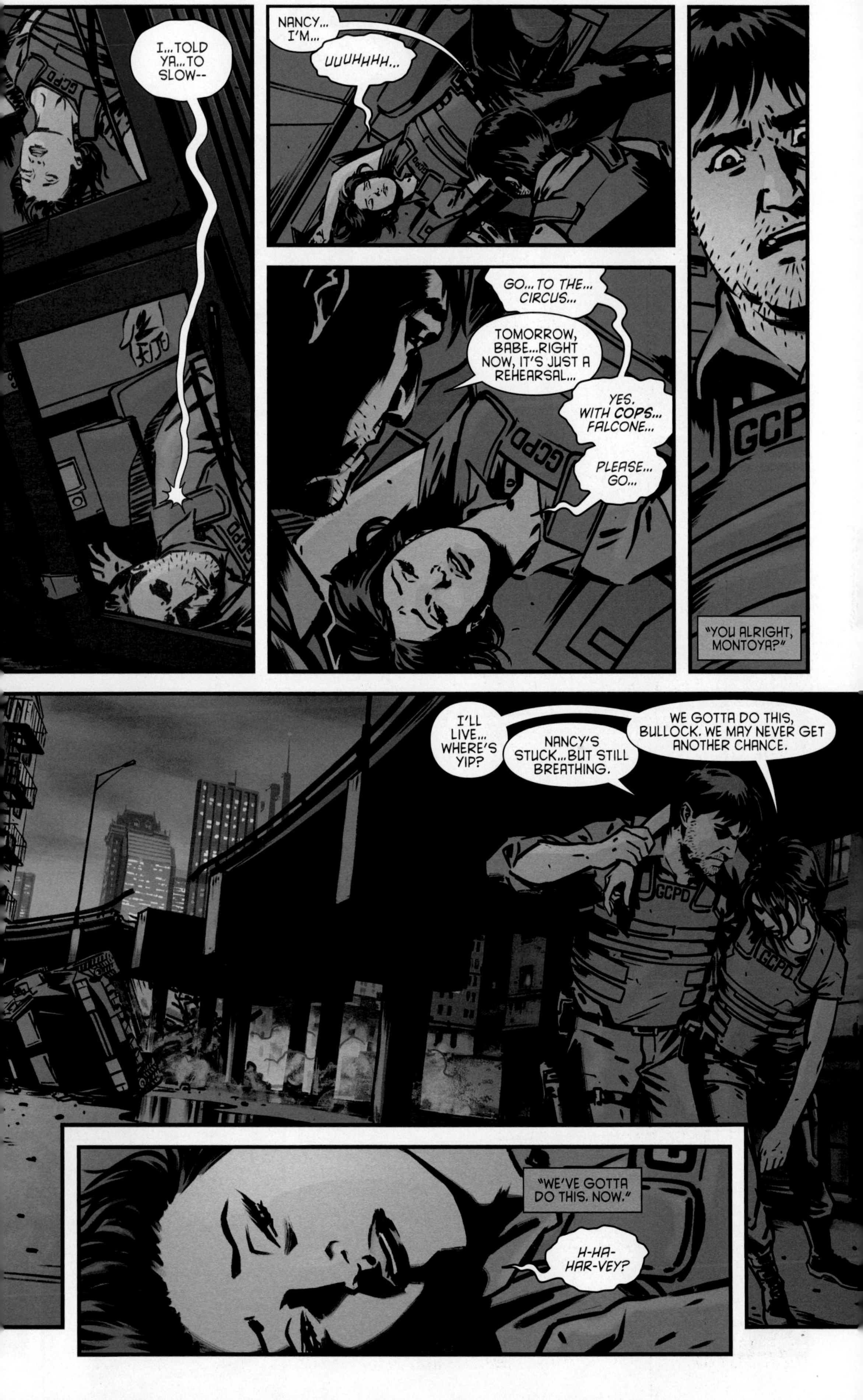
I...TOLD YA...TO SLOW--
NANCY... I'M...
UUUHHHH...
GO...TO THE... CIRCUS...
TOMORROW, BABE...RIGHT NOW, IT'S JUST A REHEARSAL...
YES. WITH **COPS...** FALCONE...
PLEASE... GO...
GCPD
"YOU ALRIGHT, MONTOYA?"
I'LL LIVE... WHERE'S YIP?
NANCY'S STUCK...BUT STILL BREATHING.
WE GOTTA DO THIS, BULLOCK. WE MAY NEVER GET ANOTHER CHANCE.
GCPD
GCPD
"WE'VE GOTTA DO THIS. NOW."
H-HA-HAR-VEY?

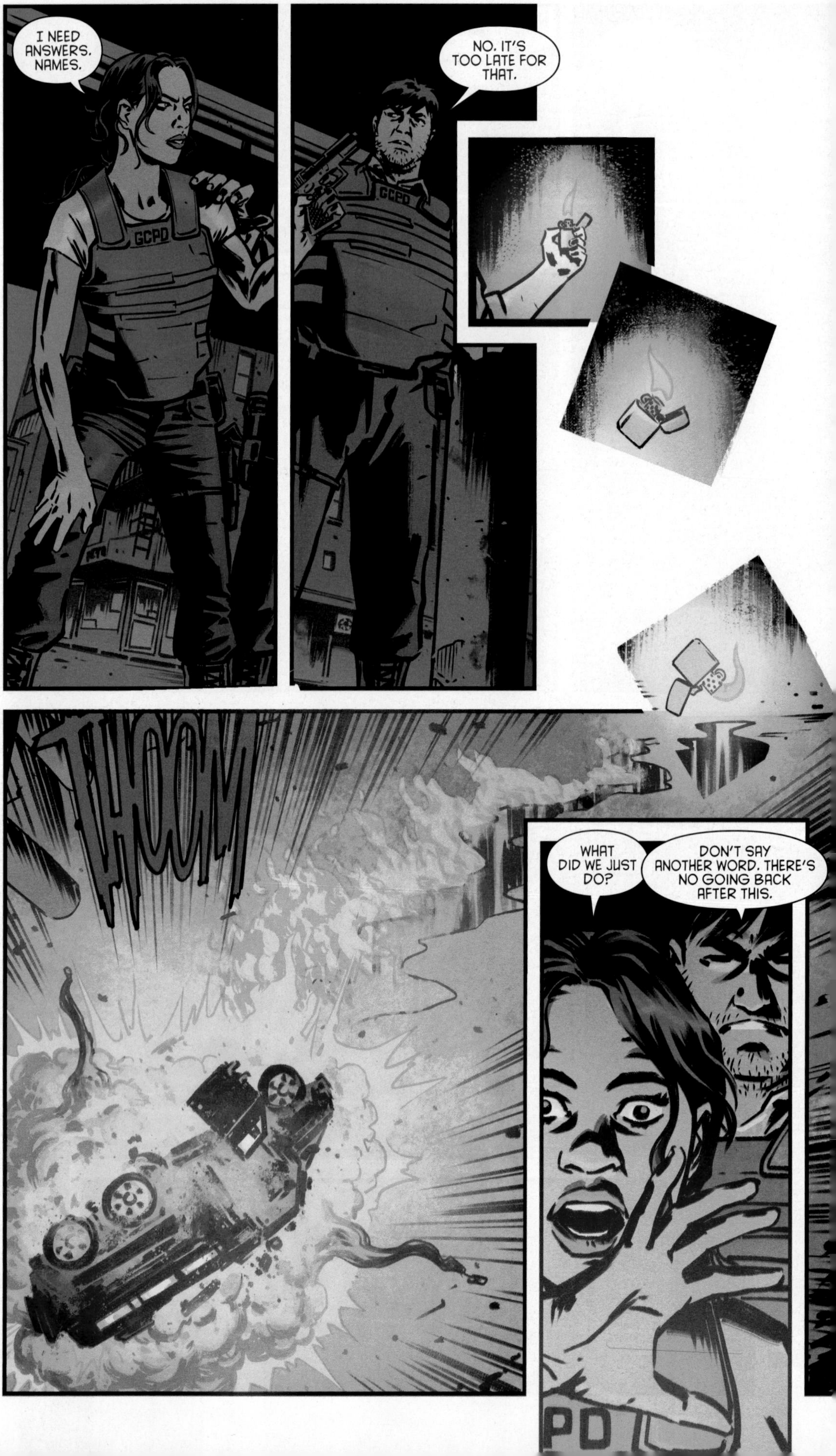
I NEED ANSWERS. NAMES.
GCPD
NO. IT'S TOO LATE FOR THAT.
GCPD
THOOM
WHAT DID WE JUST DO?
DON'T SAY ANOTHER WORD. THERE'S NO GOING BACK AFTER THIS.
PD

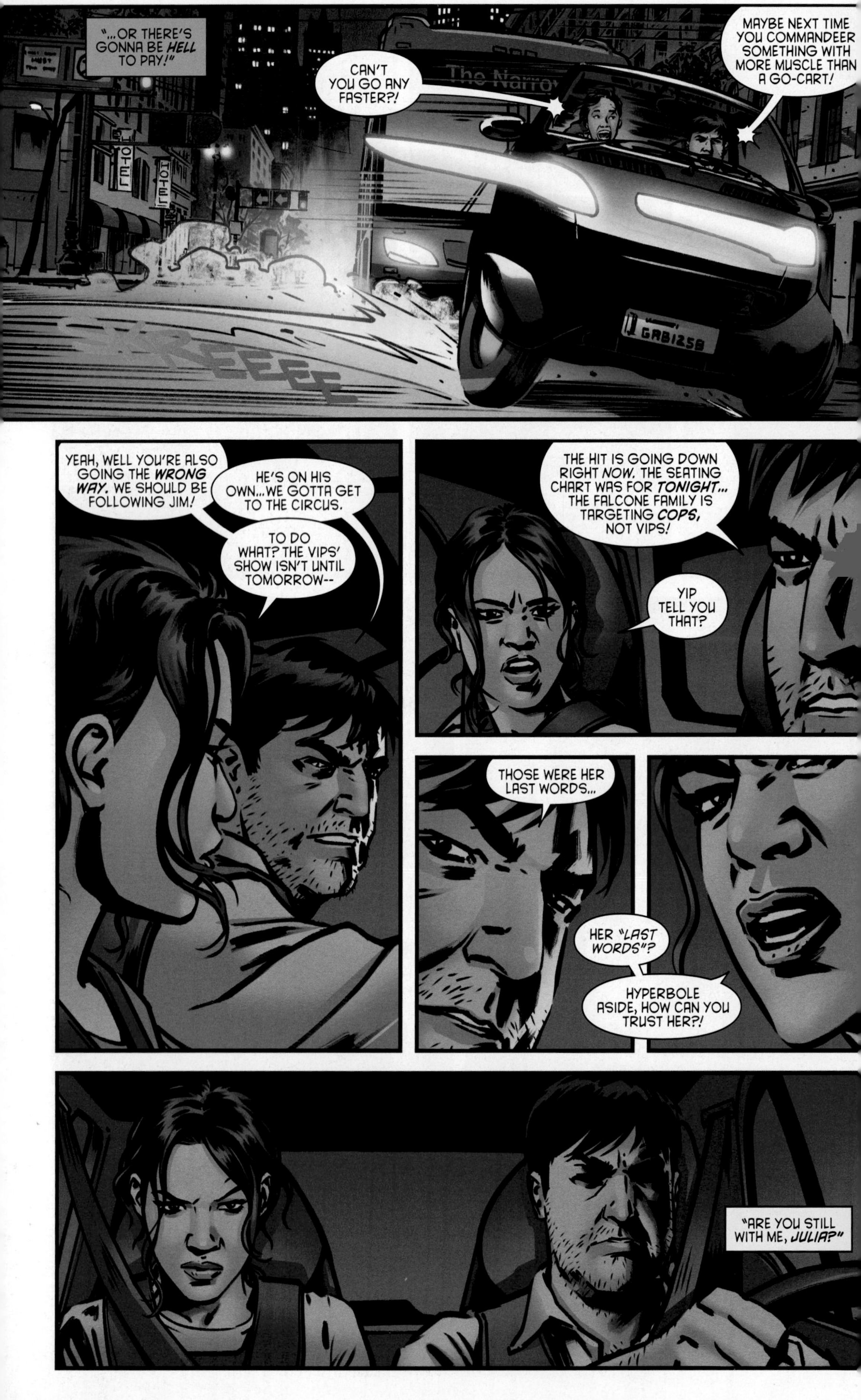
"...OR THERE'S GONNA BE *HELL* TO PAY!"
CAN'T YOU GO ANY FASTER?!
MAYBE NEXT TIME YOU COMMANDEER SOMETHING WITH MORE MUSCLE THAN A GO-CART!
YEAH, WELL YOU'RE ALSO GOING THE *WRONG WAY.* WE SHOULD BE FOLLOWING JIM!
HE'S ON HIS OWN...WE GOTTA GET TO THE CIRCUS.
TO DO WHAT? THE VIPS' SHOW ISN'T UNTIL TOMORROW--
THE HIT IS GOING DOWN RIGHT *NOW.* THE SEATING CHART WAS FOR *TONIGHT...* THE FALCONE FAMILY IS TARGETING *COPS,* NOT VIPS!
YIP TELL YOU THAT?
THOSE WERE HER LAST WORDS...
HER "*LAST WORDS*"?
HYPERBOLE ASIDE, HOW CAN YOU TRUST HER?!
"ARE YOU STILL WITH ME, *JULIA?*"

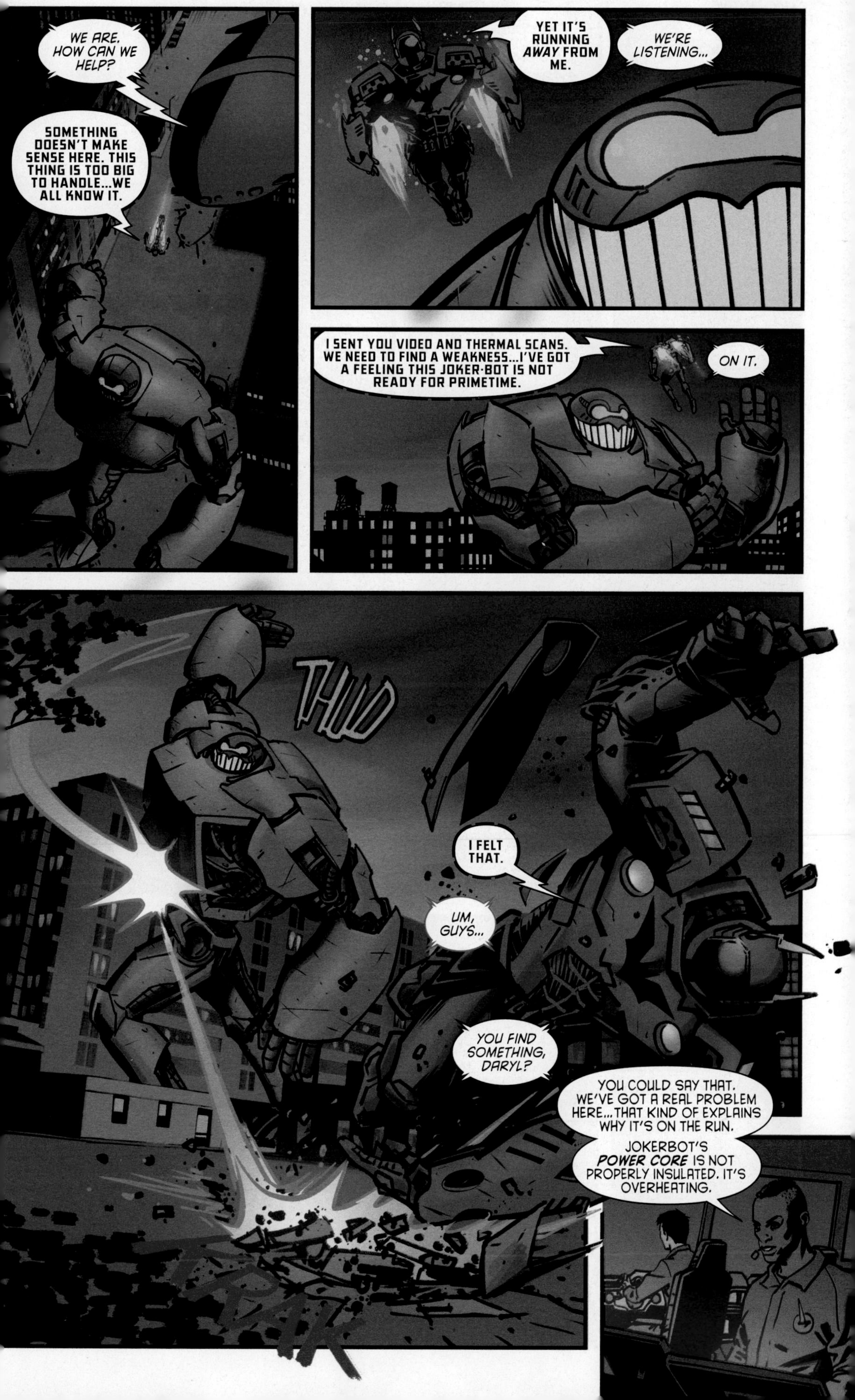
WE ARE. HOW CAN WE HELP?
SOMETHING DOESN'T MAKE SENSE HERE. THIS THING IS TOO BIG TO HANDLE...WE ALL KNOW IT.
YET IT'S RUNNING *AWAY* FROM ME.
WE'RE LISTENING...
I SENT YOU VIDEO AND THERMAL SCANS. WE NEED TO FIND A WEAKNESS...I'VE GOT A FEELING THIS JOKER-BOT IS NOT READY FOR PRIMETIME.
ON IT.
THUD
I FELT THAT.
UM, GUYS...
YOU FIND SOMETHING, DARYL?
YOU COULD SAY THAT. WE'VE GOT A REAL PROBLEM HERE...THAT KIND OF EXPLAINS WHY IT'S ON THE RUN.
JOKERBOT'S ***POWER CORE*** IS NOT PROPERLY INSULATED. IT'S OVERHEATING.
KRAK

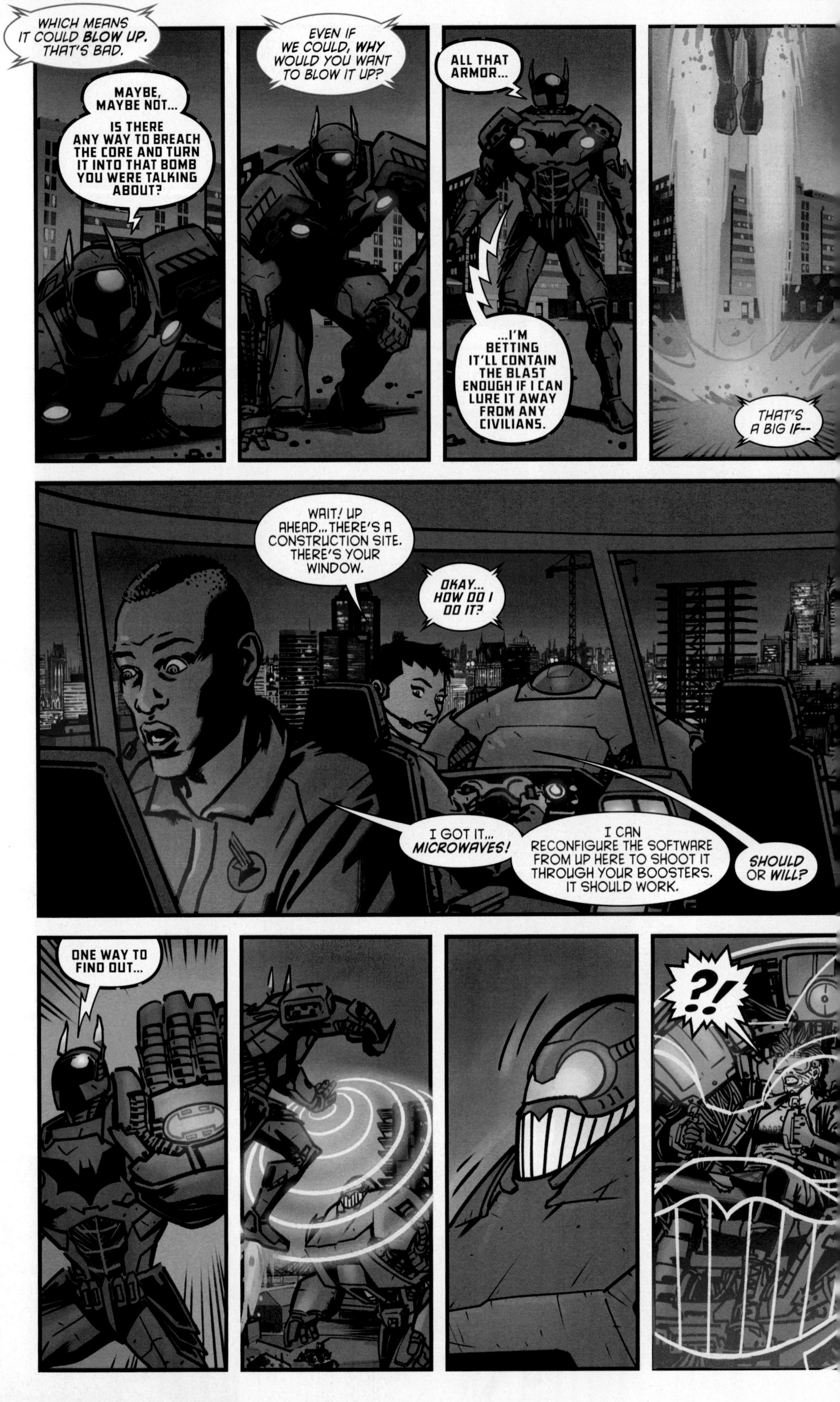
WHICH MEANS IT COULD BLOW UP. THAT'S BAD.
MAYBE, MAYBE NOT... IS THERE ANY WAY TO BREACH THE CORE AND TURN IT INTO THAT BOMB YOU WERE TALKING ABOUT?
EVEN IF WE COULD, WHY WOULD YOU WANT TO BLOW IT UP?
ALL THAT ARMOR...
...I'M BETTING IT'LL CONTAIN THE BLAST ENOUGH IF I CAN LURE IT AWAY FROM ANY CIVILIANS.
THAT'S A BIG IF--
WAIT! UP AHEAD...THERE'S A CONSTRUCTION SITE. THERE'S YOUR WINDOW.
OKAY... HOW DO I DO IT?
I GOT IT... MICROWAVES!
I CAN RECONFIGURE THE SOFTWARE FROM UP HERE TO SHOOT IT THROUGH YOUR BOOSTERS. IT SHOULD WORK.
SHOULD OR WILL?
ONE WAY TO FIND OUT...
?!

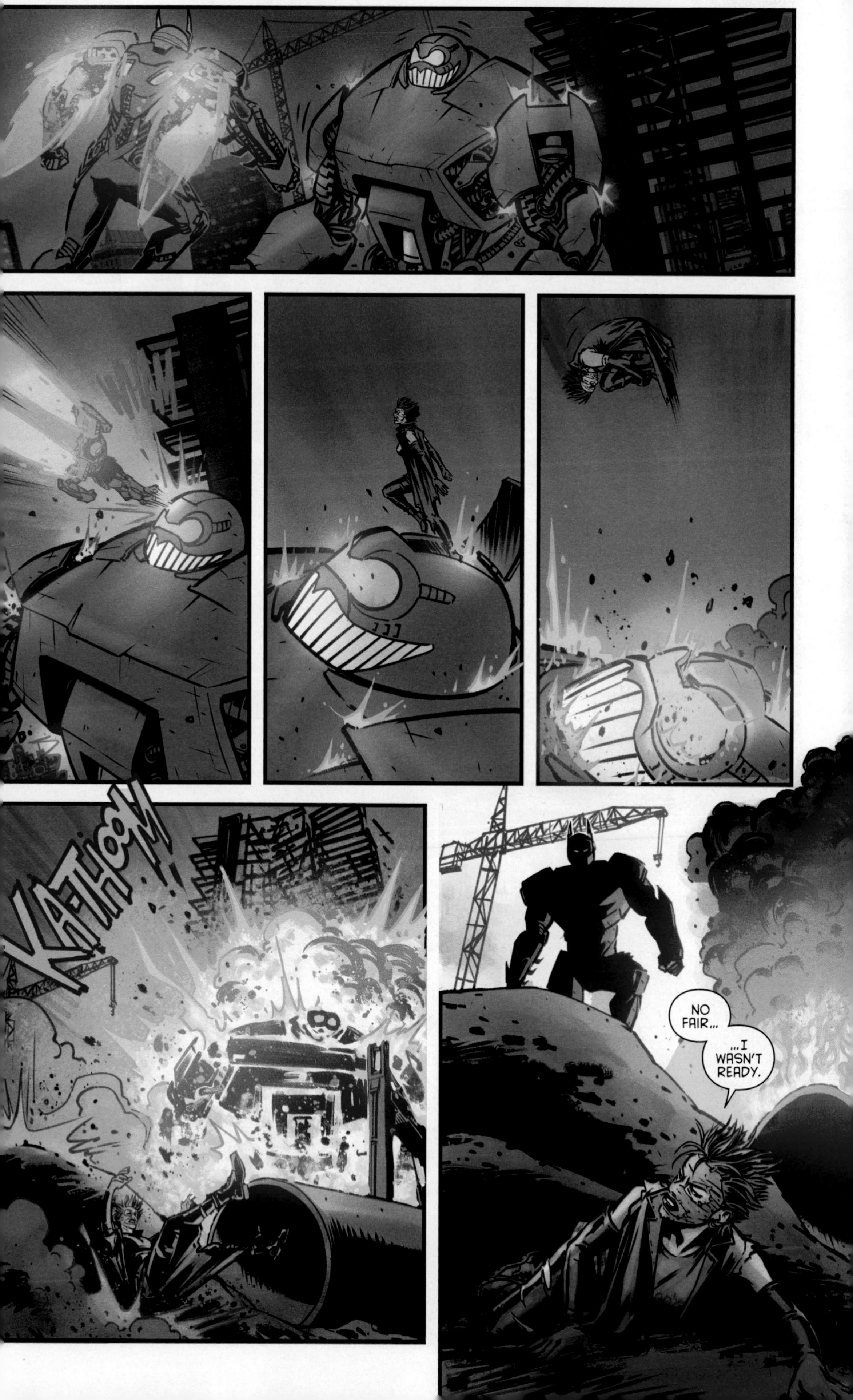
WHAM
KATHOOM
NO FAIR...
...I WASN'T READY.

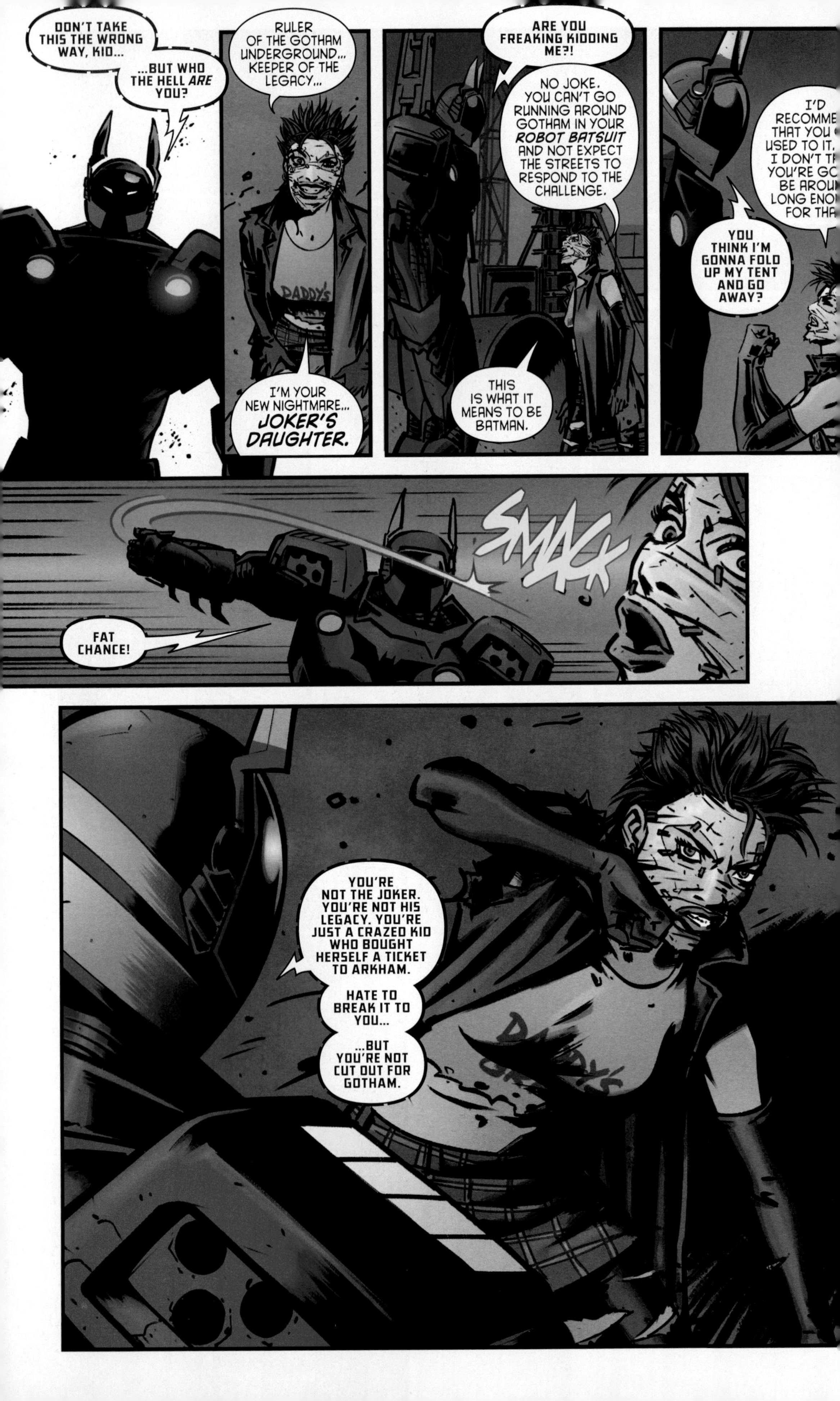
DON'T TAKE THIS THE WRONG WAY, KID...
...BUT WHO THE HELL *ARE* YOU?
RULER OF THE GOTHAM UNDERGROUND... KEEPER OF THE LEGACY...
DADDY'S
I'M YOUR NEW NIGHTMARE... ***JOKER'S DAUGHTER.***
ARE YOU FREAKING KIDDING ME?!
NO JOKE. YOU CAN'T GO RUNNING AROUND GOTHAM IN YOUR ***ROBOT BATSUIT*** AND NOT EXPECT THE STREETS TO RESPOND TO THE CHALLENGE.
THIS IS WHAT IT MEANS TO BE BATMAN.
I'D RECOMME THAT YOU USED TO IT, I DON'T T YOU'RE GO BE AROU LONG ENO FOR THA
YOU THINK I'M GONNA FOLD UP MY TENT AND GO AWAY?
FAT CHANCE!
SMACK
YOU'RE NOT THE JOKER. YOU'RE NOT HIS LEGACY. YOU'RE JUST A CRAZED KID WHO BOUGHT HERSELF A TICKET TO ARKHAM.
HATE TO BREAK IT TO YOU...
...BUT YOU'RE NOT CUT OUT FOR GOTHAM.

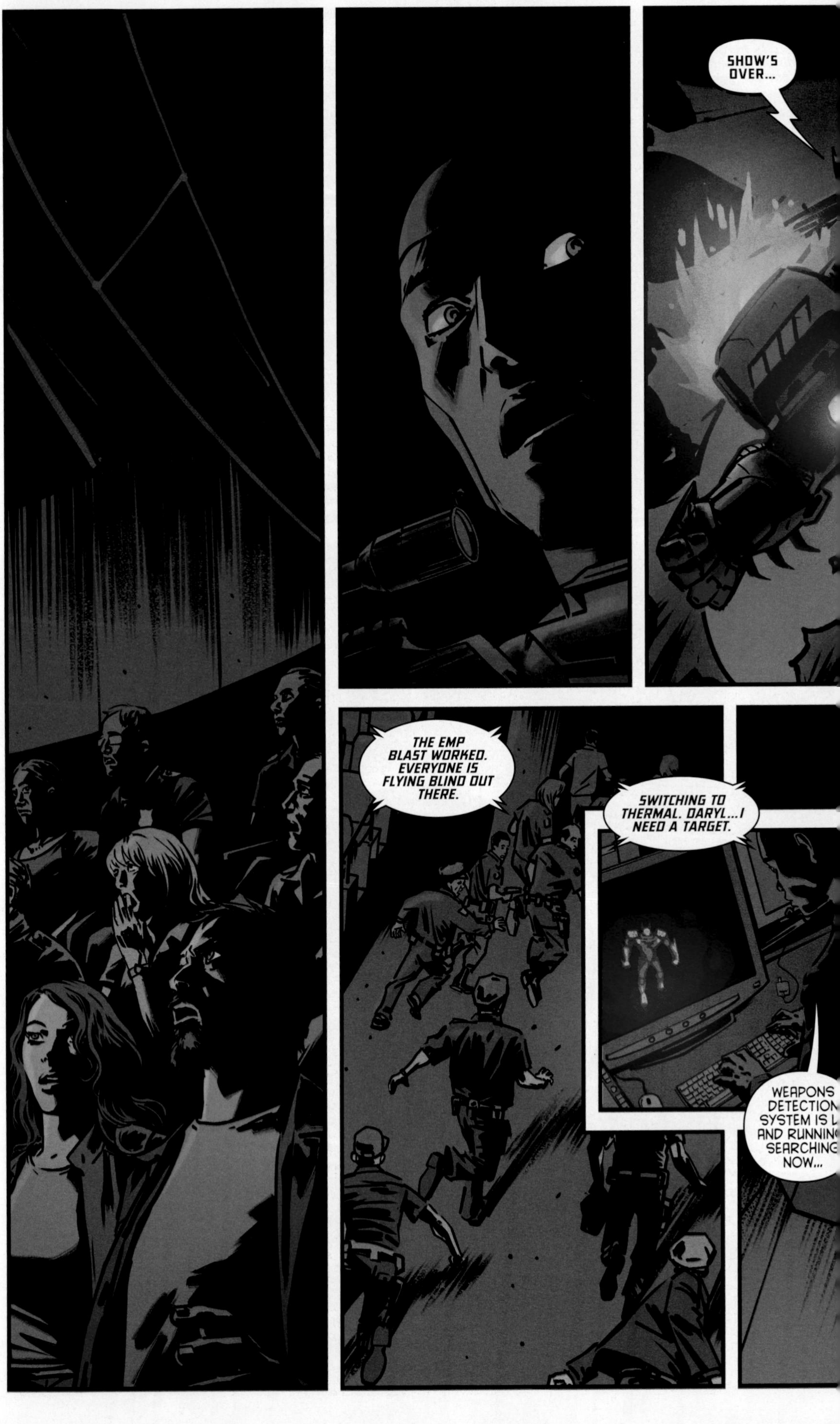
SHOW'S OVER...
THE EMP BLAST WORKED. EVERYONE IS FLYING BLIND OUT THERE.
SWITCHING TO THERMAL. DARYL...I NEED A TARGET.
WEAPONS DETECTION SYSTEM IS L AND RUNNIN SEARCHING NOW...

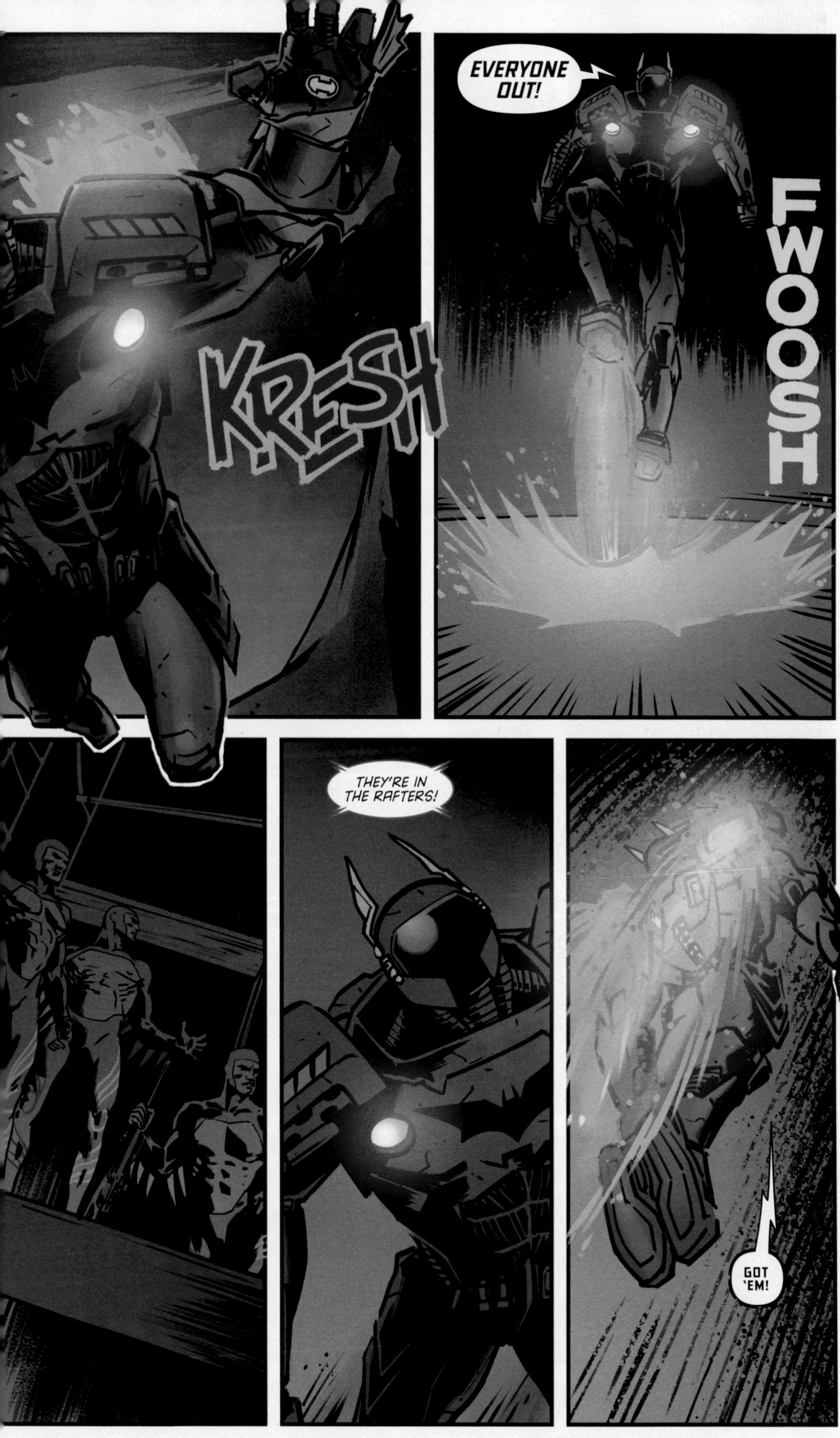
KRESH
EVERYONE OUT!
FWOOSH
THEY'RE IN THE RAFTERS!
GOT 'EM!

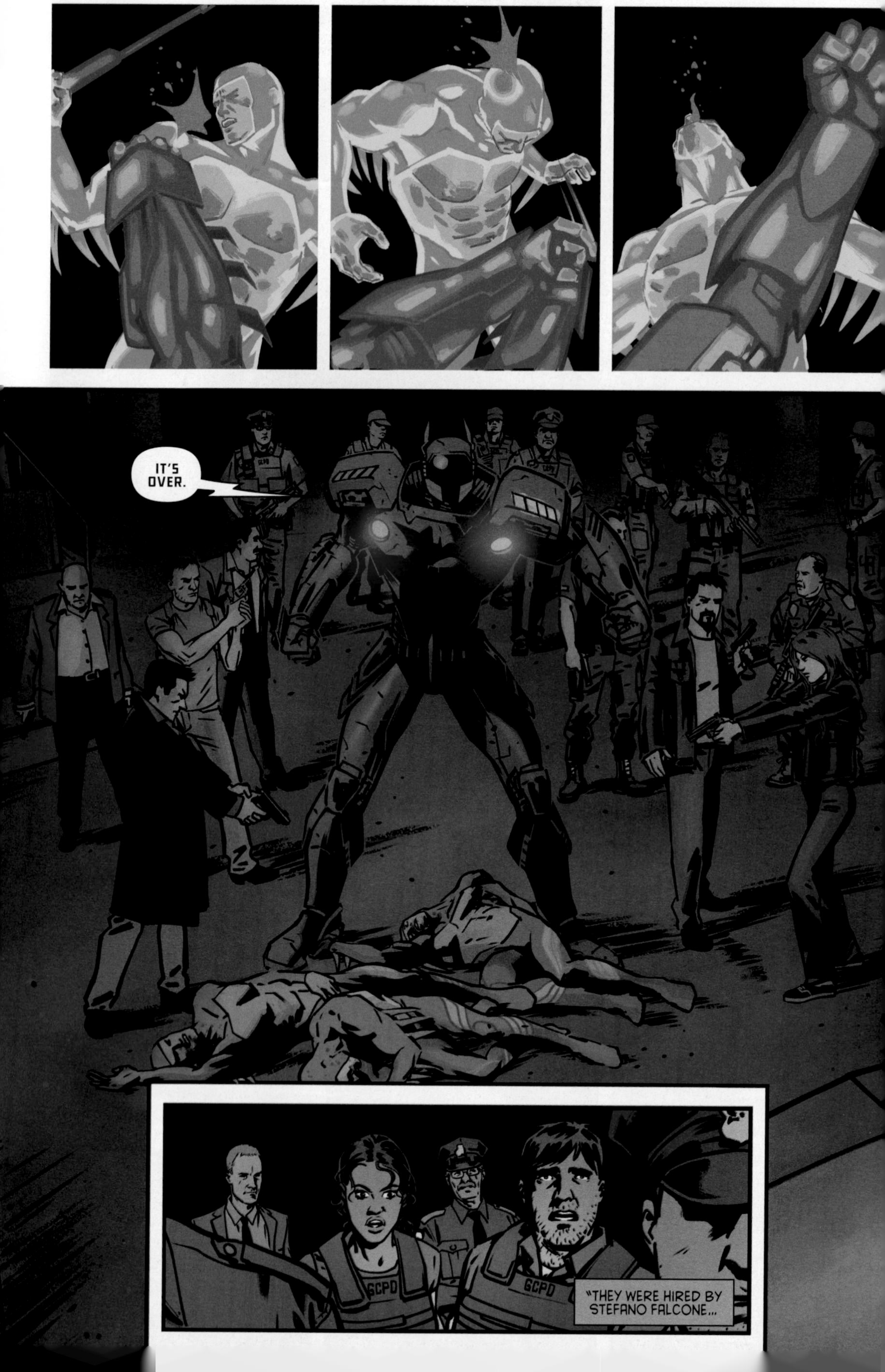
IT'S OVER.
"THEY WERE HIRED BY STEFANO FALCONE...

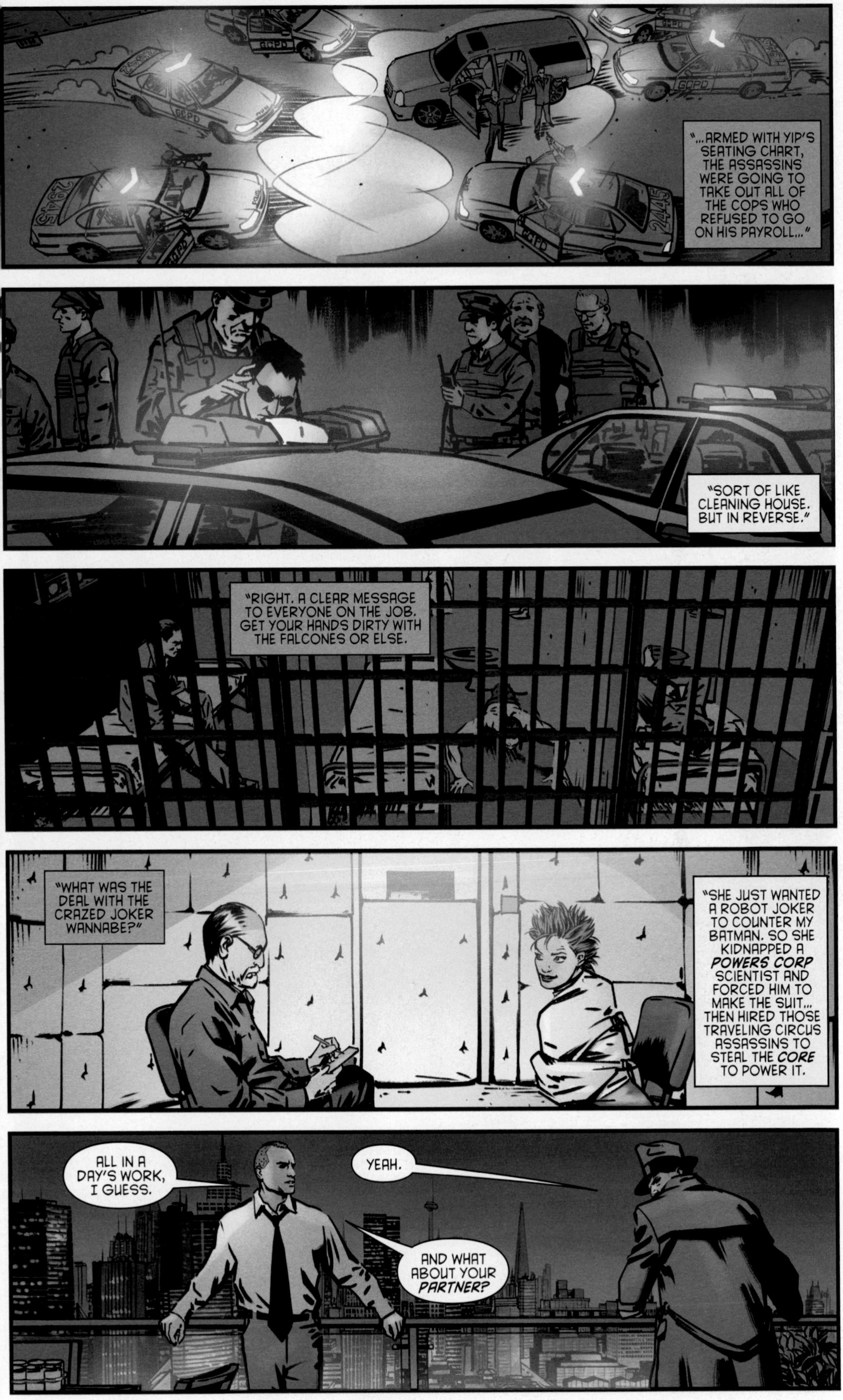
"...ARMED WITH YIP'S SEATING CHART, THE ASSASSINS WERE GOING TO TAKE OUT ALL OF THE COPS WHO REFUSED TO GO ON HIS PAYROLL..."
"SORT OF LIKE CLEANING HOUSE. BUT IN REVERSE."
"RIGHT. A CLEAR MESSAGE TO EVERYONE ON THE JOB. GET YOUR HANDS DIRTY WITH THE FALCONES OR ELSE.
"WHAT WAS THE DEAL WITH THE CRAZED JOKER WANNABE?"
"SHE JUST WANTED A ROBOT JOKER TO COUNTER MY BATMAN. SO SHE KIDNAPPED A *POWERS CORP* SCIENTIST AND FORCED HIM TO MAKE THE SUIT... THEN HIRED THOSE TRAVELING CIRCUS ASSASSINS TO STEAL THE *CORE* TO POWER IT.
ALL IN A DAY'S WORK, I GUESS.
YEAH.
AND WHAT ABOUT YOUR *PARTNER?*

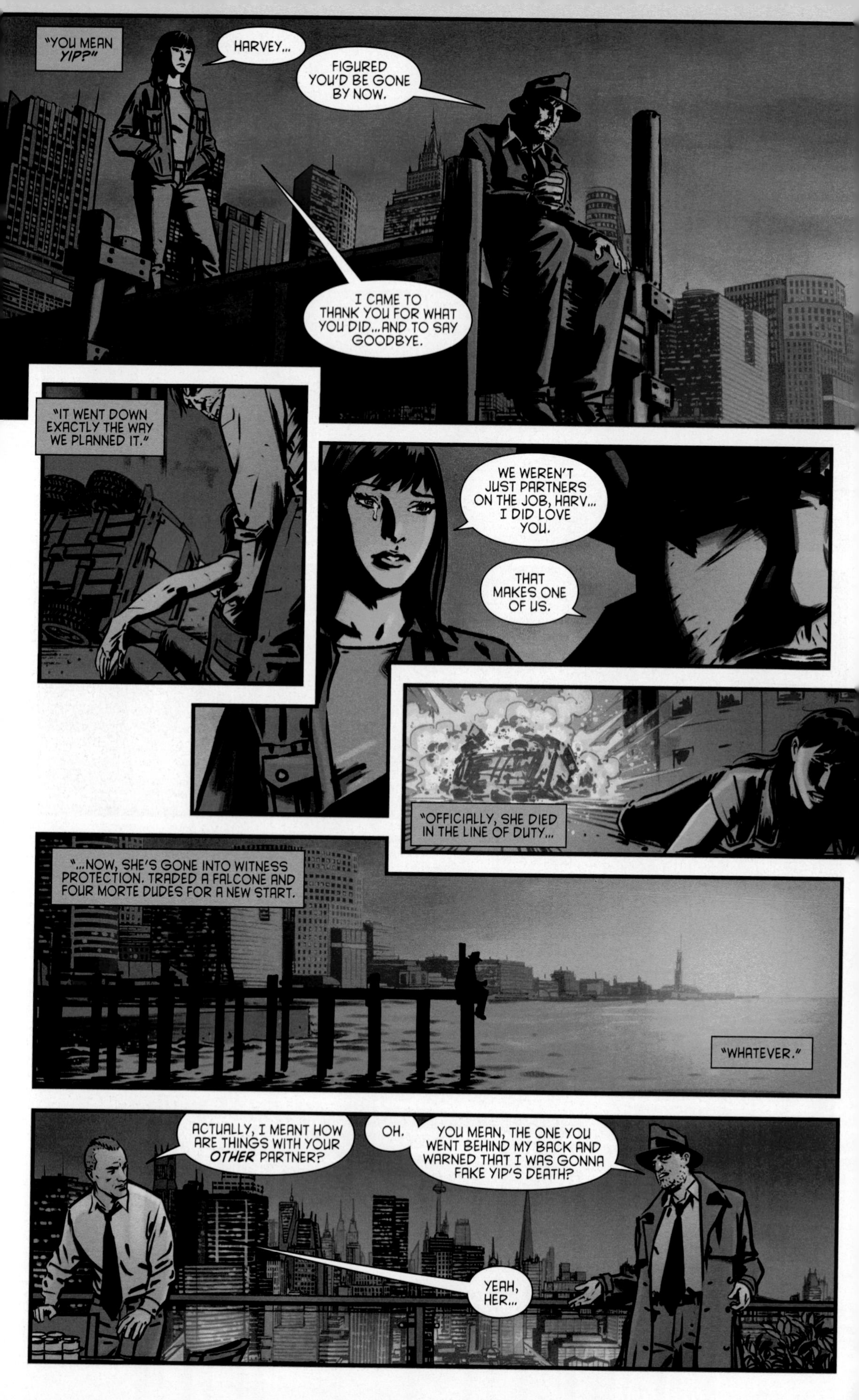
"YOU MEAN *YIP?*"
HARVEY...
FIGURED YOU'D BE GONE BY NOW.
I CAME TO THANK YOU FOR WHAT YOU DID...AND TO SAY GOODBYE.
"IT WENT DOWN EXACTLY THE WAY WE PLANNED IT."
WE WEREN'T JUST PARTNERS ON THE JOB, HARV... I DID LOVE YOU.
THAT MAKES ONE OF US.
"OFFICIALLY, SHE DIED IN THE LINE OF DUTY...
"...NOW, SHE'S GONE INTO WITNESS PROTECTION. TRADED A FALCONE AND FOUR MORTE DUDES FOR A NEW START.
"WHATEVER."
ACTUALLY, I MEANT HOW ARE THINGS WITH YOUR *OTHER* PARTNER?
OH.
YOU MEAN, THE ONE YOU WENT BEHIND MY BACK AND WARNED THAT I WAS GONNA FAKE YIP'S DEATH?
YEAH, HER...

DIDN'T MEAN TO PULL ONE OVER ON YOU, MONTOYA...

I GET IT...

YOU DIDN'T KNOW WHAT ELSE TO DO...BUT YOU'RE NEVER GONNA LIE TO ME AGAIN, RIGHT?

BECAUSE YOU KNOW HOW SACRED PARTNERSHIPS ARE.

SOMETHING LIKE THAT.

CAN I TELL YOU SOMETHING?

HAVE I EVER BEEN ABLE TO STOP YOU?

YOU REALLY WERE THE BEST TRAINING OFFICER A ROOKIE COULD HAVE. AND THE BEST *PARTNER.* I LEARNED A LOT FROM YOUR UGLY ASS...*SO* MUCH. I COULDN'T HAVE GONE OFF AND ACCOMPLISHED ALL THE THINGS I DID IN BLÜDHAVEN IF IT WASN'T FOR YOU.

BUT AT THE SAME TIME, I ALSO COULDN'T DO IT ALL *WITH* YOU. I HAD TO GO MY OWN WAY.

WE BOTH DID.

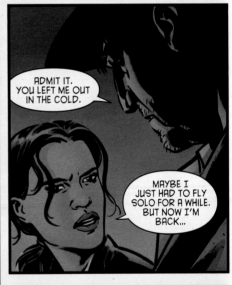

ADMIT IT. YOU LEFT ME OUT IN THE COLD.

MAYBE I JUST HAD TO FLY SOLO FOR A WHILE. BUT NOW I'M BACK...

SOMETHING LIKE THAT.

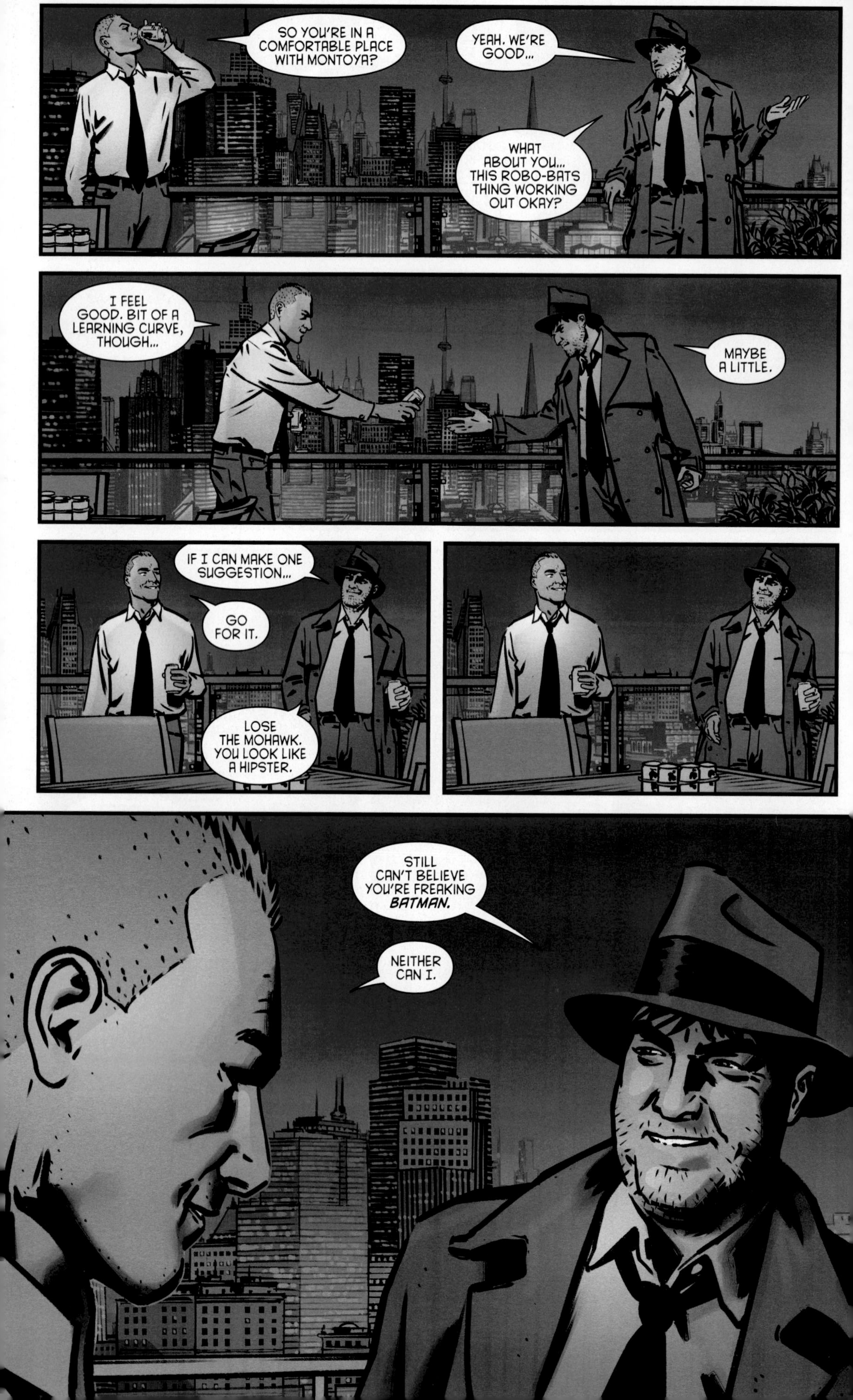
SO YOU'RE IN A COMFORTABLE PLACE WITH MONTOYA?
YEAH. WE'RE GOOD...
WHAT ABOUT YOU... THIS ROBO-BATS THING WORKING OUT OKAY?
I FEEL GOOD. BIT OF A LEARNING CURVE, THOUGH...
MAYBE A LITTLE.
IF I CAN MAKE ONE SUGGESTION...
GO FOR IT.
LOSE THE MOHAWK. YOU LOOK LIKE A HIPSTER.
STILL CAN'T BELIEVE YOU'RE FREAKING *BATMAN.*
NEITHER CAN I.

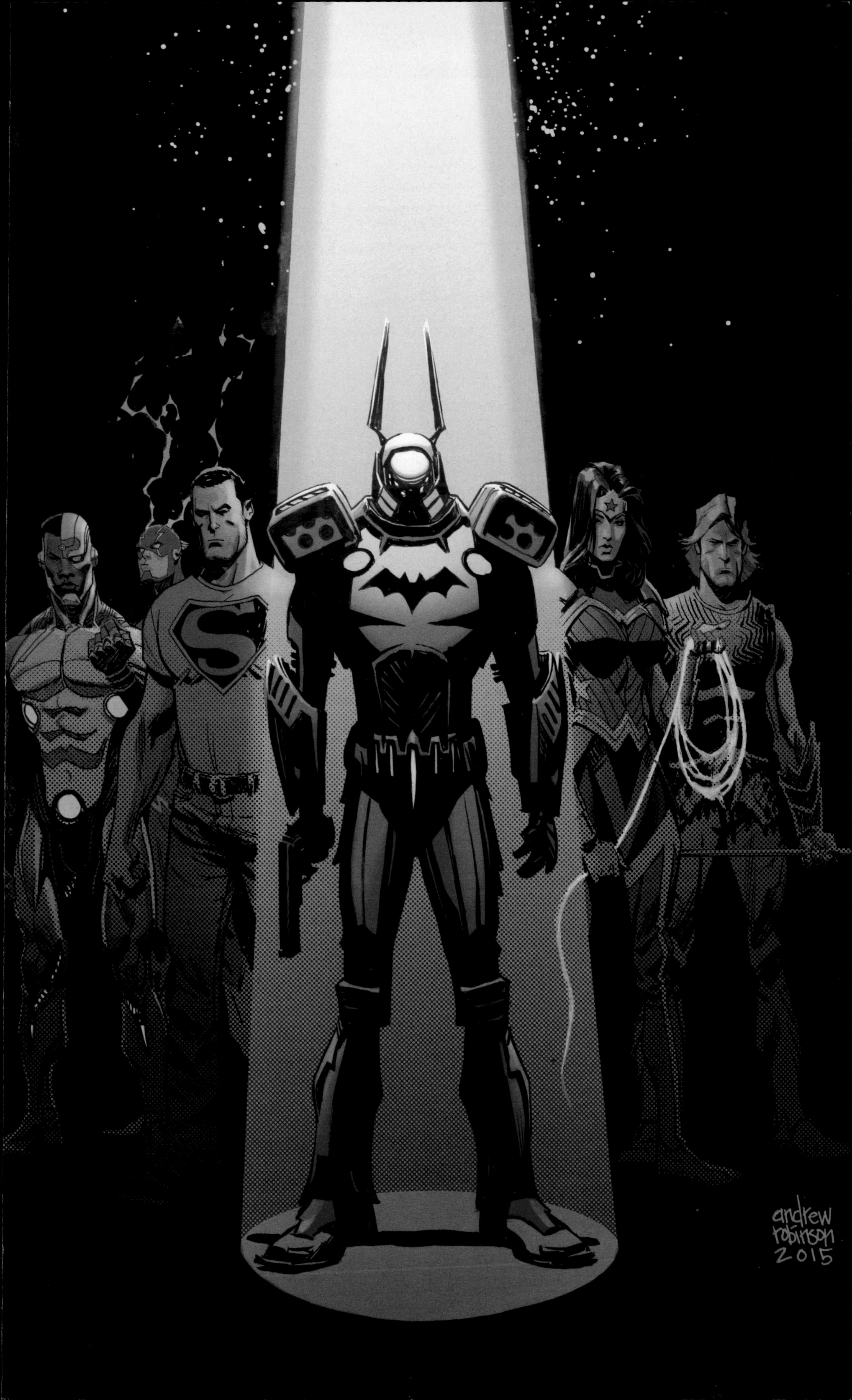
andrew robinson 2015

OF GIANTS AND MEN

PETER J. TOMASI writer MARCIO TAKARA artist CHRIS SOTOMAYOR colorist WES ABBOTT letterer ANDREW ROBINSON cover

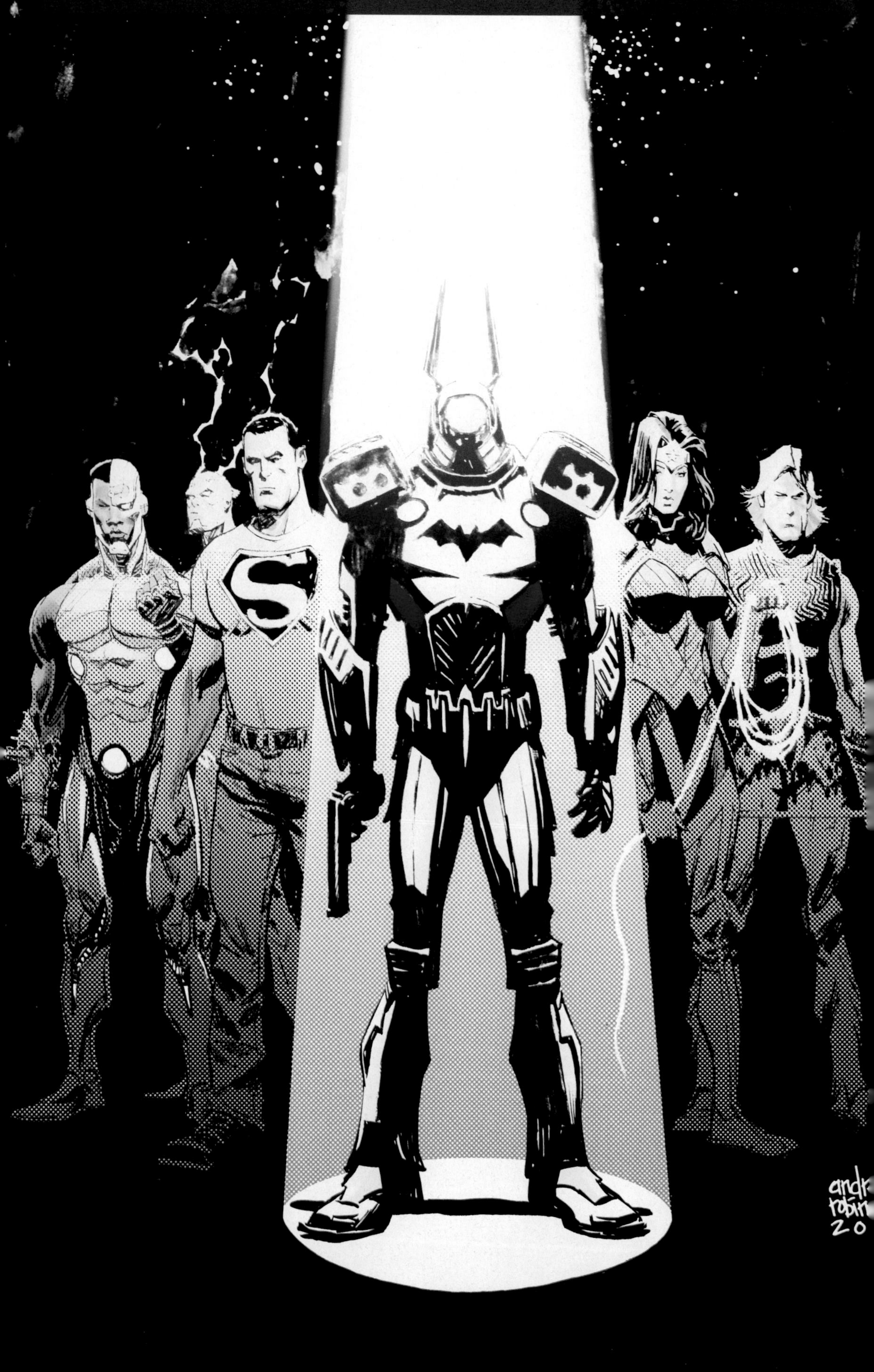

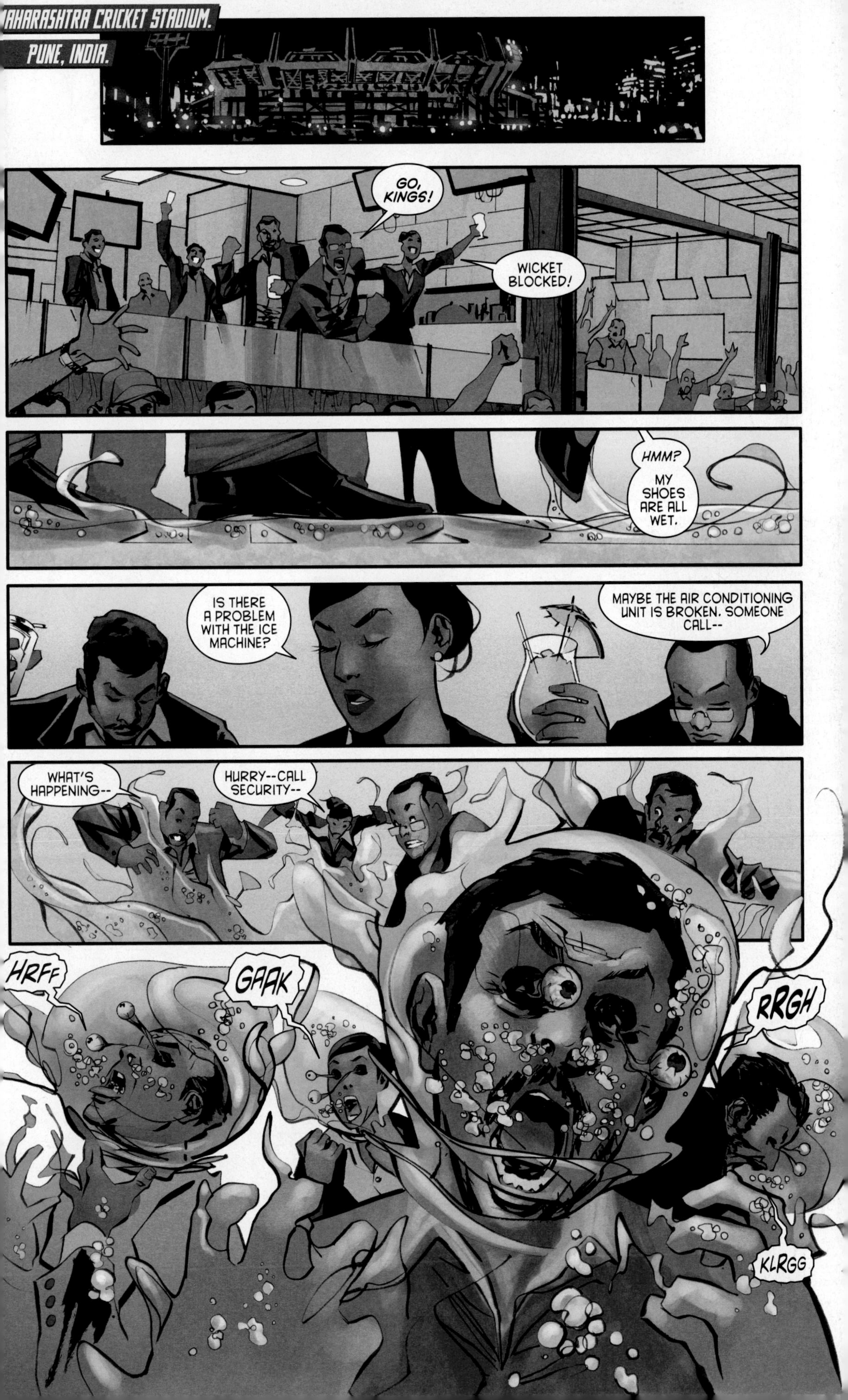
AHARASHTRA CRICKET STADIUM.
PUNE, INDIA.
GO, KINGS!
WICKET BLOCKED!
HMM?
MY SHOES ARE ALL WET.
IS THERE A PROBLEM WITH THE ICE MACHINE?
MAYBE THE AIR CONDITIONING UNIT IS BROKEN. SOMEONE CALL--
WHAT'S HAPPENING--
HURRY--CALL SECURITY--
HRFF
GAAK
RRGH
KLRGG

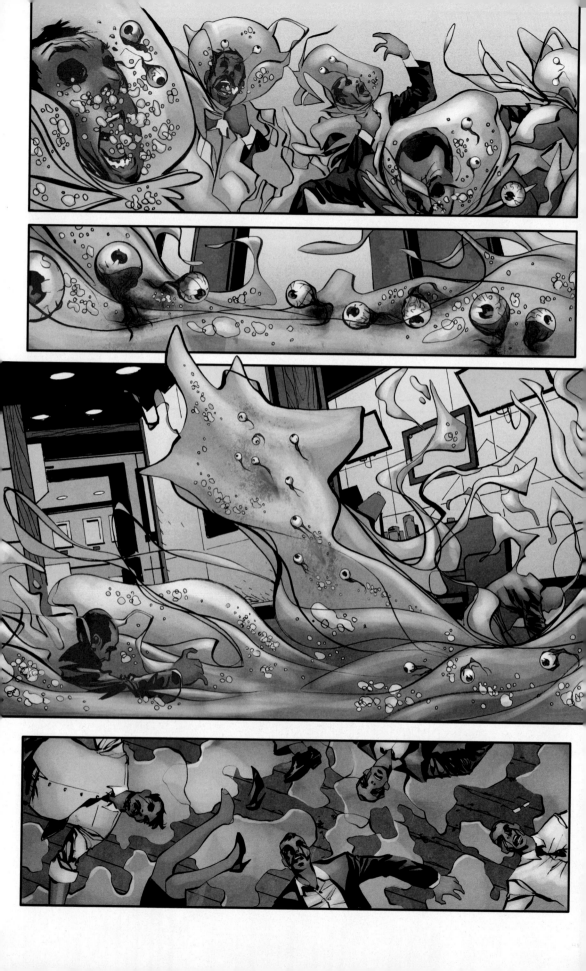

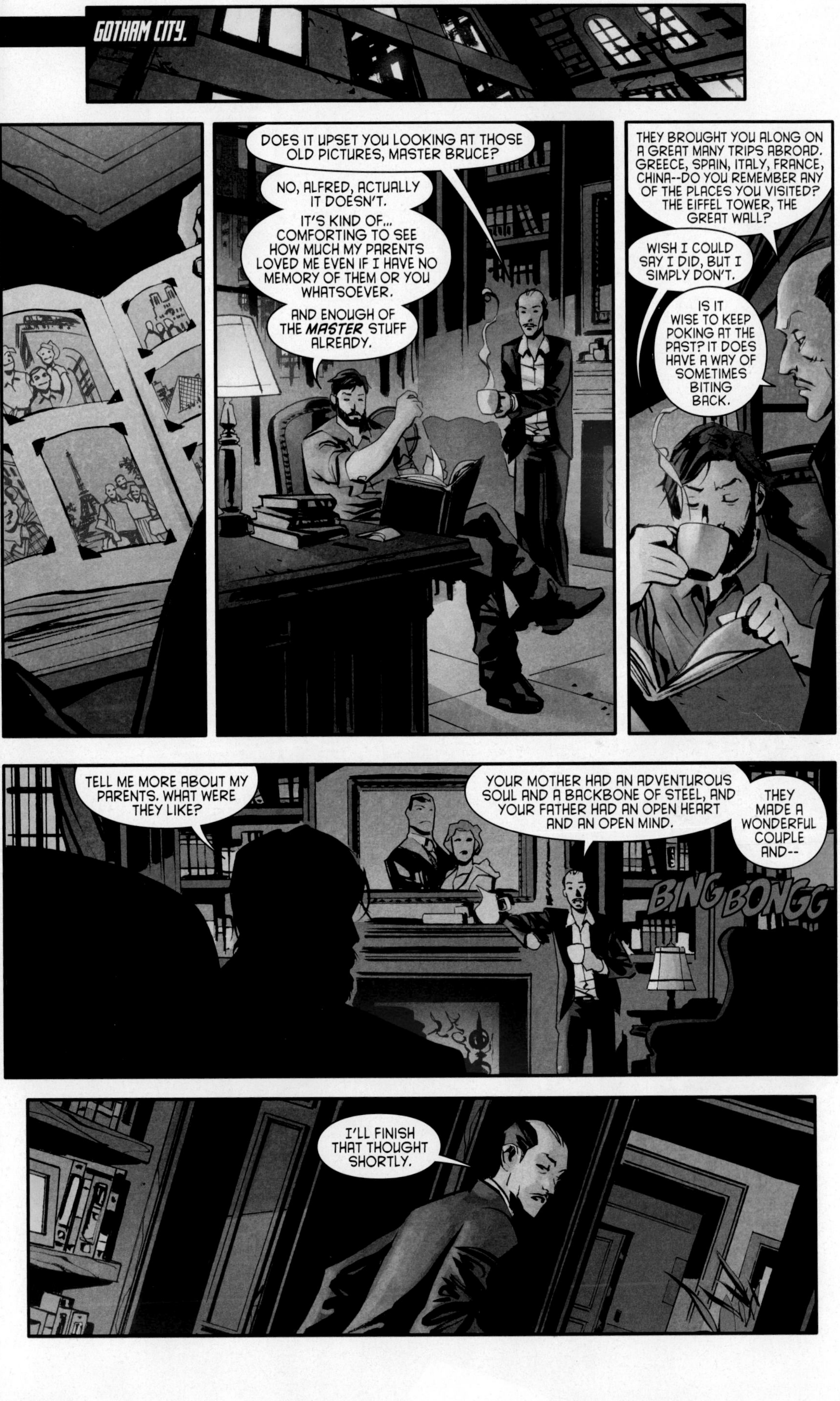
GOTHAM CITY.
DOES IT UPSET YOU LOOKING AT THOSE OLD PICTURES, MASTER BRUCE?
NO, ALFRED, ACTUALLY IT DOESN'T.
IT'S KIND OF... COMFORTING TO SEE HOW MUCH MY PARENTS LOVED ME EVEN IF I HAVE NO MEMORY OF THEM OR YOU WHATSOEVER.
AND ENOUGH OF THE *MASTER* STUFF ALREADY.
THEY BROUGHT YOU ALONG ON A GREAT MANY TRIPS ABROAD. GREECE, SPAIN, ITALY, FRANCE, CHINA--DO YOU REMEMBER ANY OF THE PLACES YOU VISITED? THE EIFFEL TOWER, THE GREAT WALL?
WISH I COULD SAY I DID, BUT I SIMPLY DON'T.
IS IT WISE TO KEEP POKING AT THE PAST? IT DOES HAVE A WAY OF SOMETIMES BITING BACK.
TELL ME MORE ABOUT MY PARENTS. WHAT WERE THEY LIKE?
YOUR MOTHER HAD AN ADVENTUROUS SOUL AND A BACKBONE OF STEEL, AND YOUR FATHER HAD AN OPEN HEART AND AN OPEN MIND.
THEY MADE A WONDERFUL COUPLE AND--
BING BONGG
I'LL FINISH THAT THOUGHT SHORTLY.

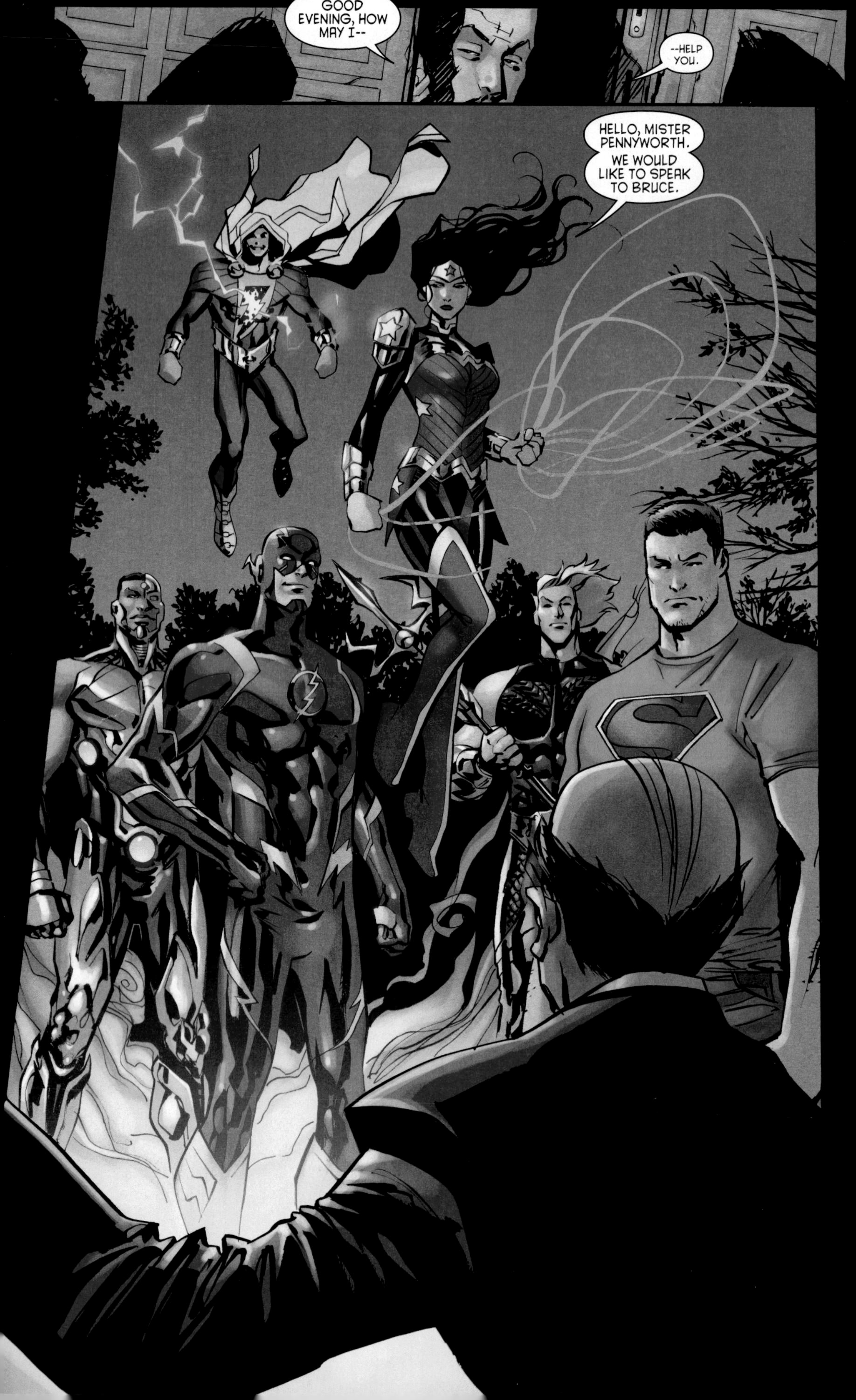
GOOD EVENING, HOW MAY I--
--HELP YOU.
HELLO, MISTER PENNYWORTH. WE WOULD LIKE TO SPEAK TO BRUCE.

I DO NOT MEAN TO SOUND BRUSQUE, BUT AS I TOLD SUPERMAN SEVERAL DAYS AGO, THERE'S A GREAT MANY REASONS WHY MASTER BRUCE CANNOT HONOR HIS JUSTICE LEAGUE RESPONSIBILITIES ANY LONGER.

SOMETHING'S COME UP SINCE THEN, ALFRED.

A CRISIS, I ASSUME, OF *EPIC* PROPORTIONS?

COULD DAMN WELL BE, BUT LET'S HOPE NOT.

HATE TO ADMIT IT, BUT WE'RE STRONGER WITH BATMAN ON OUR SIDE, ESPECIALLY IN FULL-OUT *DETECTIVE MODE,* WHICH IS EXACTLY WHAT WE NEED RIGHT NOW.

SO GETTING HIM BACK SOONER RATHER THAN LATER IS VITAL.

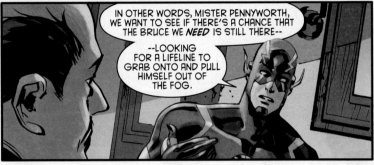

IN OTHER WORDS, MISTER PENNYWORTH, WE WANT TO SEE IF THERE'S A CHANCE THAT THE BRUCE WE *NEED* IS STILL THERE--

--LOOKING FOR A LIFELINE TO GRAB ONTO AND PULL HIMSELF OUT OF THE FOG.

WHAT BRUCE HAS BEEN GIVEN IS A *LIFELINE OF ANONYMITY*--NO HISTORY, NO BAGGAGE, NO TRAGEDY...*NO ENTANGLEMENTS.*

HE'S TRULY FREE TO WALK IN THE LIGHT AND START OVER.

AND AS MUCH AS YOU DON'T WANT TO FACE IT, THE BRUCE WAYNE YOU'RE LOOKING FOR IS SIMPLY NO LONGER THERE.

IF WE DIDN'T BELIEVE THE *DIRE SITUATION* WE'VE DISCOVERED WARRANTED KNOCKING ON YOUR FRONT DOOR, YOU KNOW WE WOULDN'T EVEN BE HERE, ALFRED.

WE'RE ASKING FOR PERMISSION TO REACH OUT TO BRUCE ONE LAST TIME TO HELP SAVE COUNTLESS LIVES.

WELL THEN MAYBE YOU SHOULD BE ASKING *ME* INSTEAD OF ALFRED?

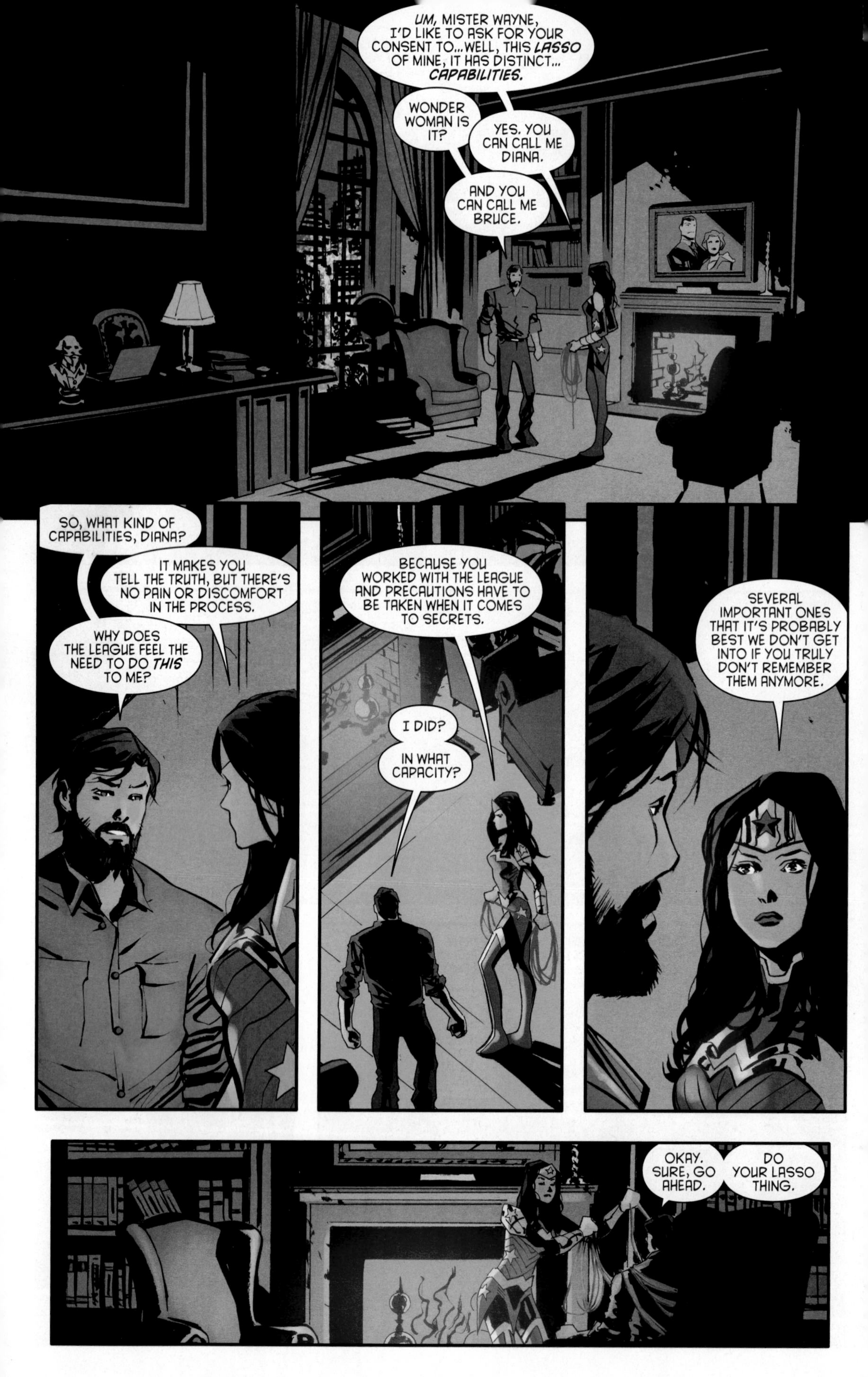

UM, MISTER WAYNE, I'D LIKE TO ASK FOR YOUR CONSENT TO...WELL, THIS LASSO OF MINE, IT HAS DISTINCT... CAPABILITIES.
WONDER WOMAN IS IT?
YES. YOU CAN CALL ME DIANA.
AND YOU CAN CALL ME BRUCE.
SO, WHAT KIND OF CAPABILITIES, DIANA?
IT MAKES YOU TELL THE TRUTH, BUT THERE'S NO PAIN OR DISCOMFORT IN THE PROCESS.
WHY DOES THE LEAGUE FEEL THE NEED TO DO THIS TO ME?
BECAUSE YOU WORKED WITH THE LEAGUE AND PRECAUTIONS HAVE TO BE TAKEN WHEN IT COMES TO SECRETS.
I DID?
IN WHAT CAPACITY?
SEVERAL IMPORTANT ONES THAT IT'S PROBABLY BEST WE DON'T GET INTO IF YOU TRULY DON'T REMEMBER THEM ANYMORE.
OKAY. SURE, GO AHEAD.
DO YOUR LASSO THING.

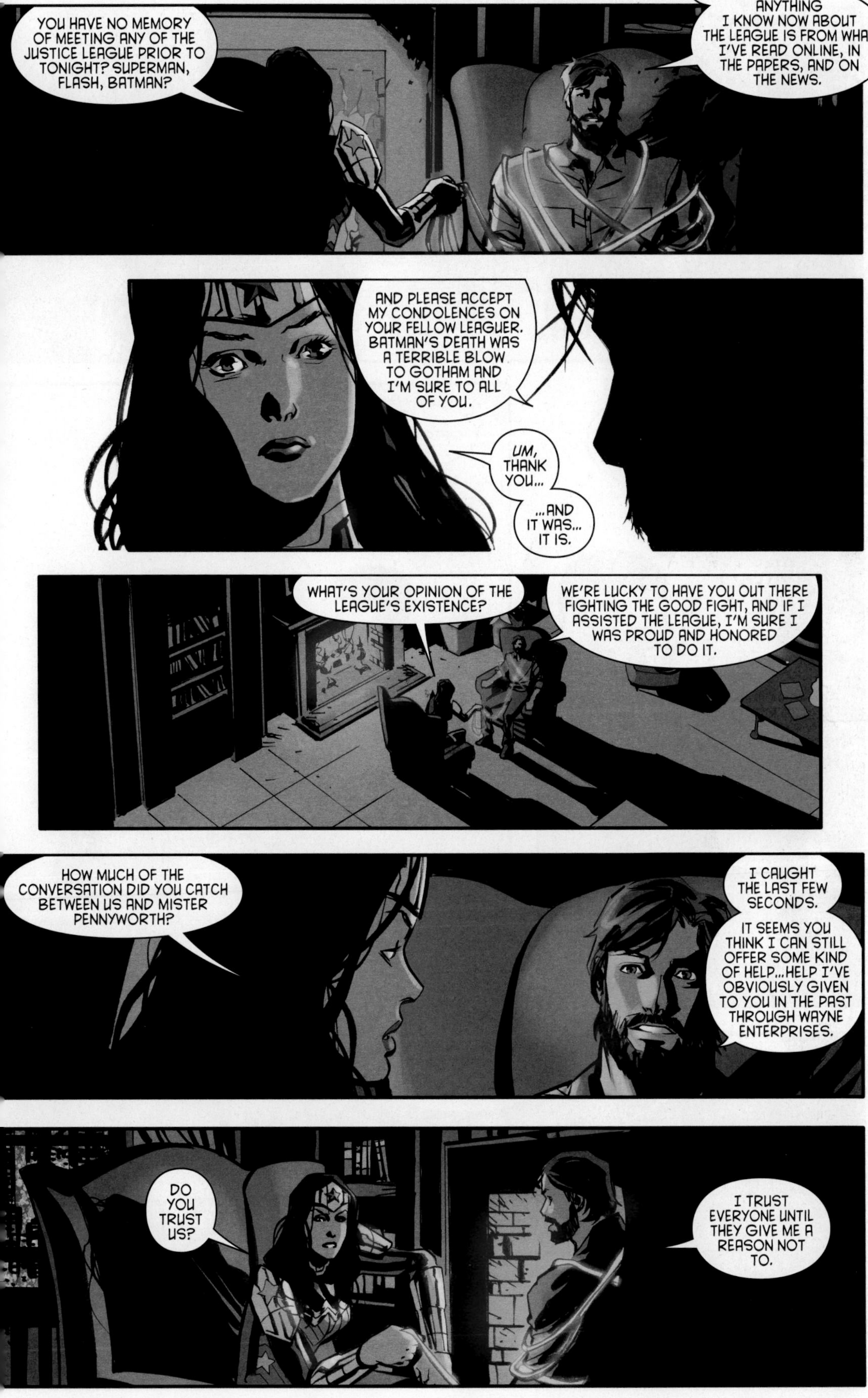
YOU HAVE NO MEMORY OF MEETING ANY OF THE JUSTICE LEAGUE PRIOR TO TONIGHT? SUPERMAN, FLASH, BATMAN?
NO.
ANYTHING I KNOW NOW ABOUT THE LEAGUE IS FROM WHAT I'VE READ ONLINE, IN THE PAPERS, AND ON THE NEWS.
AND PLEASE ACCEPT MY CONDOLENCES ON YOUR FELLOW LEAGUER. BATMAN'S DEATH WAS A TERRIBLE BLOW TO GOTHAM AND I'M SURE TO ALL OF YOU.
UM, THANK YOU...
...AND IT WAS... IT IS.
WHAT'S YOUR OPINION OF THE LEAGUE'S EXISTENCE?
WE'RE LUCKY TO HAVE YOU OUT THERE FIGHTING THE GOOD FIGHT, AND IF I ASSISTED THE LEAGUE, I'M SURE I WAS PROUD AND HONORED TO DO IT.
HOW MUCH OF THE CONVERSATION DID YOU CATCH BETWEEN US AND MISTER PENNYWORTH?
I CAUGHT THE LAST FEW SECONDS.
IT SEEMS YOU THINK I CAN STILL OFFER SOME KIND OF HELP...HELP I'VE OBVIOUSLY GIVEN TO YOU IN THE PAST THROUGH WAYNE ENTERPRISES.
DO YOU TRUST US?
I TRUST EVERYONE UNTIL THEY GIVE ME A REASON NOT TO.

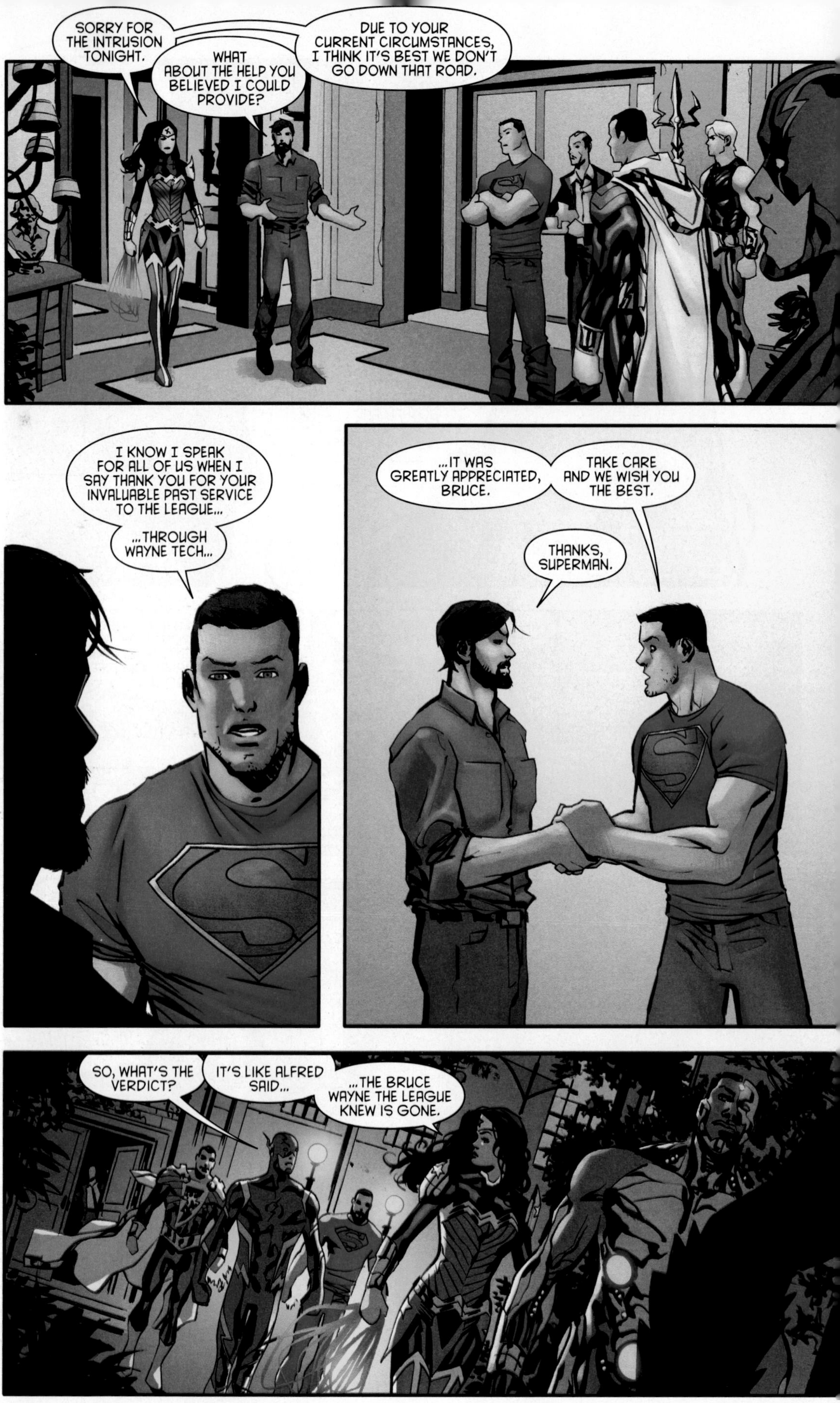
SORRY FOR THE INTRUSION TONIGHT.
WHAT ABOUT THE HELP YOU BELIEVED I COULD PROVIDE?
DUE TO YOUR CURRENT CIRCUMSTANCES, I THINK IT'S BEST WE DON'T GO DOWN THAT ROAD.
I KNOW I SPEAK FOR ALL OF US WHEN I SAY THANK YOU FOR YOUR INVALUABLE PAST SERVICE TO THE LEAGUE...
...THROUGH WAYNE TECH...
...IT WAS GREATLY APPRECIATED, BRUCE.
TAKE CARE AND WE WISH YOU THE BEST.
THANKS, SUPERMAN.
SO, WHAT'S THE VERDICT?
IT'S LIKE ALFRED SAID...
...THE BRUCE WAYNE THE LEAGUE KNEW IS GONE.

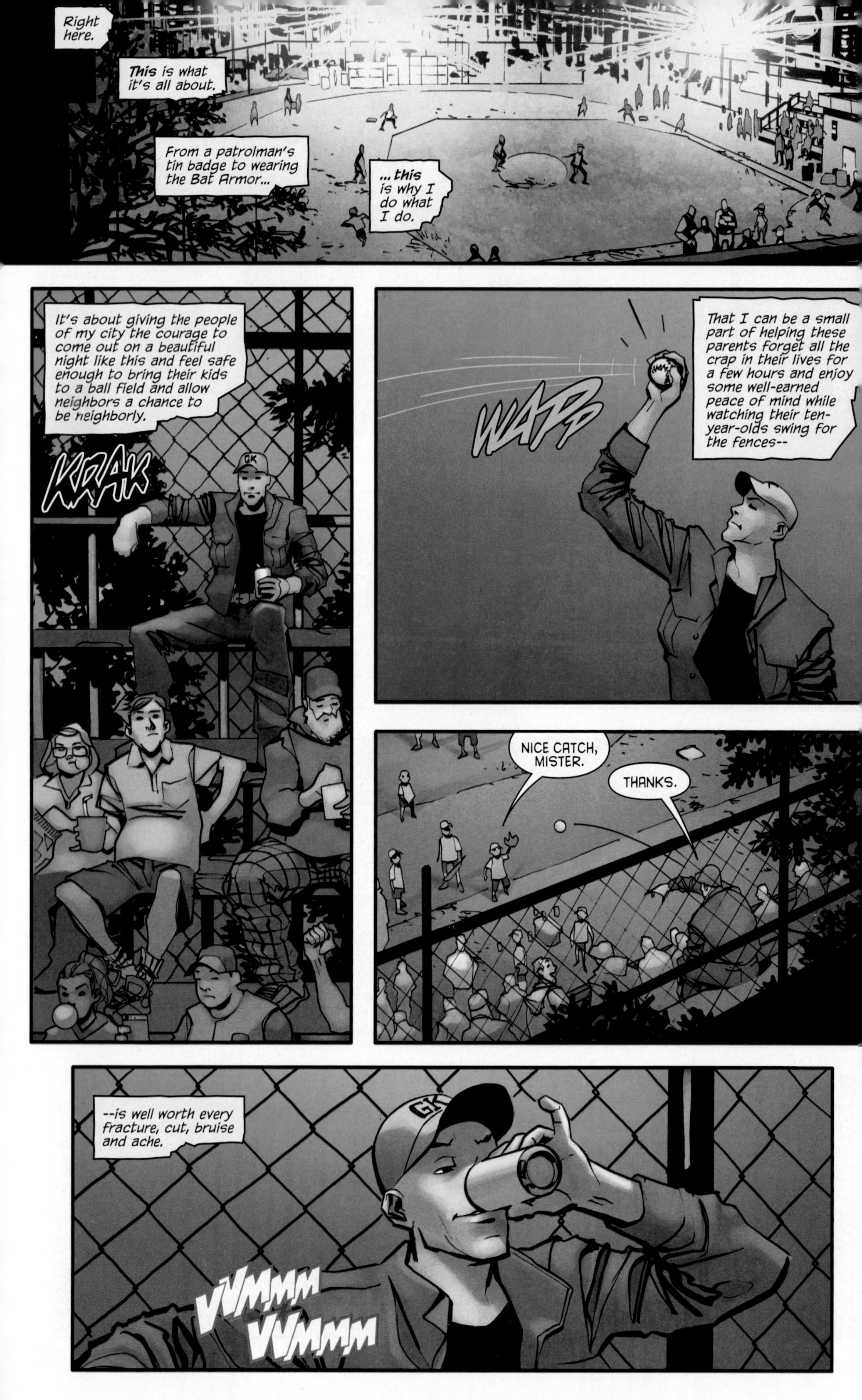

Right here.
This is what it's all about.
From a patrolman's tin badge to wearing the Bat Armor...
...this is why I do what I do.
It's about giving the people of my city the courage to come out on a beautiful night like this and feel safe enough to bring their kids to a ball field and allow neighbors a chance to be neighborly.
KRAK
GK
WAPP
That I can be a small part of helping these parents forget all the crap in their lives for a few hours and enjoy some well-earned peace of mind while watching their ten-year-olds swing for the fences--
NICE CATCH, MISTER.
THANKS.
--is well worth every fracture, cut, bruise and ache.
GK
VVMMM VVMMM

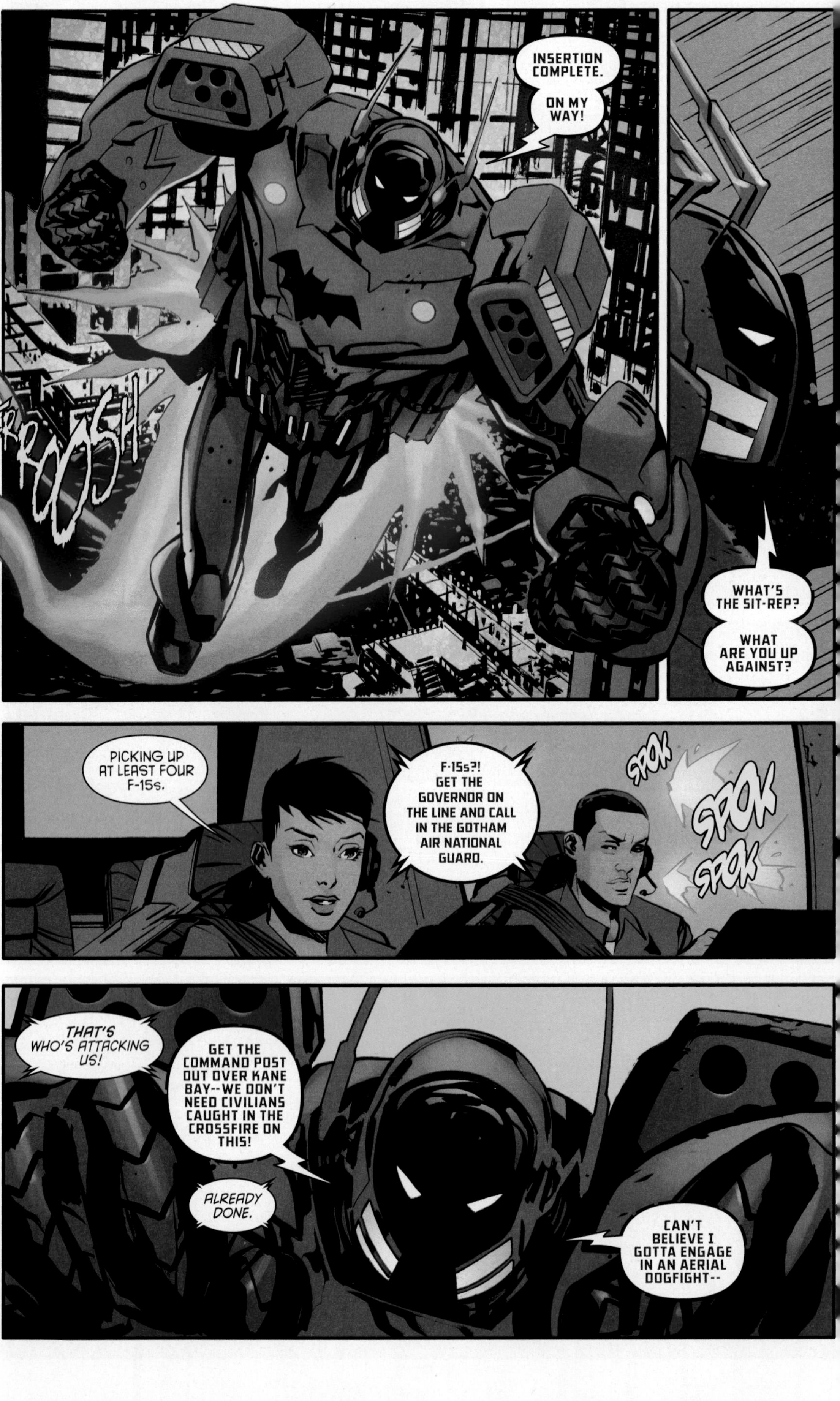
INSERTION COMPLETE.
ON MY WAY!
FRROOSH
WHAT'S THE SIT-REP?
WHAT ARE YOU UP AGAINST?
PICKING UP AT LEAST FOUR F-15s.
F-15s?! GET THE GOVERNOR ON THE LINE AND CALL IN THE GOTHAM AIR NATIONAL GUARD.
SPOK
SPOK
SPOK
THAT'S WHO'S ATTACKING US!
GET THE COMMAND POST OUT OVER KANE BAY--WE DON'T NEED CIVILIANS CAUGHT IN THE CROSSFIRE ON THIS!
ALREADY DONE.
CAN'T BELIEVE I GOTTA ENGAGE IN AN AERIAL DOGFIGHT--

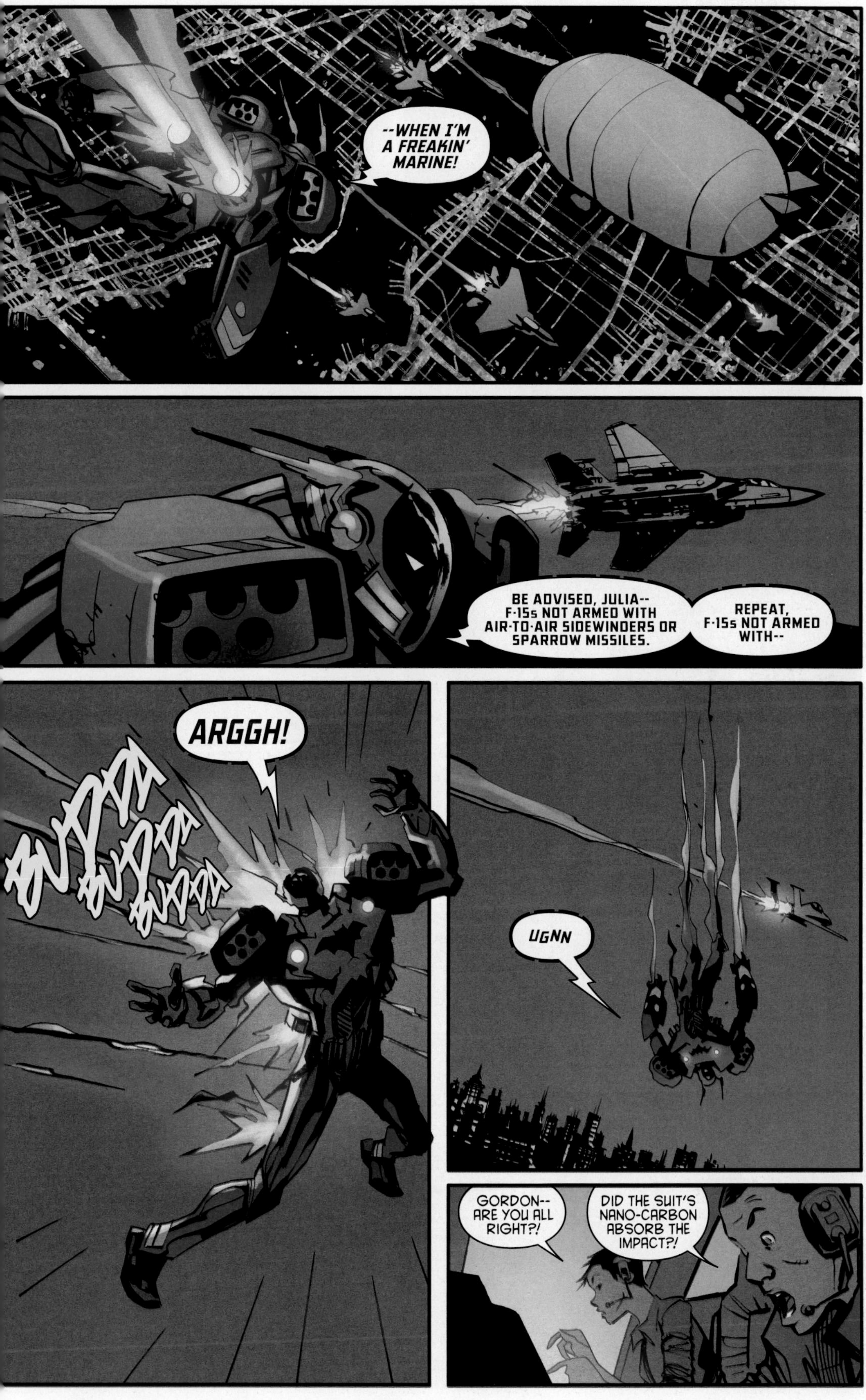
--WHEN I'M A FREAKIN' MARINE!
BE ADVISED, JULIA-- F-15s NOT ARMED WITH AIR-TO-AIR SIDEWINDERS OR SPARROW MISSILES.
REPEAT, F-15s NOT ARMED WITH--
ARGGH!
UGNN
GORDON-- ARE YOU ALL RIGHT?!
DID THE SUIT'S NANO-CARBON ABSORB THE IMPACT?!

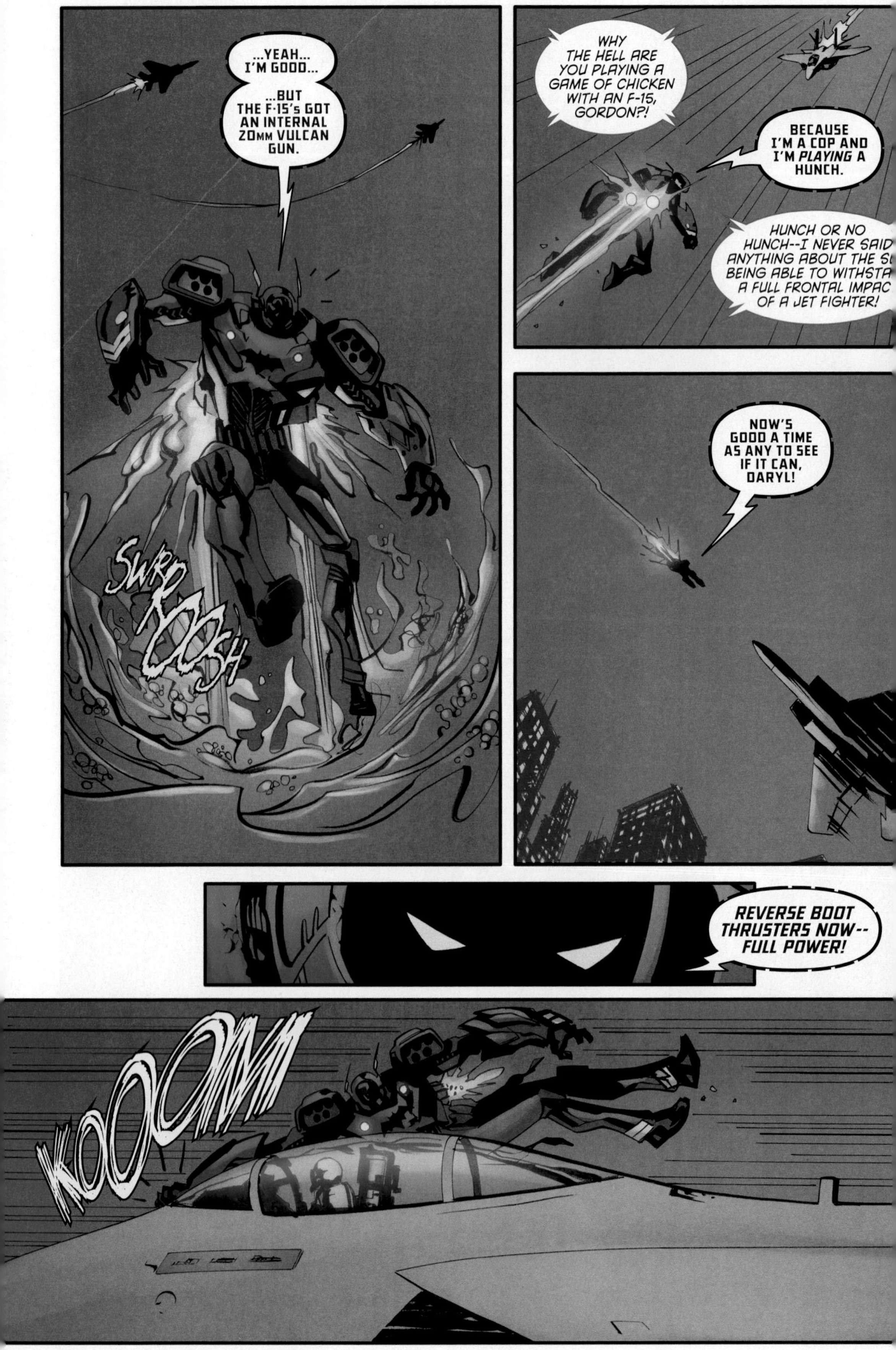
...YEAH... I'M GOOD...
...BUT THE F-15's GOT AN INTERNAL 20MM VULCAN GUN.
SWROOSH
WHY THE HELL ARE YOU PLAYING A GAME OF CHICKEN WITH AN F-15, GORDON?!
BECAUSE I'M A COP AND I'M *PLAYING* A HUNCH.
NOW'S GOOD A TIME AS ANY TO SEE IF IT CAN, DARYL!
REVERSE BOOT THRUSTERS NOW-- FULL POWER!
KOOOM

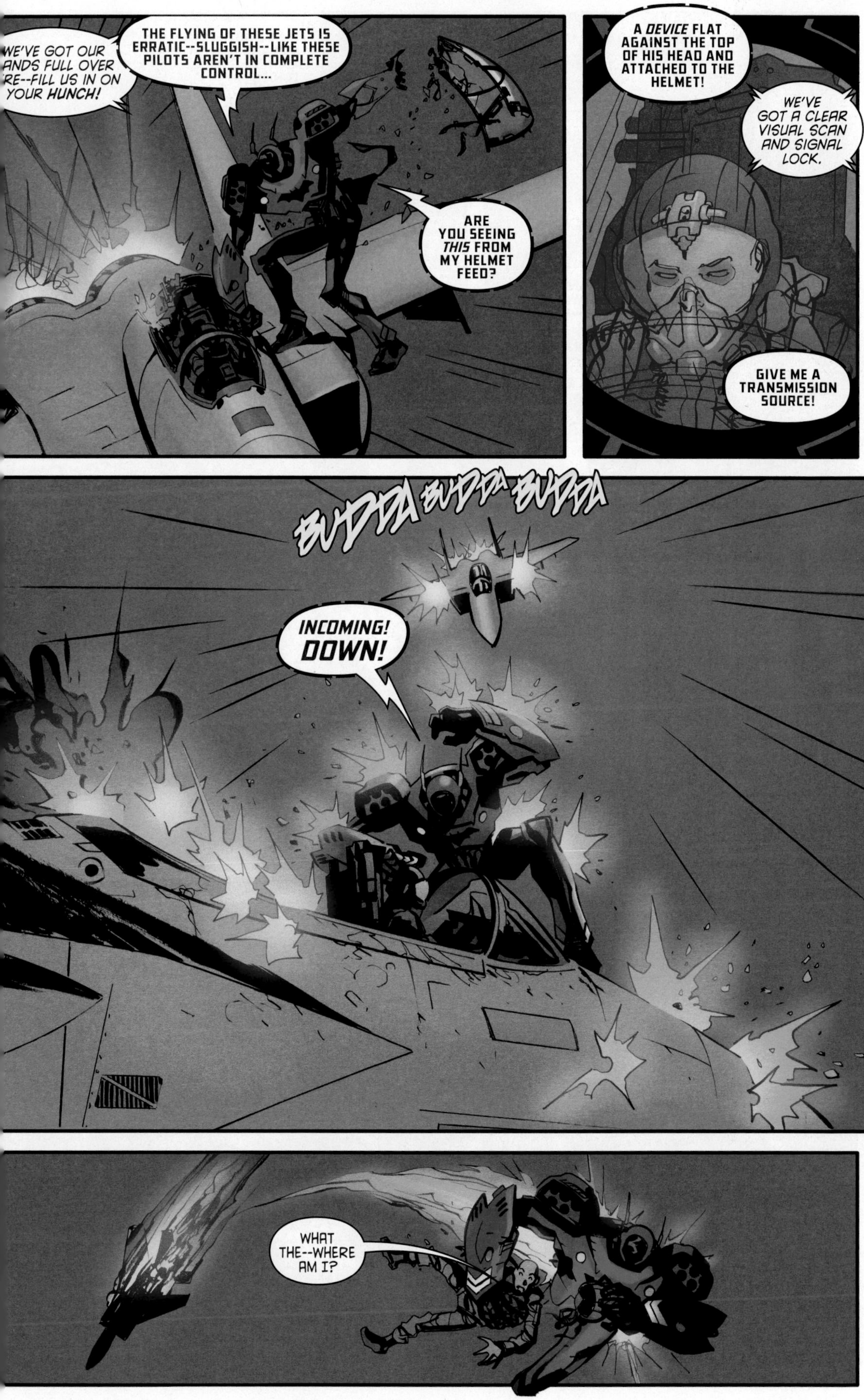
WE'VE GOT OUR ANDS FULL OVER RE--FILL US IN ON YOUR HUNCH!
THE FLYING OF THESE JETS IS ERRATIC--SLUGGISH--LIKE THESE PILOTS AREN'T IN COMPLETE CONTROL...
ARE YOU SEEING THIS FROM MY HELMET FEED?
A DEVICE FLAT AGAINST THE TOP OF HIS HEAD AND ATTACHED TO THE HELMET!
WE'VE GOT A CLEAR VISUAL SCAN AND SIGNAL LOCK.
GIVE ME A TRANSMISSION SOURCE!
BUDDA BUDDA BUDDA
INCOMING! DOWN!
WHAT THE--WHERE AM I?

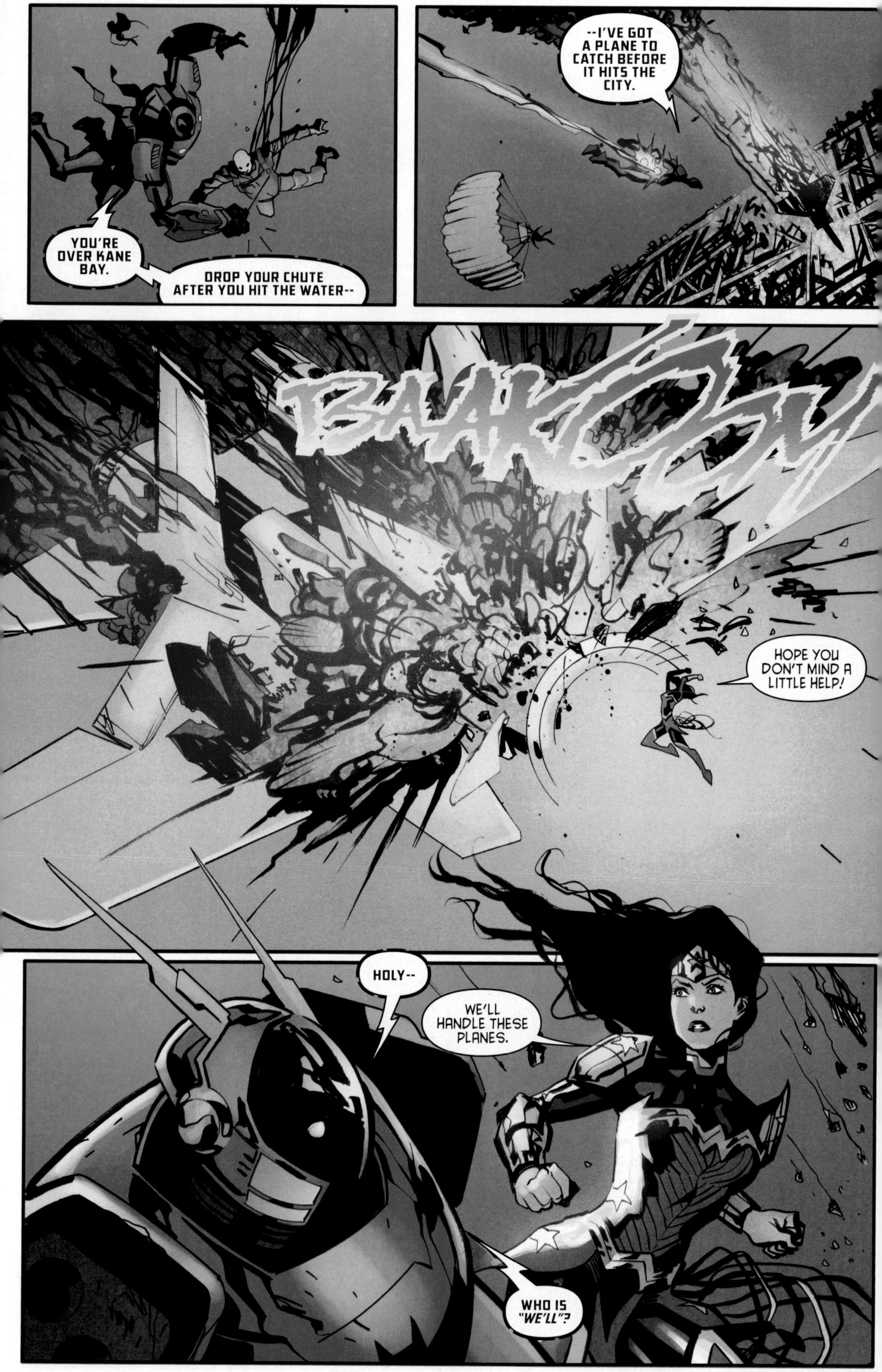
YOU'RE OVER KANE BAY.
DROP YOUR CHUTE AFTER YOU HIT THE WATER--
--I'VE GOT A PLANE TO CATCH BEFORE IT HITS THE CITY.
BAAKOOM
HOPE YOU DON'T MIND A LITTLE HELP!
HOLY--
WE'LL HANDLE THESE PLANES.
WHO IS "WE'LL"?

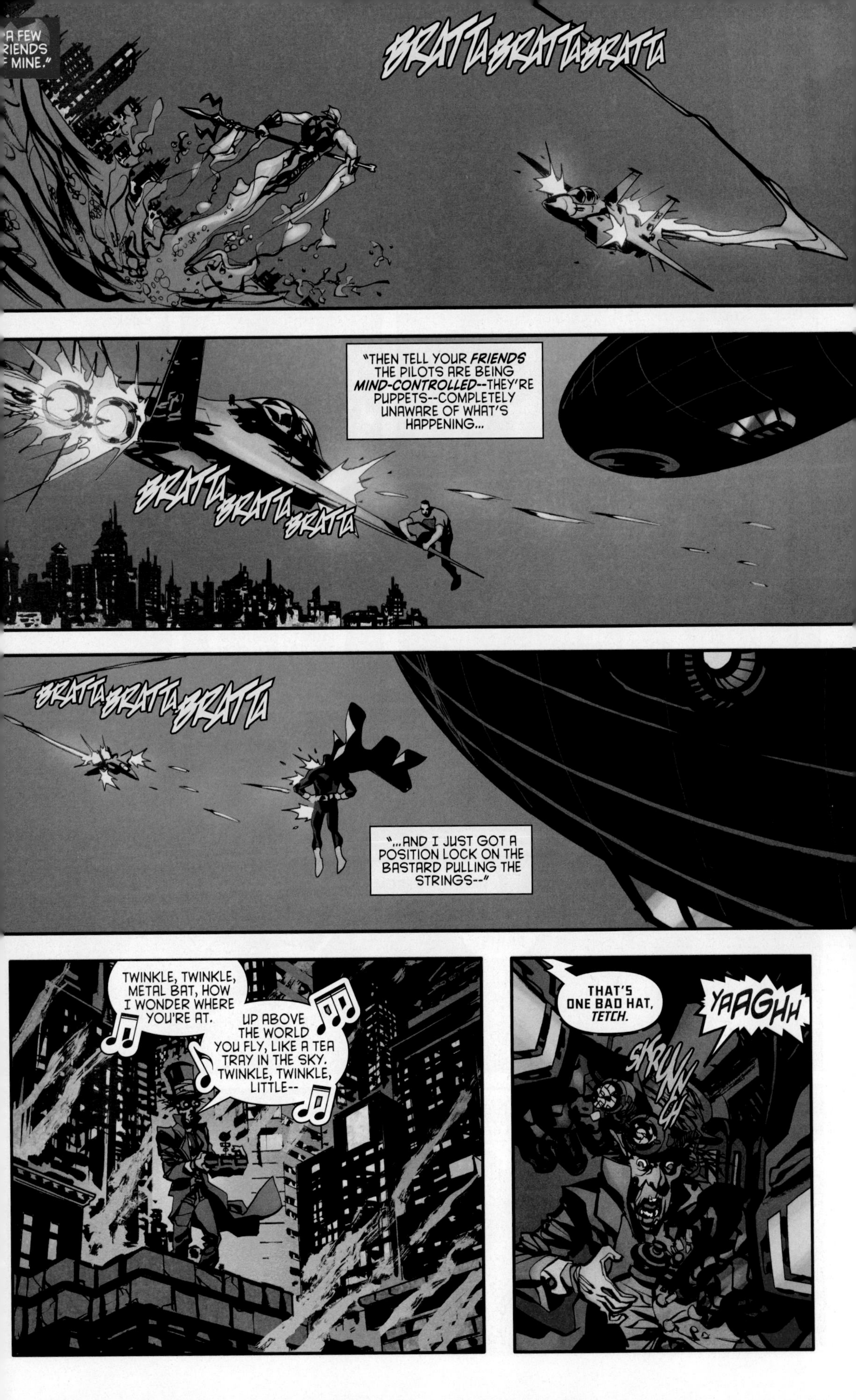
"A FEW
RIENDS
F MINE."
BRATTABRATTABRATTA
"THEN TELL YOUR *FRIENDS* THE PILOTS ARE BEING *MIND-CONTROLLED*--THEY'RE PUPPETS--COMPLETELY UNAWARE OF WHAT'S HAPPENING...
BRATTA BRATTA BRATTA
BRATTA BRATTA BRATTA
"...AND I JUST GOT A POSITION LOCK ON THE BASTARD PULLING THE STRINGS--"
TWINKLE, TWINKLE, METAL BAT, HOW I WONDER WHERE YOU'RE AT.
UP ABOVE THE WORLD YOU FLY, LIKE A TEA TRAY IN THE SKY. TWINKLE, TWINKLE, LITTLE--
THAT'S ONE BAD HAT, *TETCH.*
YAAGHH
SKRUNNCH

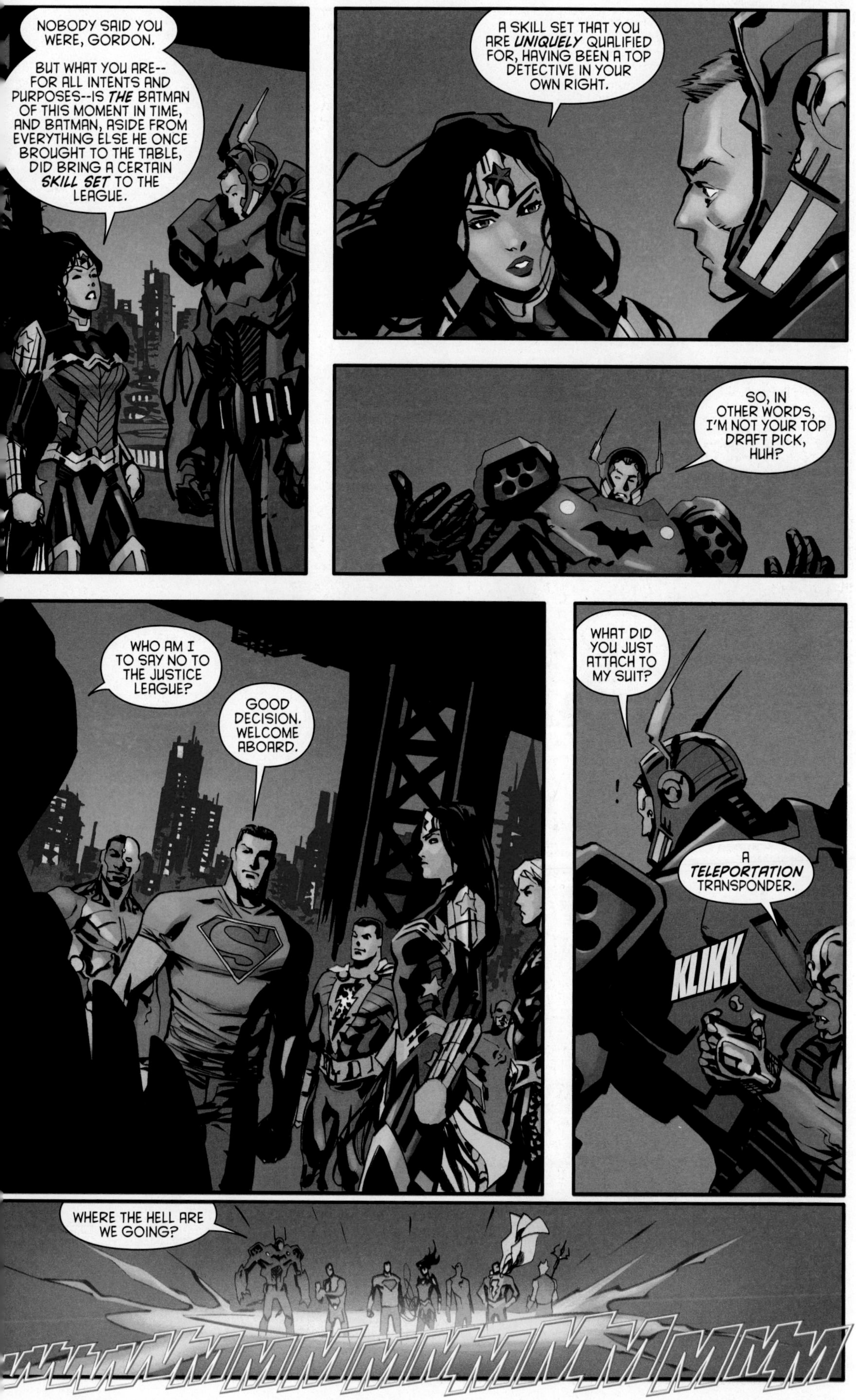
NOBODY SAID YOU WERE, GORDON.
BUT WHAT YOU ARE--FOR ALL INTENTS AND PURPOSES--IS *THE* BATMAN OF THIS MOMENT IN TIME, AND BATMAN, ASIDE FROM EVERYTHING ELSE HE ONCE BROUGHT TO THE TABLE, DID BRING A CERTAIN *SKILL SET* TO THE LEAGUE.
A SKILL SET THAT YOU ARE *UNIQUELY* QUALIFIED FOR, HAVING BEEN A TOP DETECTIVE IN YOUR OWN RIGHT.
SO, IN OTHER WORDS, I'M NOT YOUR TOP DRAFT PICK, HUH?
WHO AM I TO SAY NO TO THE JUSTICE LEAGUE?
GOOD DECISION. WELCOME ABOARD.
WHAT DID YOU JUST ATTACH TO MY SUIT?
!
A *TELEPORTATION* TRANSPONDER.
KLIKK
WHERE THE HELL ARE WE GOING?
WWWMMMMMMMMMMMMM

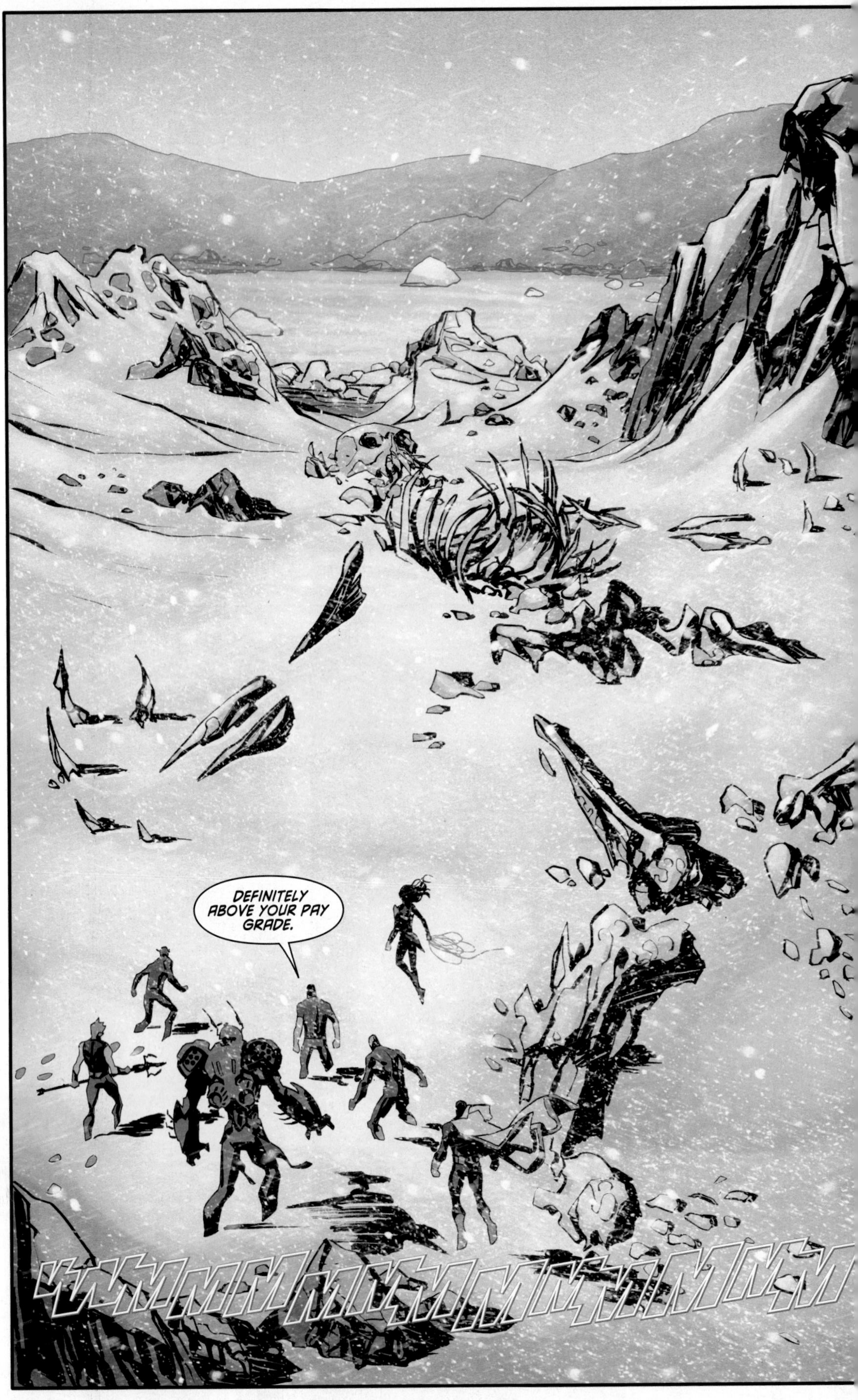
DEFINITELY ABOVE YOUR PAY GRADE.
VMMMMMMMMMMMMMMM

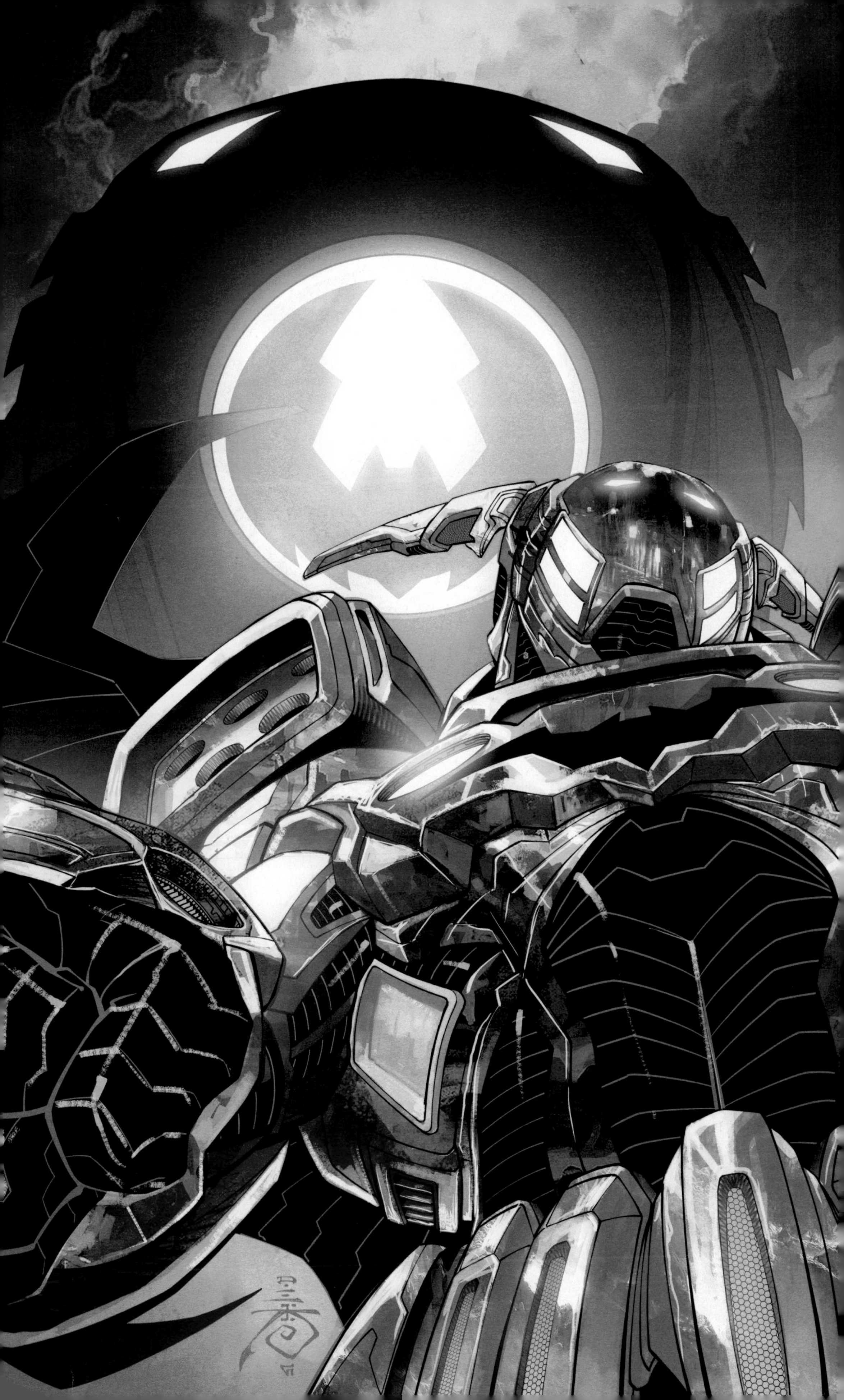

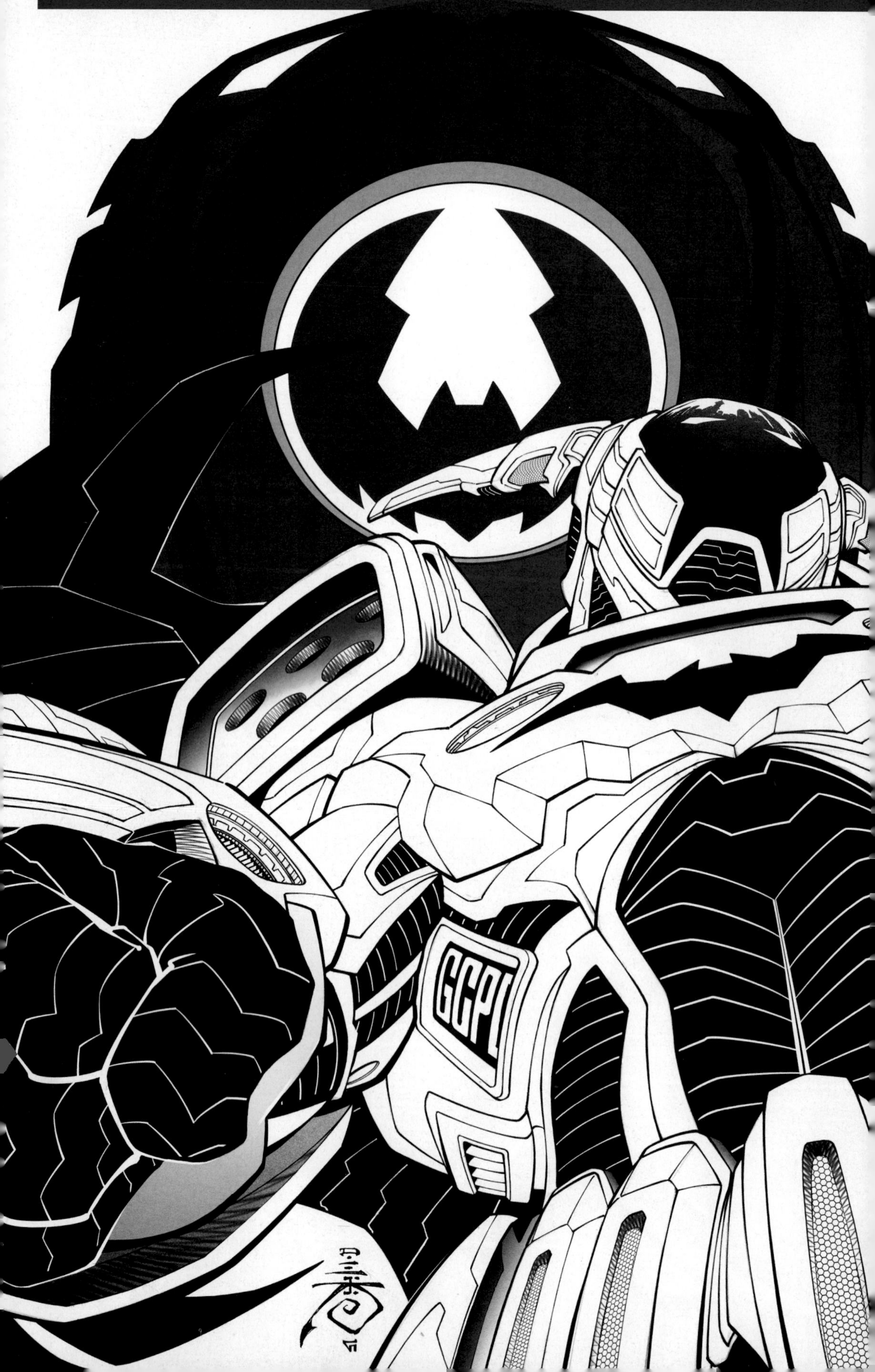
GCP

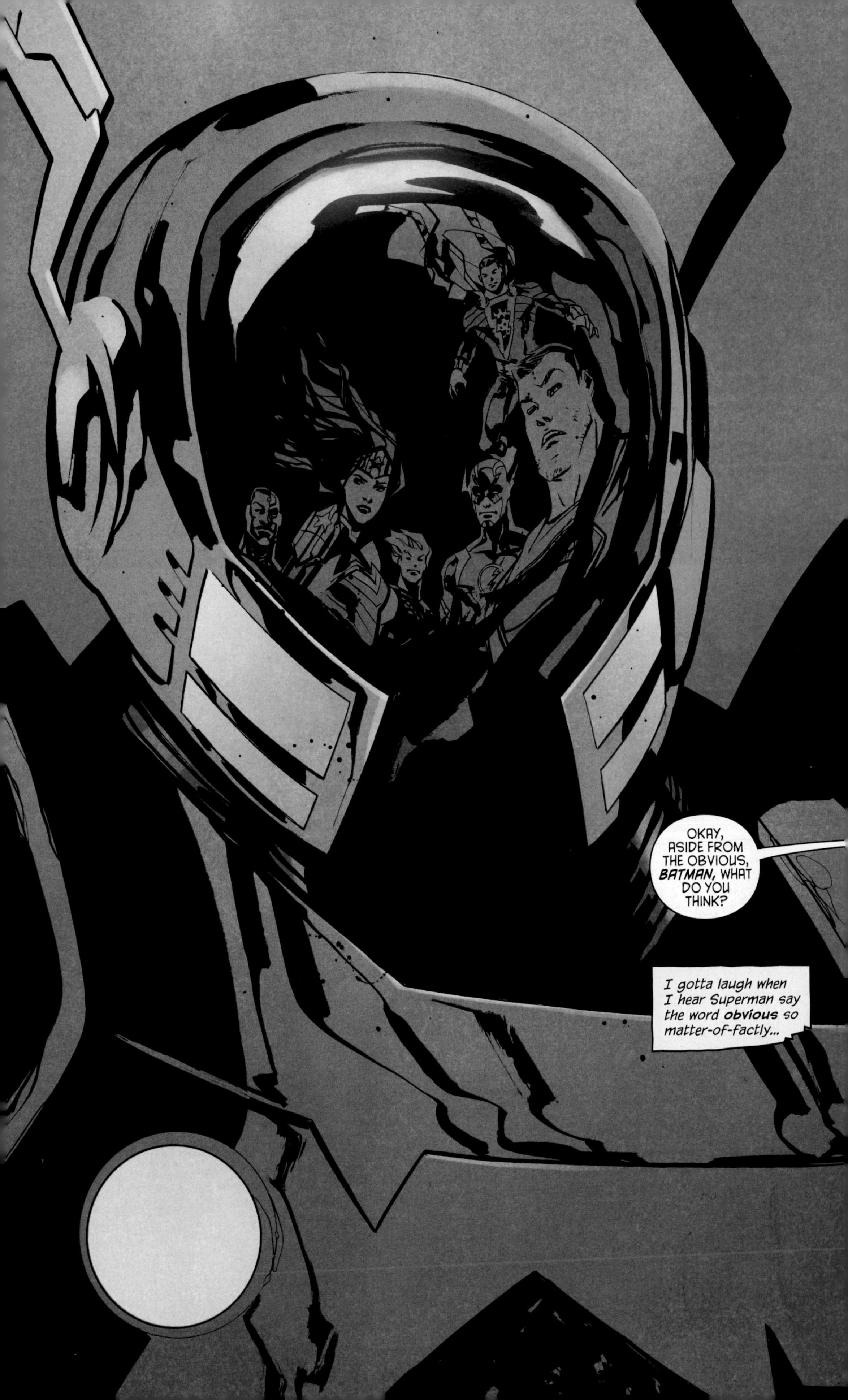
OKAY, ASIDE FROM THE OBVIOUS, BATMAN, WHAT DO YOU THINK?
I gotta laugh when I hear Superman say the word obvious so matter-of-factly...

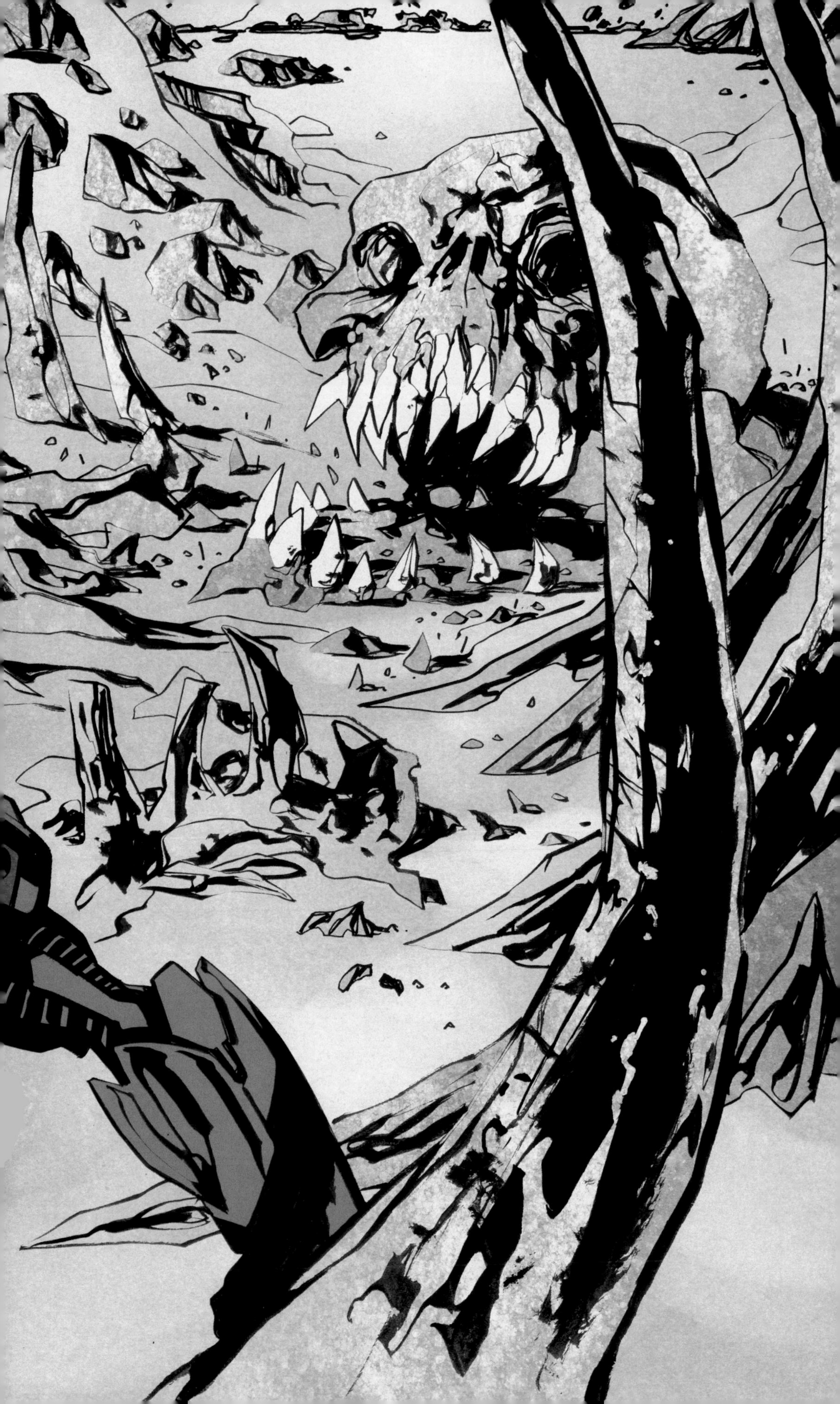

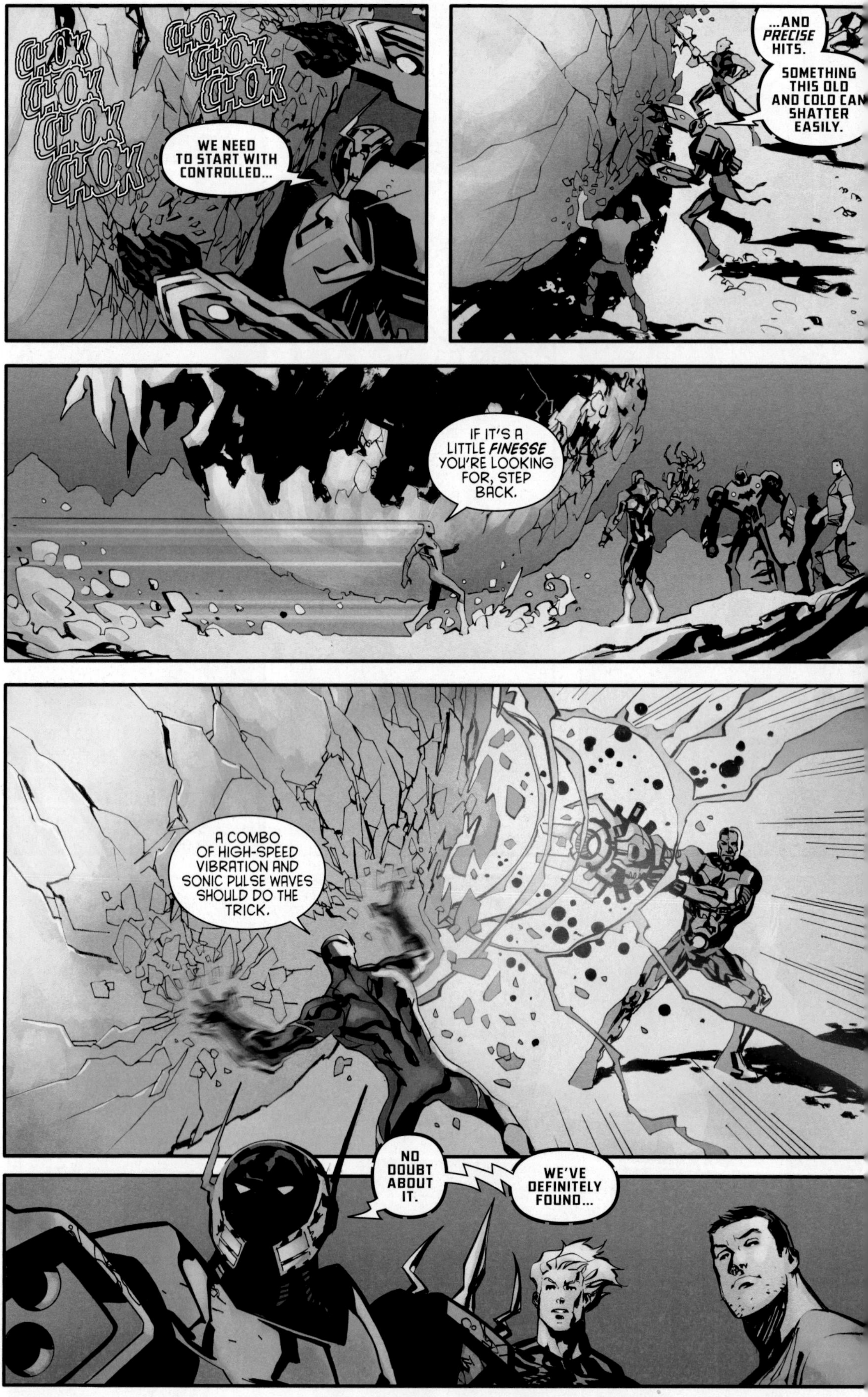
CHOK CHOK CHOK CHOK
CHOK CHOK CHOK
WE NEED TO START WITH CONTROLLED...
...AND PRECISE HITS.
SOMETHING THIS OLD AND COLD CAN SHATTER EASILY.
IF IT'S A LITTLE FINESSE YOU'RE LOOKING FOR, STEP BACK.
A COMBO OF HIGH-SPEED VIBRATION AND SONIC PULSE WAVES SHOULD DO THE TRICK.
NO DOUBT ABOUT IT.
WE'VE DEFINITELY FOUND...

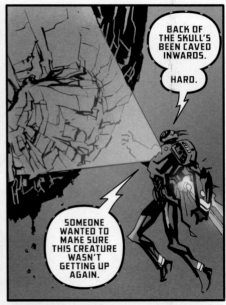

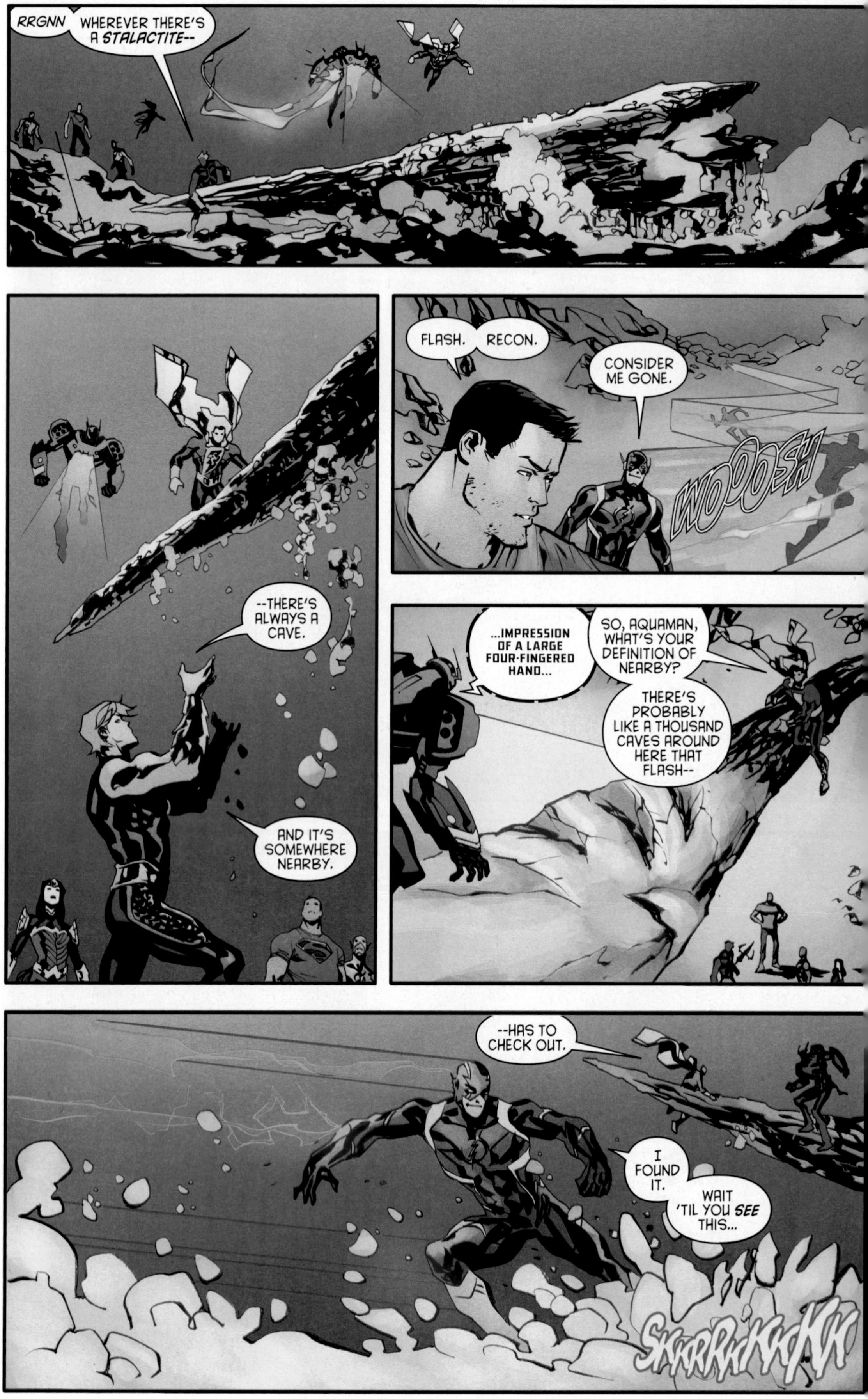

RRGNN
WHEREVER THERE'S A STALACTITE--
--THERE'S ALWAYS A CAVE.
AND IT'S SOMEWHERE NEARBY.
FLASH.
RECON.
CONSIDER ME GONE.
WOOOSH
...IMPRESSION OF A LARGE FOUR-FINGERED HAND...
SO, AQUAMAN, WHAT'S YOUR DEFINITION OF NEARBY?
THERE'S PROBABLY LIKE A THOUSAND CAVES AROUND HERE THAT FLASH--
--HAS TO CHECK OUT.
I FOUND IT.
WAIT 'TIL YOU SEE THIS...
SKRRRKKKKKK

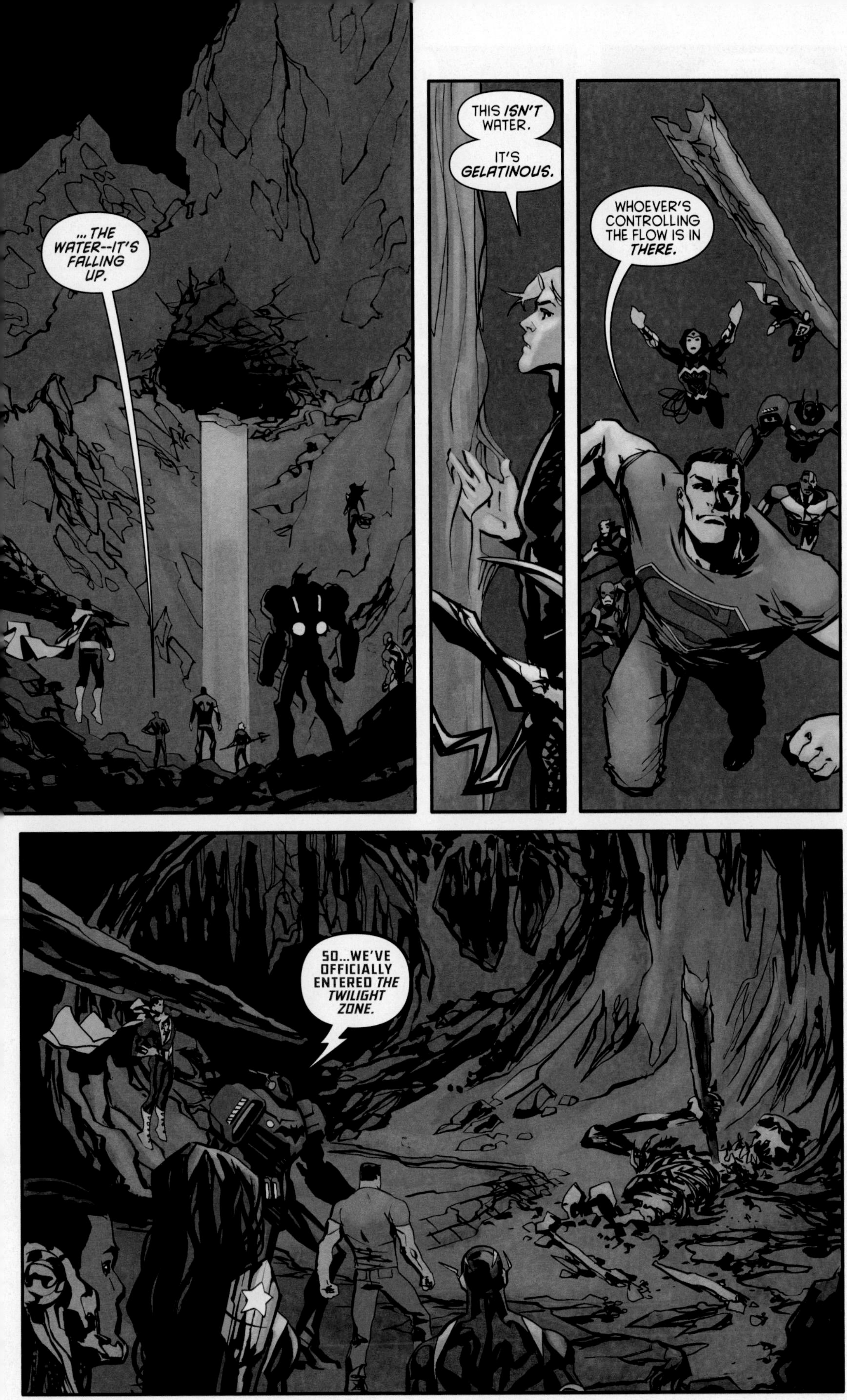
...THE WATER--IT'S FALLING UP.
THIS ISN'T WATER.
IT'S GELATINOUS.
WHOEVER'S CONTROLLING THE FLOW IS IN THERE.
SO...WE'VE OFFICIALLY ENTERED THE TWILIGHT ZONE.

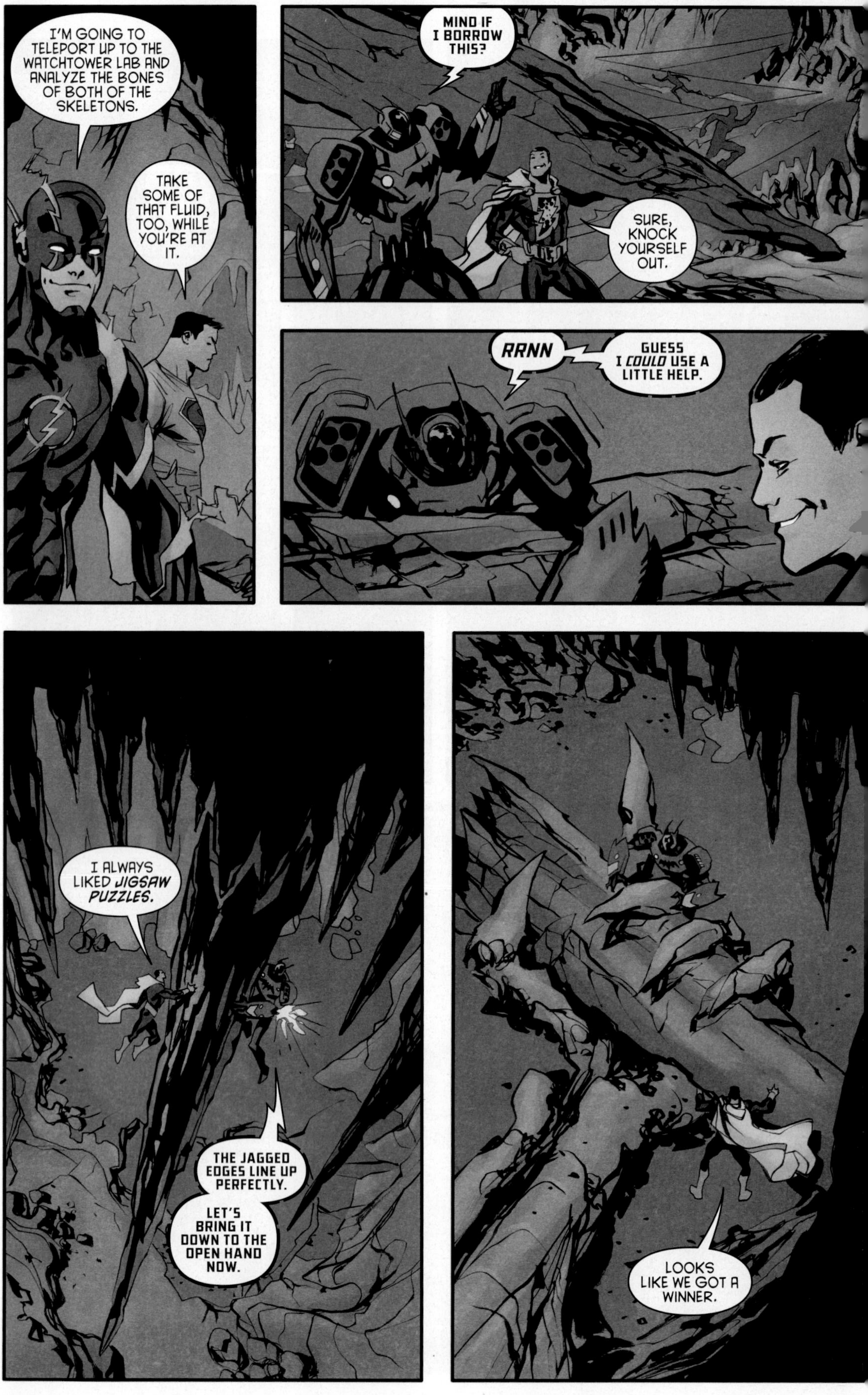
I'M GOING TO TELEPORT UP TO THE WATCHTOWER LAB AND ANALYZE THE BONES OF BOTH OF THE SKELETONS.
TAKE SOME OF THAT FLUID, TOO, WHILE YOU'RE AT IT.
MIND IF I BORROW THIS?
SURE, KNOCK YOURSELF OUT.
RRNN
GUESS I *COULD* USE A LITTLE HELP.
I ALWAYS LIKED *JIGSAW PUZZLES.*
THE JAGGED EDGES LINE UP PERFECTLY.
LET'S BRING IT DOWN TO THE OPEN HAND NOW.
LOOKS LIKE WE GOT A WINNER.

AND IT LOOKS LIKE THIS CREATURE COMMITTED *SUICIDE*.

AND IT LOOKS LIKE THE DISAPPEARANCE OF MOUNTAIN CLIMBERS IN THIS AREA JUST STOPPED BEING A COLD CASE.

OKAY, I'M BACK. THE FIRST SKELETON WE FOUND IS A MALE, AND THIS SKELETON HERE IN THE CAVE IS A FEMALE.

AND THE *LIQUID?*

VWMMMMMMMMM

AQUEOUS HUMOUR. AND IT'S *HUMAN.*

THAT TIES INTO THE MYSTERIOUS DEATHS AND LOSS OF EYES WE'VE HEARD ABOUT IN THE REGION.

AQUEOUS HUMOUR--THAT LIKE SOME KINDA ICE CREAM FROM A GOOD HUMOR TRUCK?

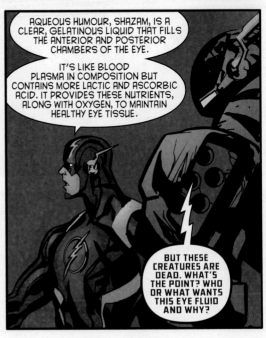

AQUEOUS HUMOUR, SHAZAM, IS A CLEAR, GELATINOUS LIQUID THAT FILLS THE ANTERIOR AND POSTERIOR CHAMBERS OF THE EYE.

IT'S LIKE BLOOD PLASMA IN COMPOSITION BUT CONTAINS MORE LACTIC AND ASCORBIC ACID. IT PROVIDES THESE NUTRIENTS, ALONG WITH OXYGEN, TO MAINTAIN HEALTHY EYE TISSUE.

BUT THESE CREATURES ARE DEAD. WHAT'S THE POINT? WHO OR WHAT WANTS THIS EYE FLUID AND WHY?

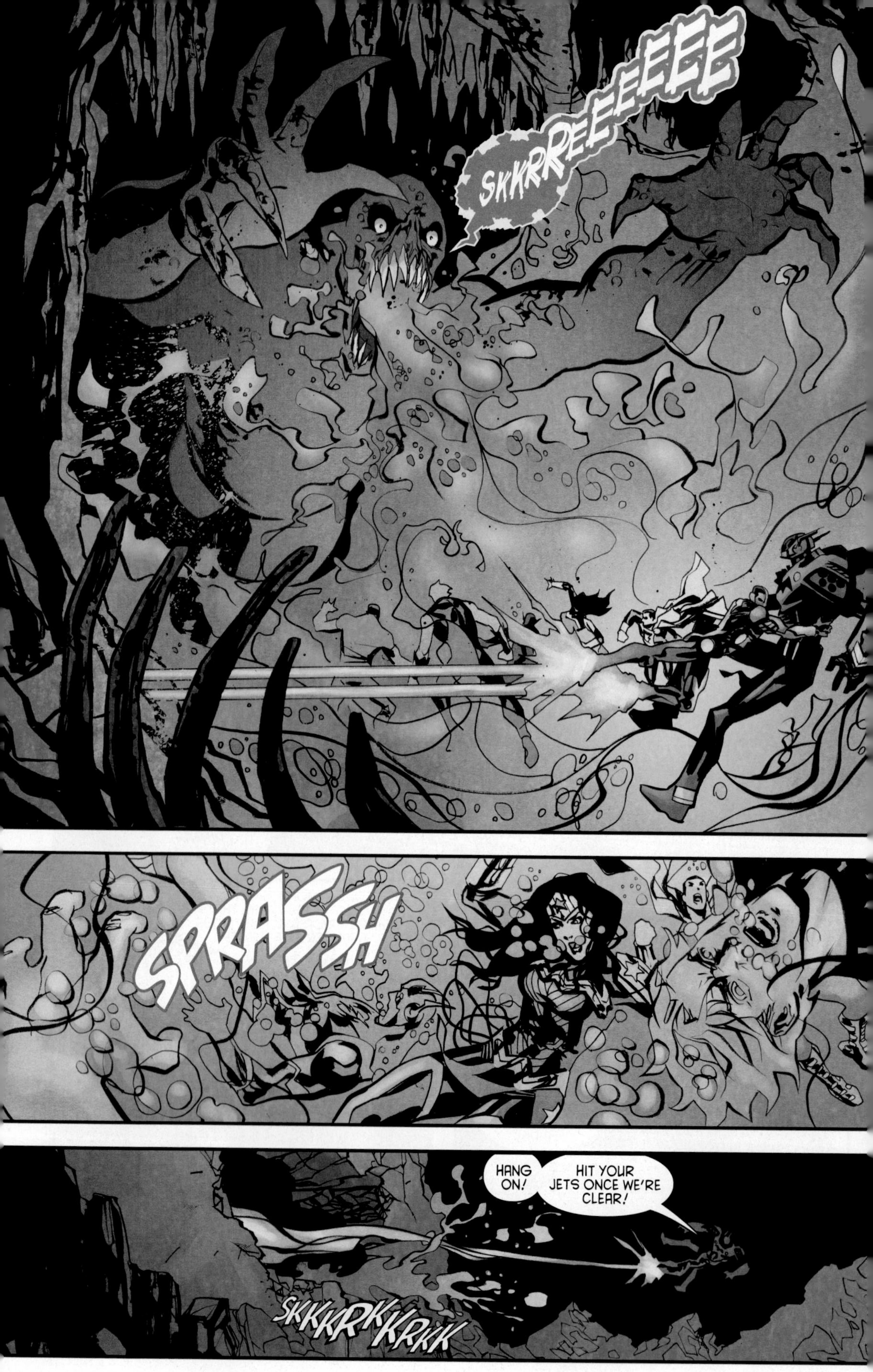
SKKRREEEEEEEE
SPRASSH
HANG ON!
HIT YOUR JETS ONCE WE'RE CLEAR!
SKKKRKKRKK

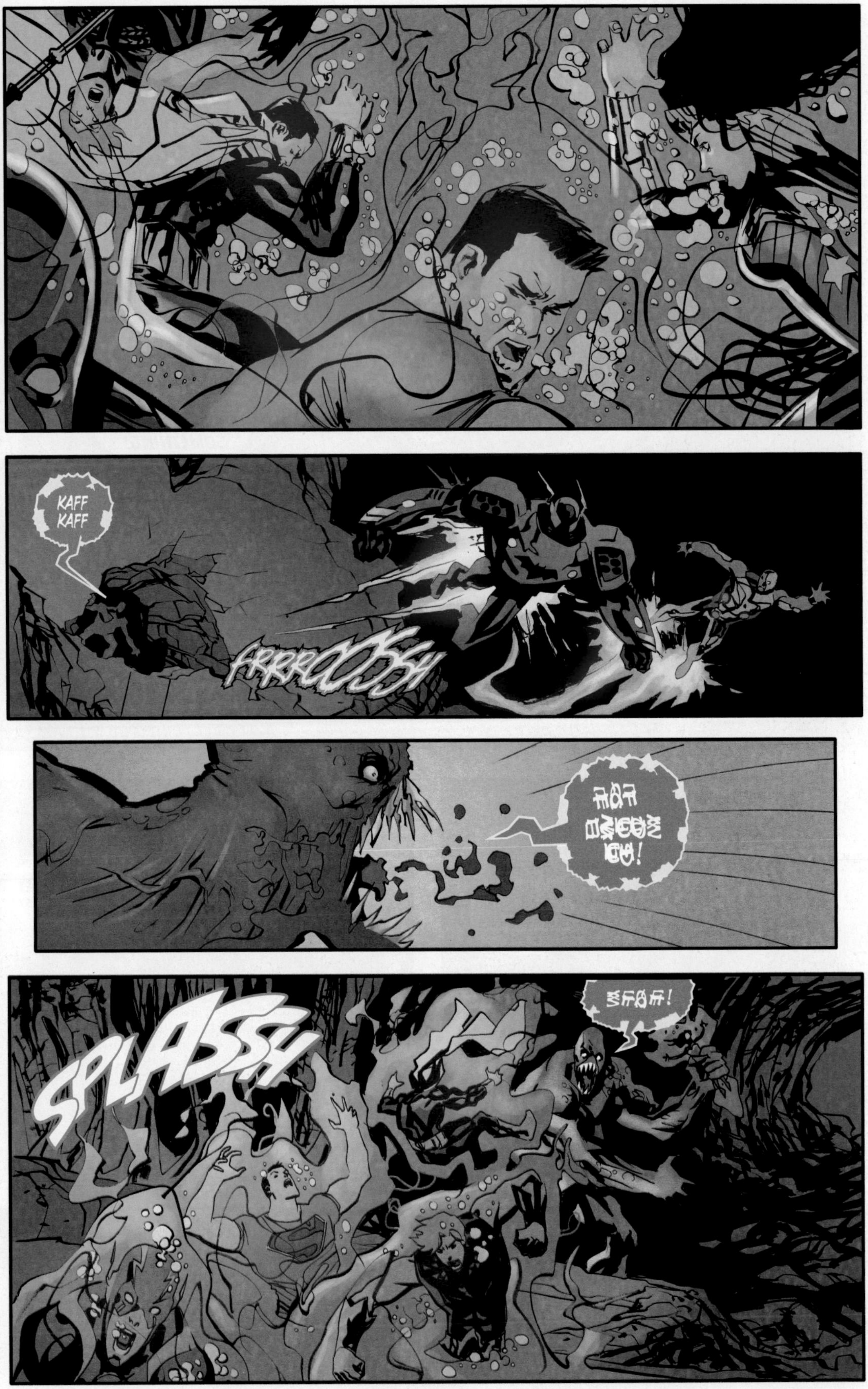
KAFF KAFF
FRRROOOSSH
SPLASSH

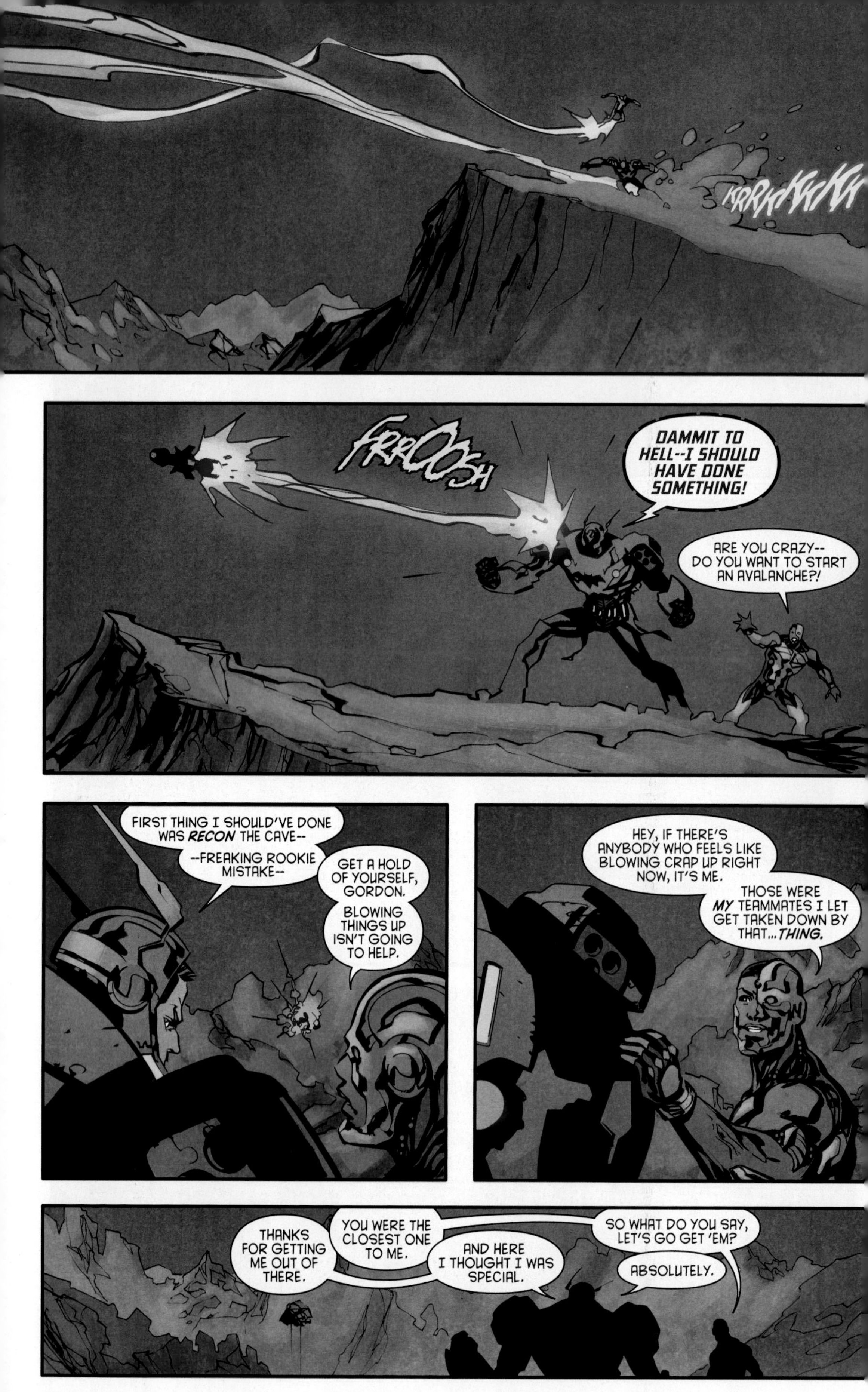
KRRKKKKKK
FRROOSH
DAMMIT TO HELL--I SHOULD HAVE DONE SOMETHING!
ARE YOU CRAZY-- DO YOU WANT TO START AN AVALANCHE?!
FIRST THING I SHOULD'VE DONE WAS RECON THE CAVE--
--FREAKING ROOKIE MISTAKE--
GET A HOLD OF YOURSELF, GORDON.
BLOWING THINGS UP ISN'T GOING TO HELP.
HEY, IF THERE'S ANYBODY WHO FEELS LIKE BLOWING CRAP UP RIGHT NOW, IT'S ME.
THOSE WERE MY TEAMMATES I LET GET TAKEN DOWN BY THAT...THING.
THANKS FOR GETTING ME OUT OF THERE.
YOU WERE THE CLOSEST ONE TO ME.
AND HERE I THOUGHT I WAS SPECIAL.
SO WHAT DO YOU SAY, LET'S GO GET 'EM?
ABSOLUTELY.

KAFF
KAFF

ӨꝾꞤ
ꝾꞤꞤꝾꝄꞤ
ꝾꝄ!

"ALL RIGHT, WE'VE
DONE OUR *RECON*...

"...SO NOW THAT BLASTING
AND SMASHING *ISN'T* PART
OF THE EQUATION...

ꝾꝄꞤꝾꞤ
ꝾꝄ...

"...LET'S ASK
OURSELVES..."

...WHAT DO
WE KNOW AND HOW
DO WE GET THE LEAGUE
OUT OF THERE?

ALL I *KNOW*
IS THAT THIS WHOLE
THING IS STARTING
TO FREAK THE HELL
OUTTA ME.

WHAT I'M
ABOUT TO SAY
SOUNDS *CRAZY*
BUT HEAR ME
OUT...

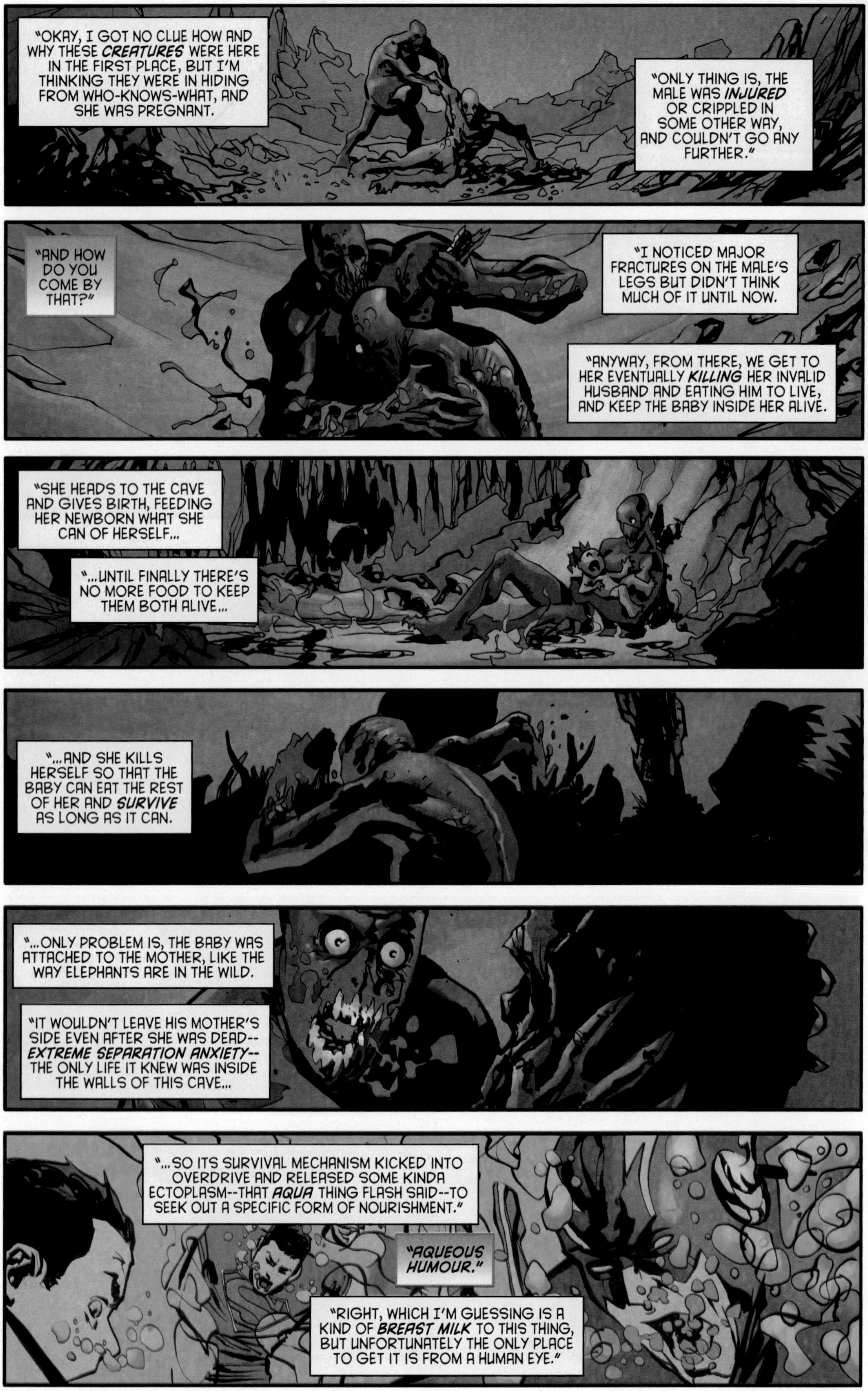
"OKAY, I GOT NO CLUE HOW AND WHY THESE *CREATURES* WERE HERE IN THE FIRST PLACE, BUT I'M THINKING THEY WERE IN HIDING FROM WHO-KNOWS-WHAT, AND SHE WAS PREGNANT.
"ONLY THING IS, THE MALE WAS *INJURED* OR CRIPPLED IN SOME OTHER WAY, AND COULDN'T GO ANY FURTHER."
"AND HOW DO YOU COME BY THAT?"
"I NOTICED MAJOR FRACTURES ON THE MALE'S LEGS BUT DIDN'T THINK MUCH OF IT UNTIL NOW.
"ANYWAY, FROM THERE, WE GET TO HER EVENTUALLY *KILLING* HER INVALID HUSBAND AND EATING HIM TO LIVE, AND KEEP THE BABY INSIDE HER ALIVE.
"SHE HEADS TO THE CAVE AND GIVES BIRTH, FEEDING HER NEWBORN WHAT SHE CAN OF HERSELF...
"...UNTIL FINALLY THERE'S NO MORE FOOD TO KEEP THEM BOTH ALIVE...
"...AND SHE KILLS HERSELF SO THAT THE BABY CAN EAT THE REST OF HER AND *SURVIVE* AS LONG AS IT CAN.
"...ONLY PROBLEM IS, THE BABY WAS ATTACHED TO THE MOTHER, LIKE THE WAY ELEPHANTS ARE IN THE WILD.
"IT WOULDN'T LEAVE HIS MOTHER'S SIDE EVEN AFTER SHE WAS DEAD-- *EXTREME SEPARATION ANXIETY*-- THE ONLY LIFE IT KNEW WAS INSIDE THE WALLS OF THIS CAVE...
"...SO ITS SURVIVAL MECHANISM KICKED INTO OVERDRIVE AND RELEASED SOME KINDA ECTOPLASM--THAT *AQUA* THING FLASH SAID--TO SEEK OUT A SPECIFIC FORM OF NOURISHMENT."
"AQUEOUS HUMOUR."
"RIGHT, WHICH I'M GUESSING IS A KIND OF *BREAST MILK* TO THIS THING, BUT UNFORTUNATELY THE ONLY PLACE TO GET IT IS FROM A HUMAN EYE."

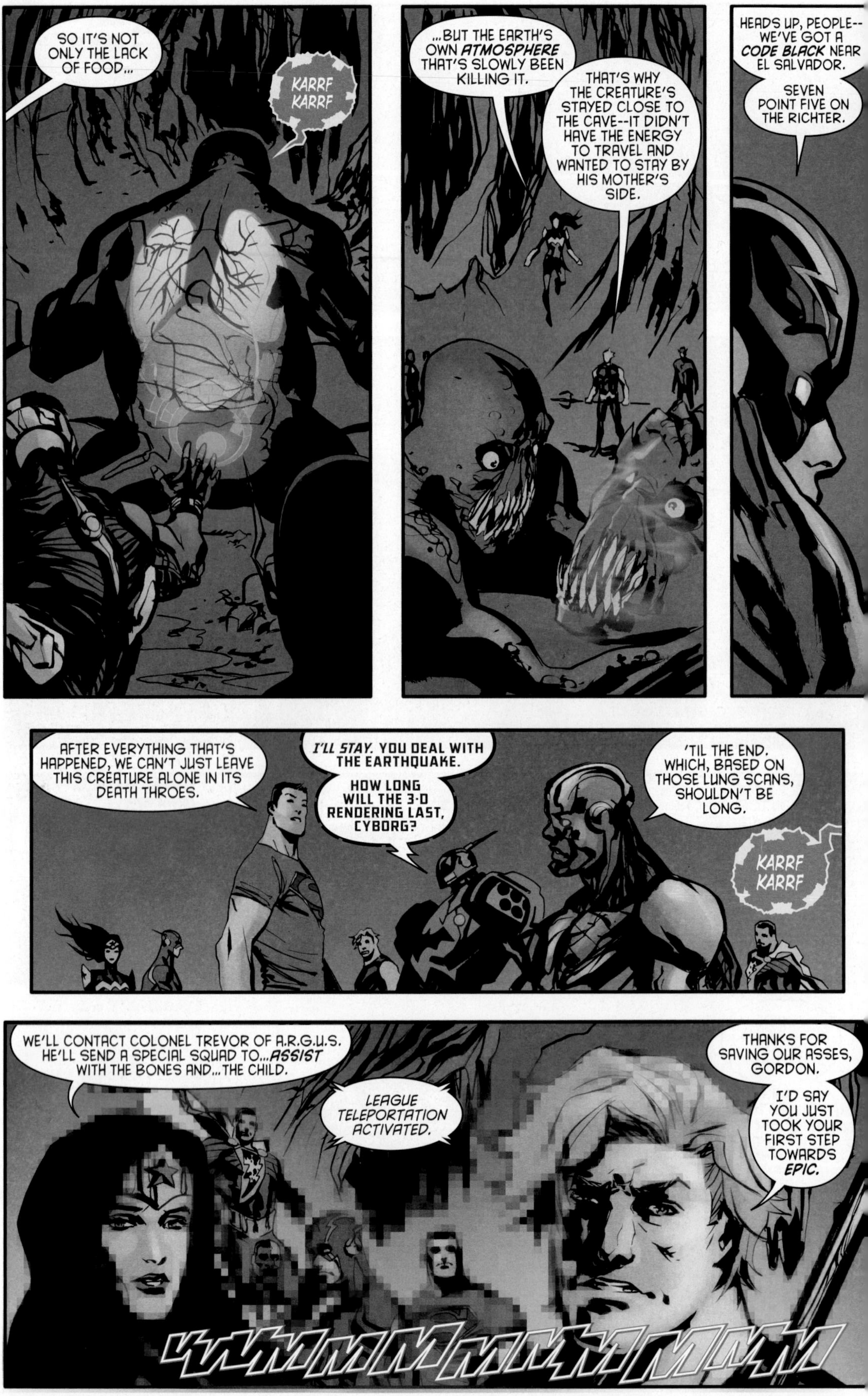
SO IT'S NOT ONLY THE LACK OF FOOD...
KARRF KARRF
...BUT THE EARTH'S OWN ATMOSPHERE THAT'S SLOWLY BEEN KILLING IT.
THAT'S WHY THE CREATURE'S STAYED CLOSE TO THE CAVE--IT DIDN'T HAVE THE ENERGY TO TRAVEL AND WANTED TO STAY BY HIS MOTHER'S SIDE.
HEADS UP, PEOPLE--WE'VE GOT A CODE BLACK NEAR EL SALVADOR.
SEVEN POINT FIVE ON THE RICHTER.
AFTER EVERYTHING THAT'S HAPPENED, WE CAN'T JUST LEAVE THIS CREATURE ALONE IN ITS DEATH THROES.
I'LL STAY. YOU DEAL WITH THE EARTHQUAKE.
HOW LONG WILL THE 3-D RENDERING LAST, CYBORG?
'TIL THE END. WHICH, BASED ON THOSE LUNG SCANS, SHOULDN'T BE LONG.
KARRF KARRF
WE'LL CONTACT COLONEL TREVOR OF A.R.G.U.S. HE'LL SEND A SPECIAL SQUAD TO...ASSIST WITH THE BONES AND...THE CHILD.
LEAGUE TELEPORTATION ACTIVATED.
THANKS FOR SAVING OUR ASSES, GORDON.
I'D SAY YOU JUST TOOK YOUR FIRST STEP TOWARDS EPIC.
VVMMMMMMMMMMMM

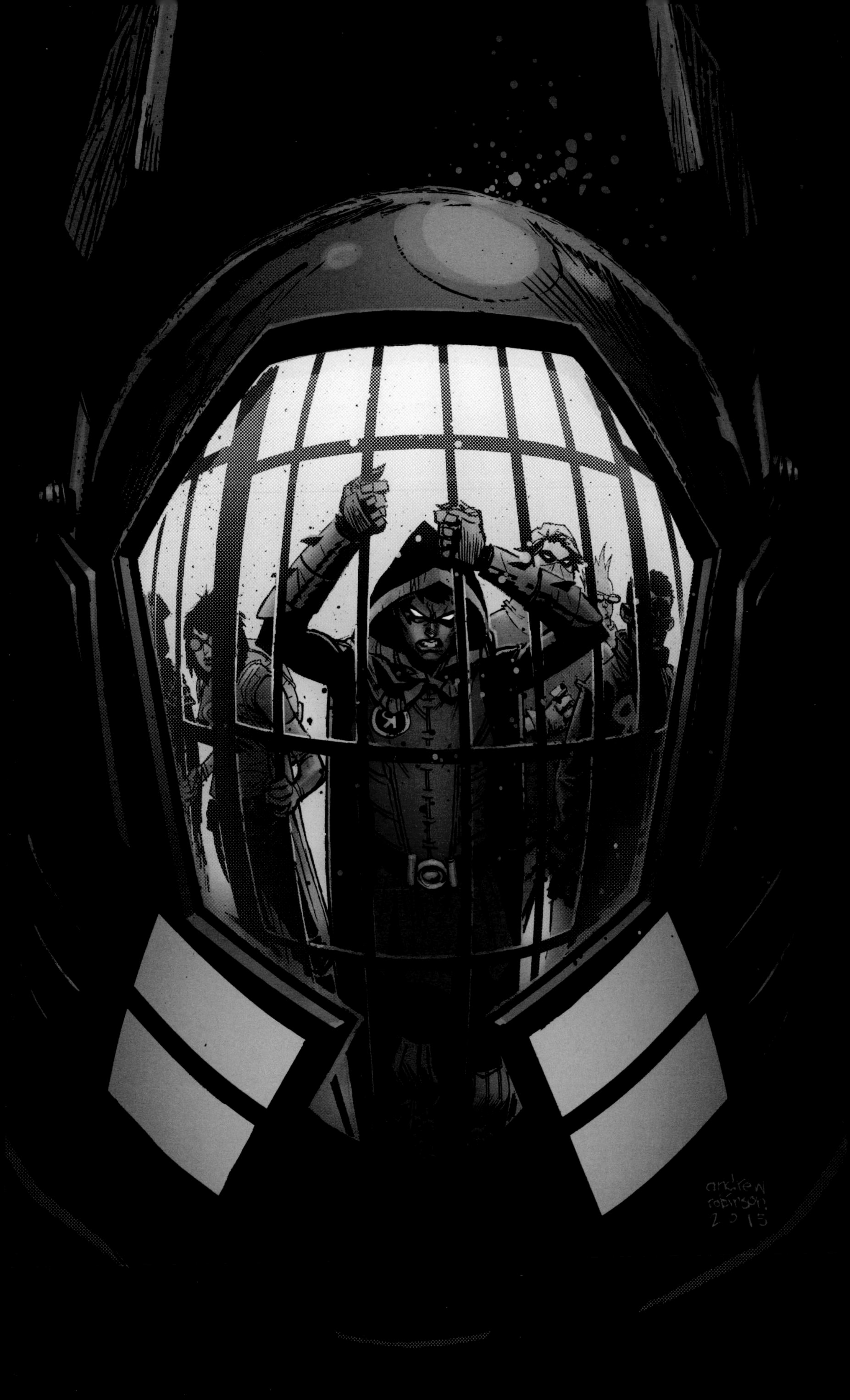
andrew robinson 2015

ROBIN WAR PART 3: GETTING DIRTY

RAY FAWKES writer STEVE PUGH artist CHRIS SOTOMAYOR colorist WES ABBOTT letterer ANDREW ROBINSON cover

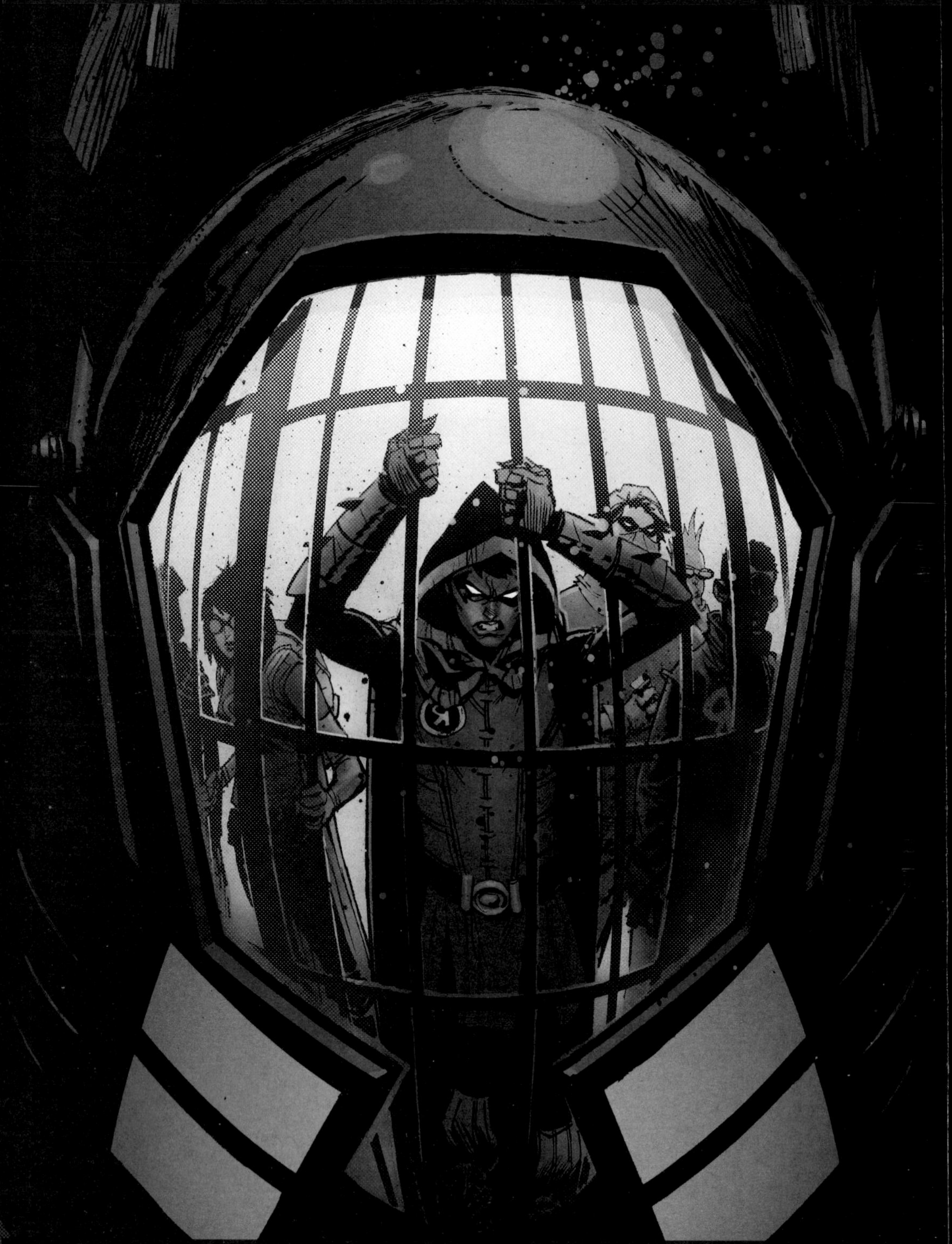

"WE ARE ROBIN."

PREVIOUSLY IN ROBIN WARS ...

There are amateur Robins in Gotham. In an effort to control the teen vigilante group, Gotham's Councilwoman Athene Noctua has put laws in place that make the wearing or possessing of Robin merchandise illegal. The vigilantes were driven underground, where they were found by the real Robin—Damian Wayne—and the three men who once called themselves Robin—Dick Grayson, Jason Todd and Tim Drake. In an effort to protect the untrained gang, Dick Grayson tipped off the Gotham police to their location, leading to the arrest of the entire group, including Damian, Jason, and Tim. Dick's intentions were to keep the children safe, but he is about to run into some serious complications, in the form of Jim Gordon, the new Batman...

ROBIN WAR was originally published in ROBIN WAR #1 GRAYSON #15, DETECTIVE COMICS #47, WE ARE ROBIN #7, ROBIN: SON OF BATMAN #7, RED HOOD/ARSENAL #7, TEEN TITANS #15, GOTHAM ACADEMY #13 and ROBIN WAR #2.

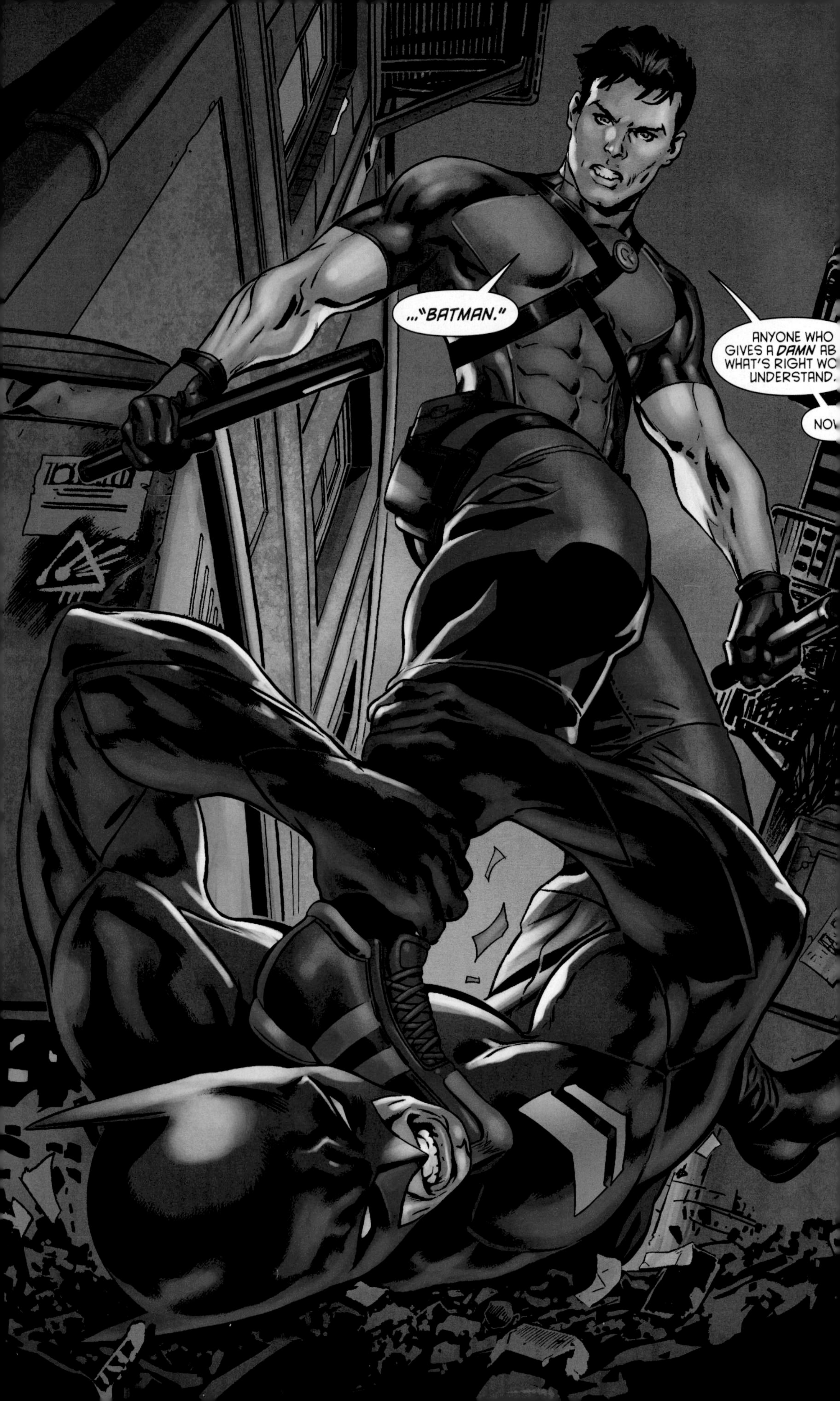
..."BATMAN."
ANYONE WHO GIVES A *DAMN* AB WHAT'S RIGHT WO UNDERSTAND.
NOW

MONTOYA CALLED IT "THE CAGE" AND IT *STUCK*.

THESE ARE *CHILDREN*, HARVEY. I BROUGHT THEM *IN*, BUT...

THEIR *PARENTS* KNOW ABOUT THIS? THEIR *LAWYERS*? HAVE THEY BEEN CHARGED WITH ANYTHING?

WHERE'S THE *DUE PROCESS*?

GOOD *QUESTIONS*. ASK COUNCILWOMAN WHATSERNAME... *NOCTUA*.

NO SMOKING IN THIS AREA

BUNCHA SCRAWNY KIDS IN TOY MASKS GETTIN' THE TERRORIST *SUPERMAX* TREATMENT. THEN AGAIN...

I COULD BRING THIS PLACE DOWN. AT SUNSET, WHEN THE SHADOWS ARE LONG.

THOSE OF US WITH *TRAINING* WOULD BE FINE.

AND TODD AND DRAKE ARE RESOURCEFUL...

YOU *IN* WITH GRAYSON ON THIS, RED ROBIN? YOU'VE GOT A *GUILTY* LOOK.

DON'T EVEN. YOU *KNOW* I WOULDN'T CALL THE COPS.

DO I KNOW THAT? WHAT I KNOW IS THAT YOU CAN BE A REAL CHICKEN--

...WE COULD RESCUE THE PRETENDERS IF WE NEED TO.

WOW. HERE'S YOU SETTING AN *AWESOME* EXAMPLE THOUGH. ALL *RATIONAL* AND *INTELLIGENT*...

...YOU ALWAYS DID GET *DUMBER* UNDER PRESSURE.

I'LL SHOW YOU *PRESSURE,* YOU CONDESCENDING LITTLE PUNK!

It's not that the kids who played robbers wanted to be *bad.* I remember Pauly Wright, his dad was *beat up* by burglars. He *hated* crooks.

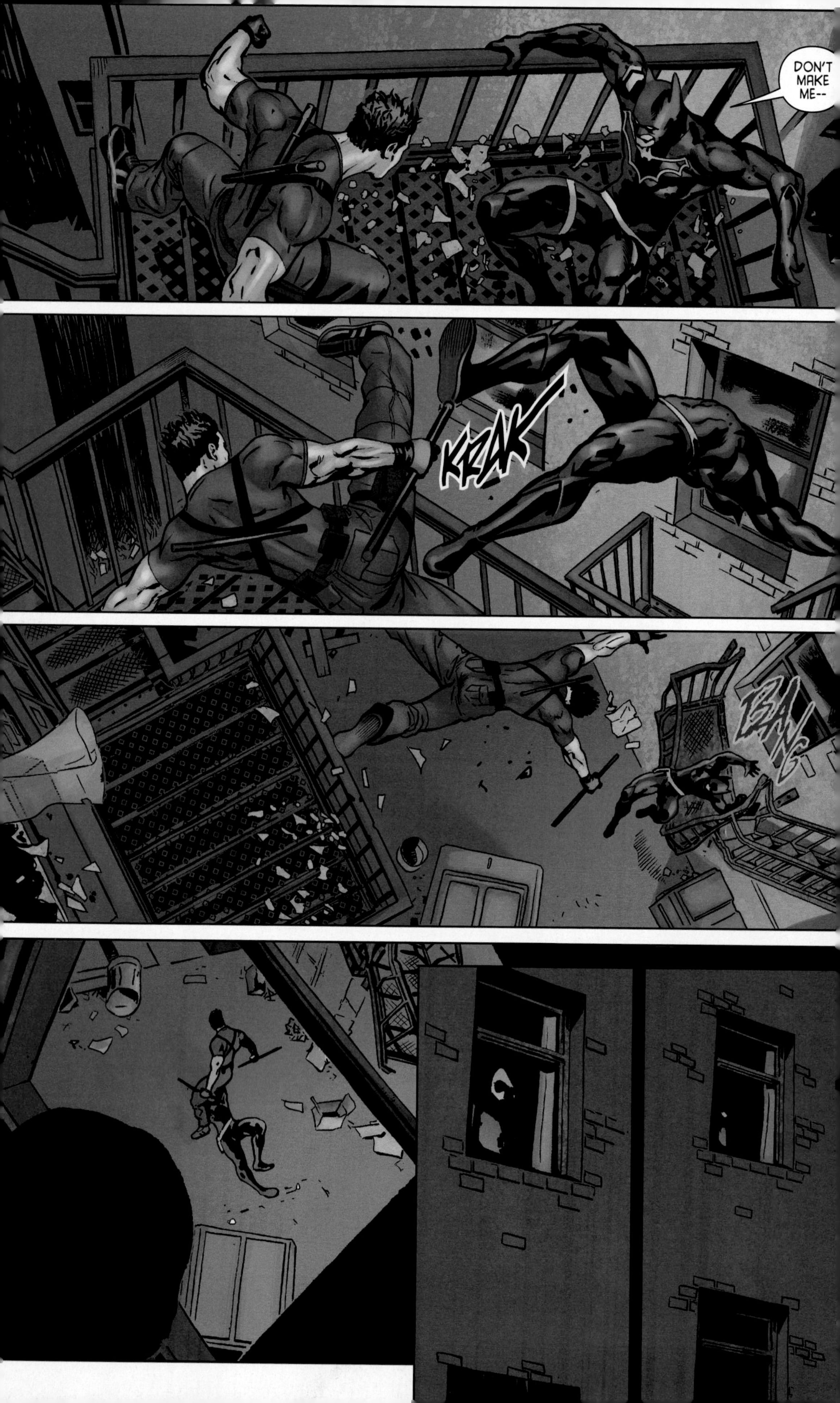
DON'T MAKE ME--
KRAK
BANG

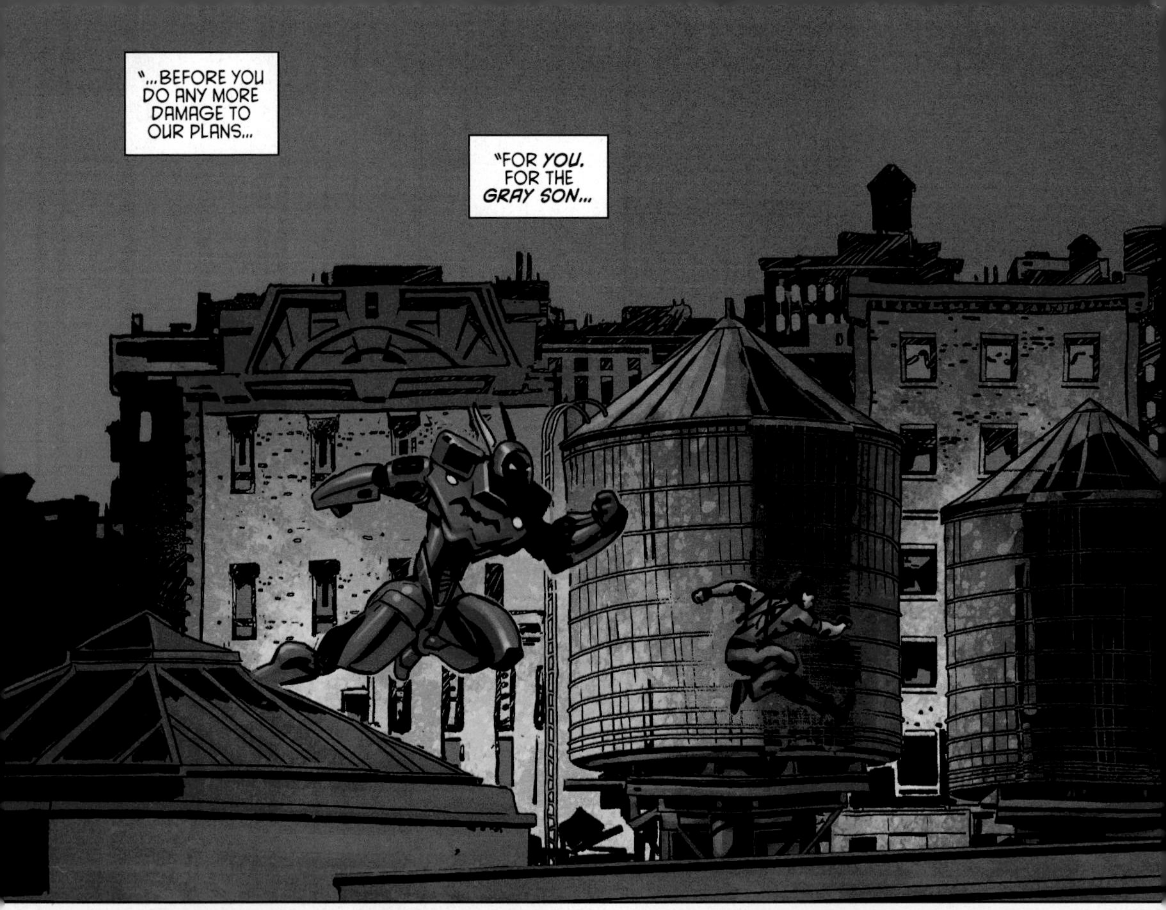
"...BEFORE YOU DO ANY MORE DAMAGE TO OUR PLANS...
"FOR YOU. FOR THE GRAY SON...
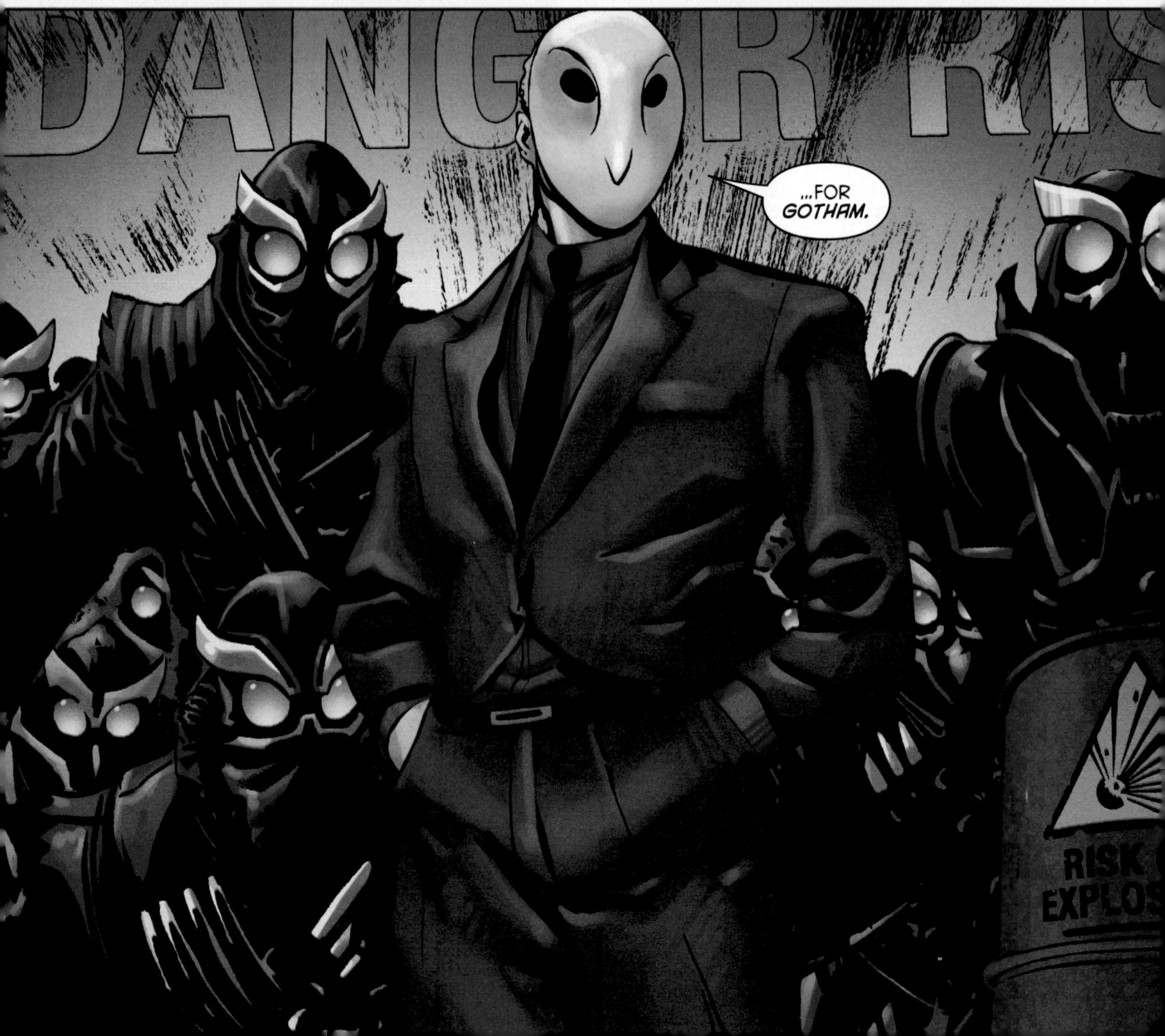
DANG R RIS
...FOR GOTHAM.
RISK EXPLOS

VARIANT COVER GALLERY

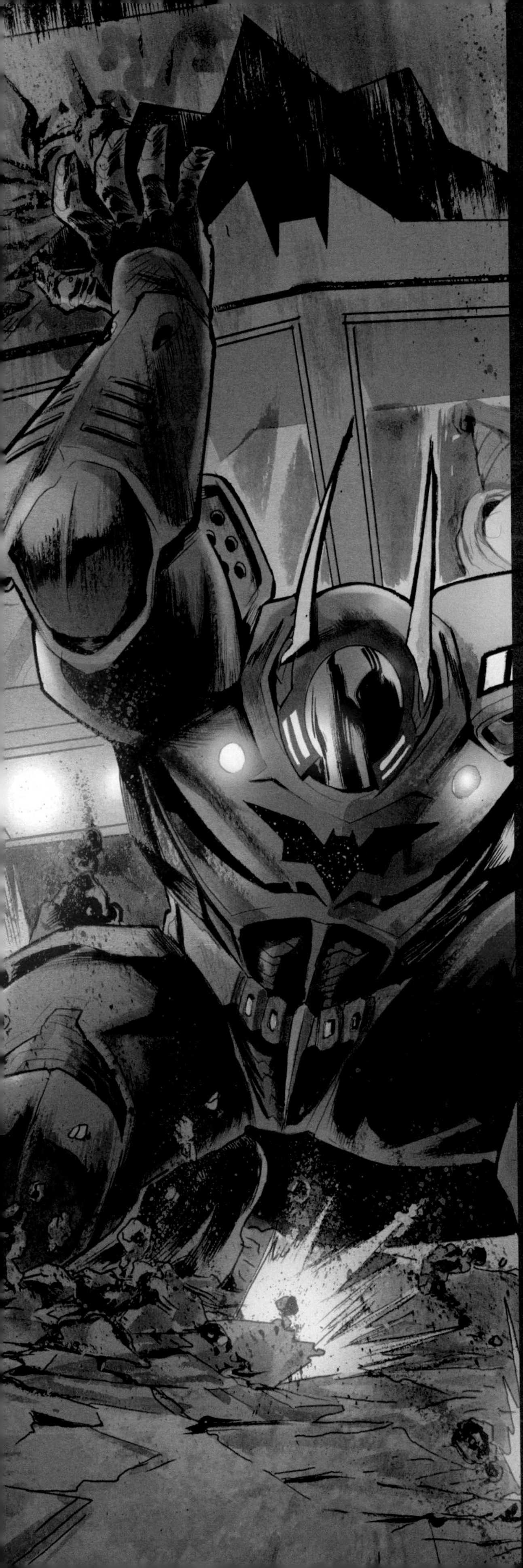

DETECTIVE COMICS #41
JOKER 75TH ANNIVERSARY
VARIANT BY PATRICK GLEASON
AND JOHN KALISZ

DETECTIVE COMICS #42
TEEN TITANS GO! VARIANT
BY DAN HIPP

DETECTIVE COMICS #43
BOMBSHELLS VARIANT
BY EMANUELA LUPACCHINO
WITH TOMEU MOREY

DETECTIVE COMICS #44
FANEXPO VARIANT
BY FRANCIS MANAPUL

DETECTIVE COMICS #44
GREEN LANTERN 75TH
ANNIVERSARY VARIANT
BY CLIFF CHIANG

DETECTIVE COMICS #45
MONSTER VARIANT
BY BILL SIENKIEWICZ

DETECTIVE COMICS #45
NEW YORK COMIC CON VARIANT
BY ANDREW ROBINSON

DETECTIVE COMICS #46
LOONEY TUNES VARIANT BY
BEN CALDWELL AND WARNER
BROTHERS ANIMATION

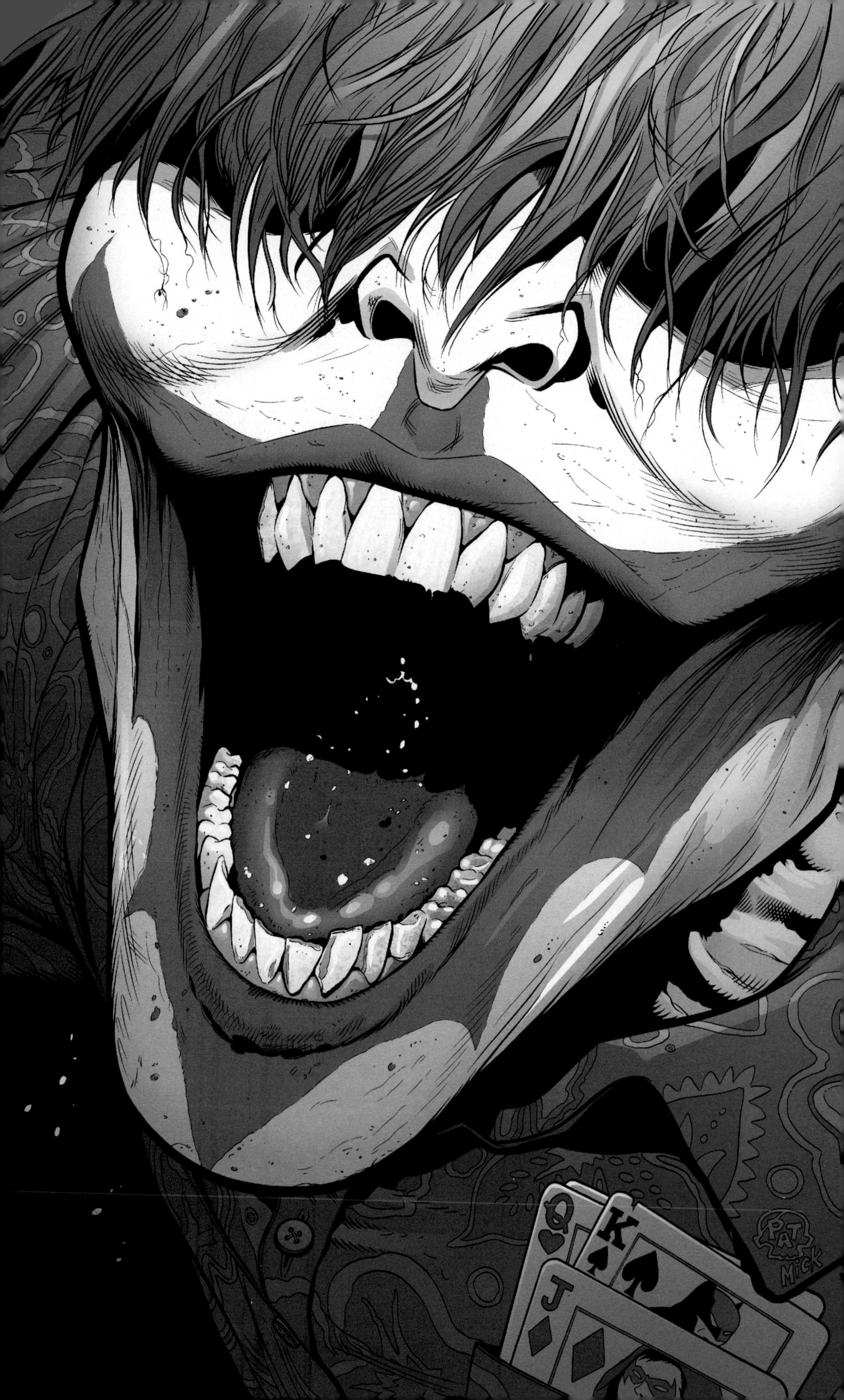
PAT MICK

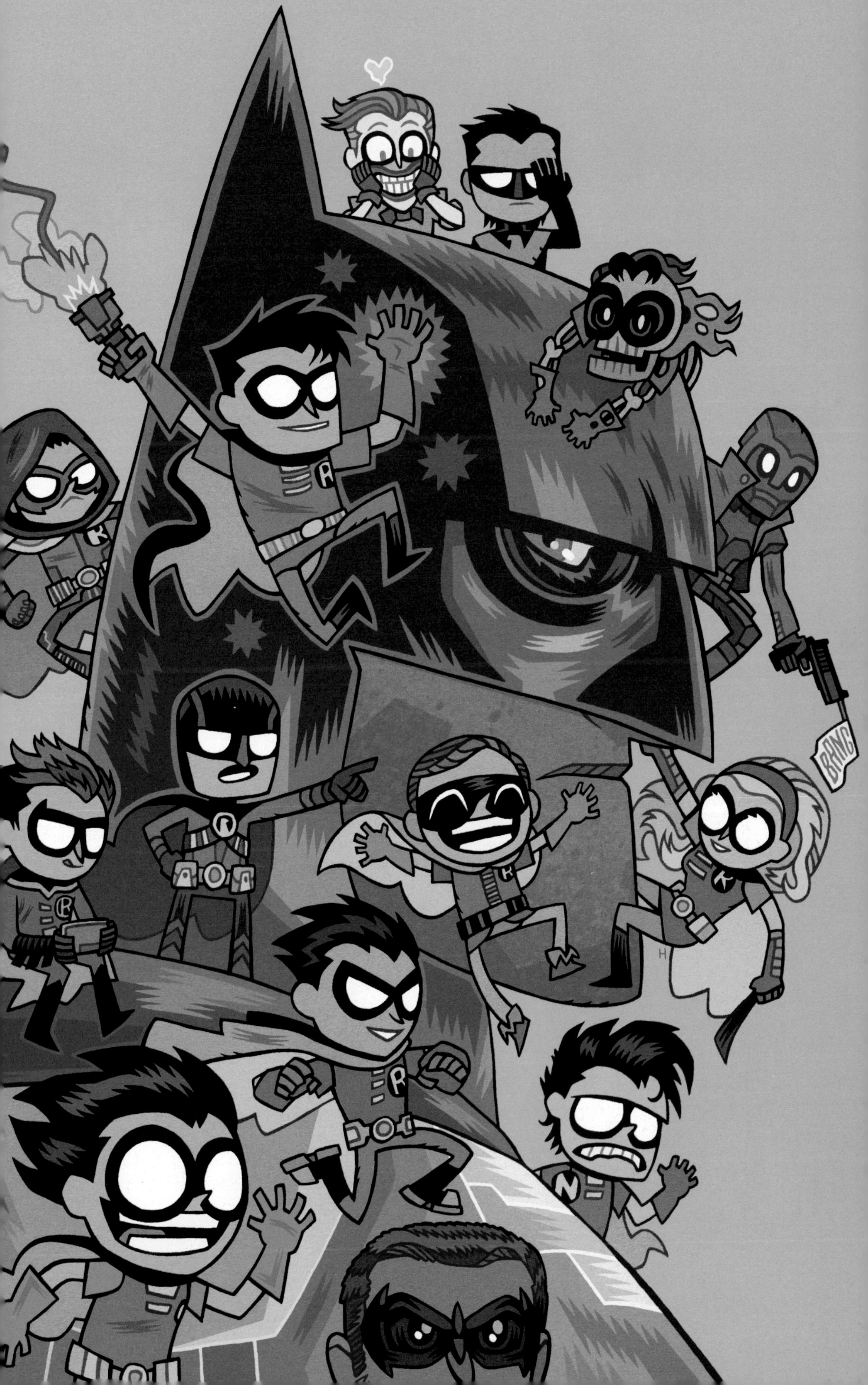
BANG

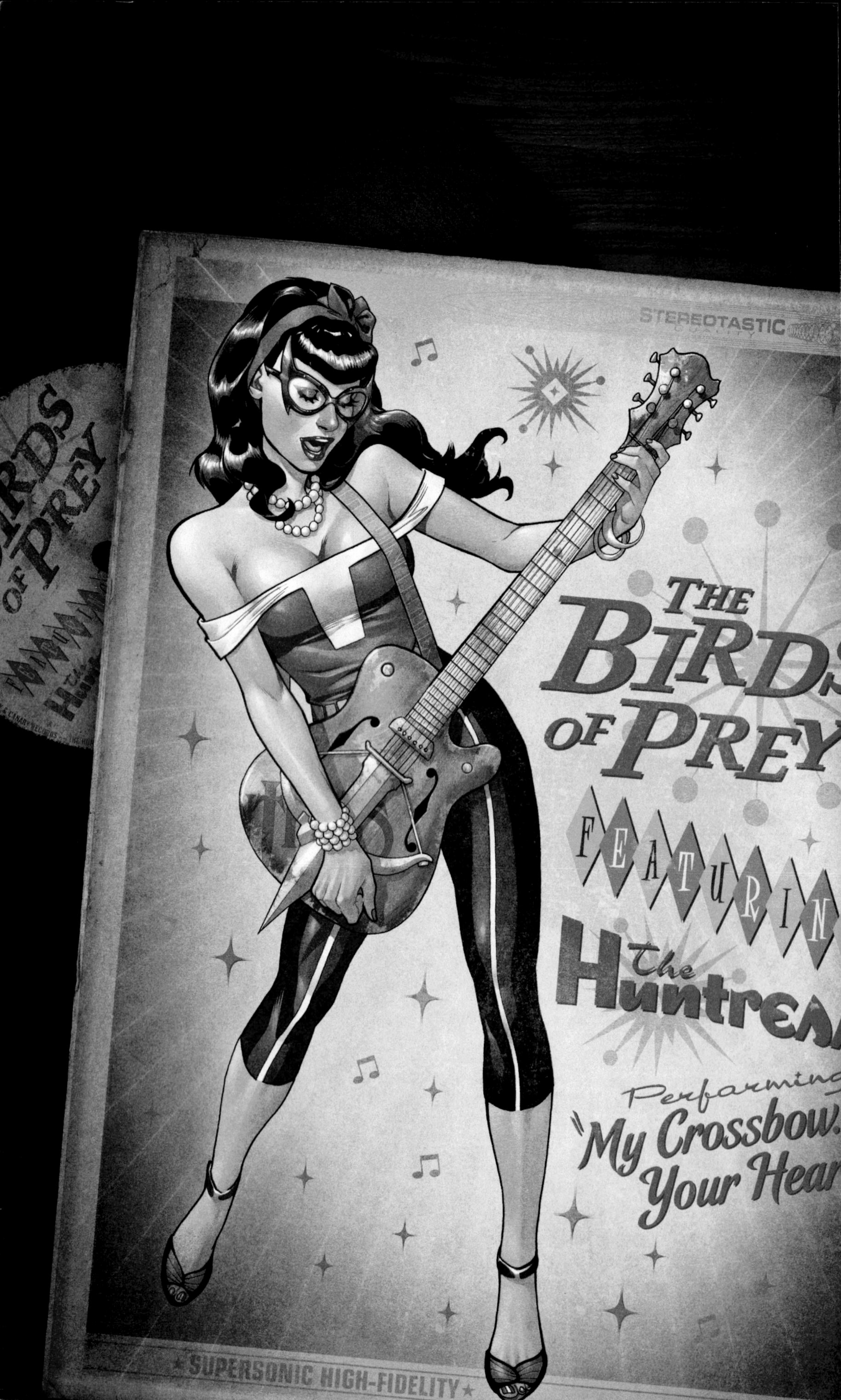
STEREOTASTIC
THE
BIRDS
OF PREY
FEATURIN
The
Huntres
Performin
"My Crossbow.
Your Hear
SUPERSONIC HIGH-FIDELITY

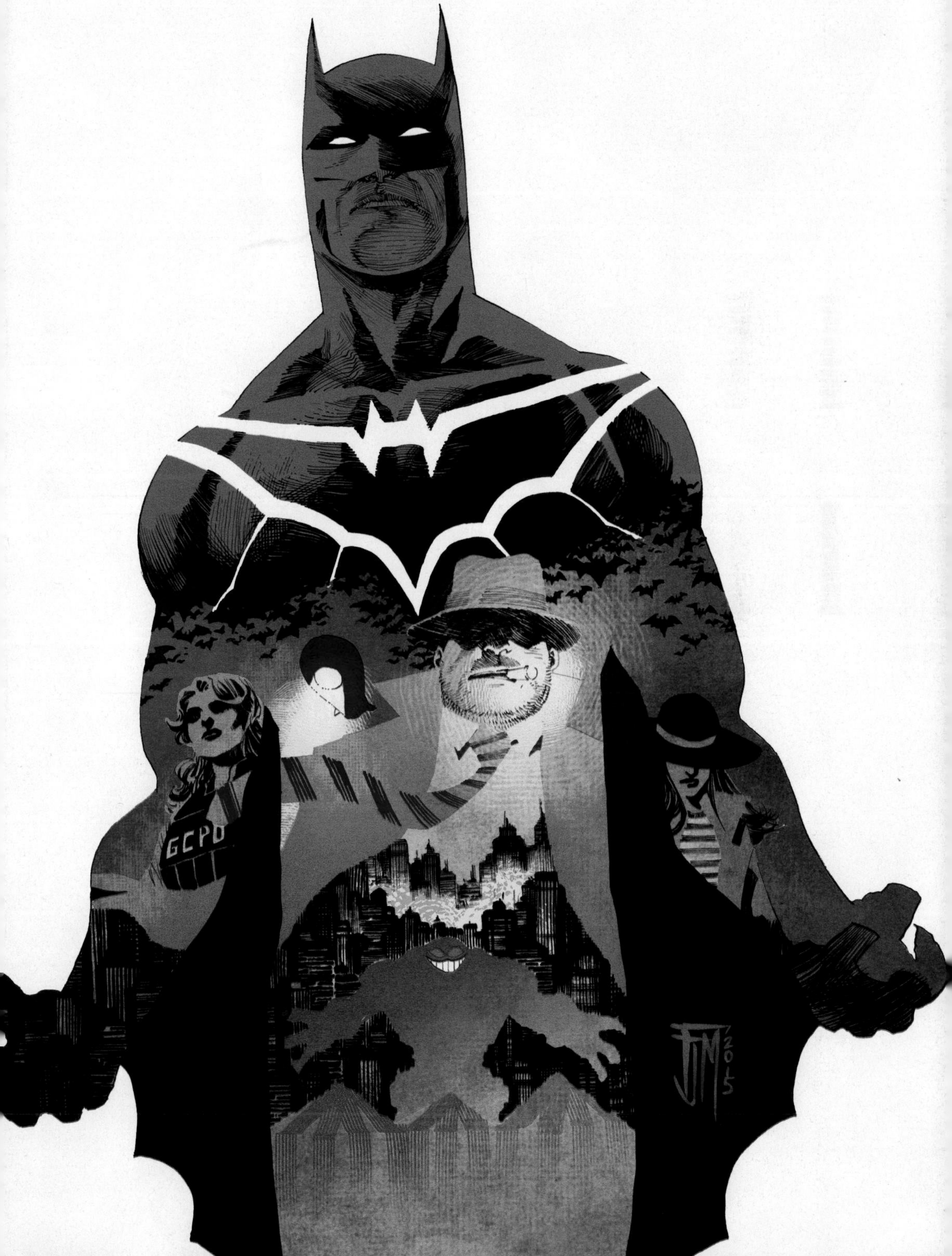
GCPD

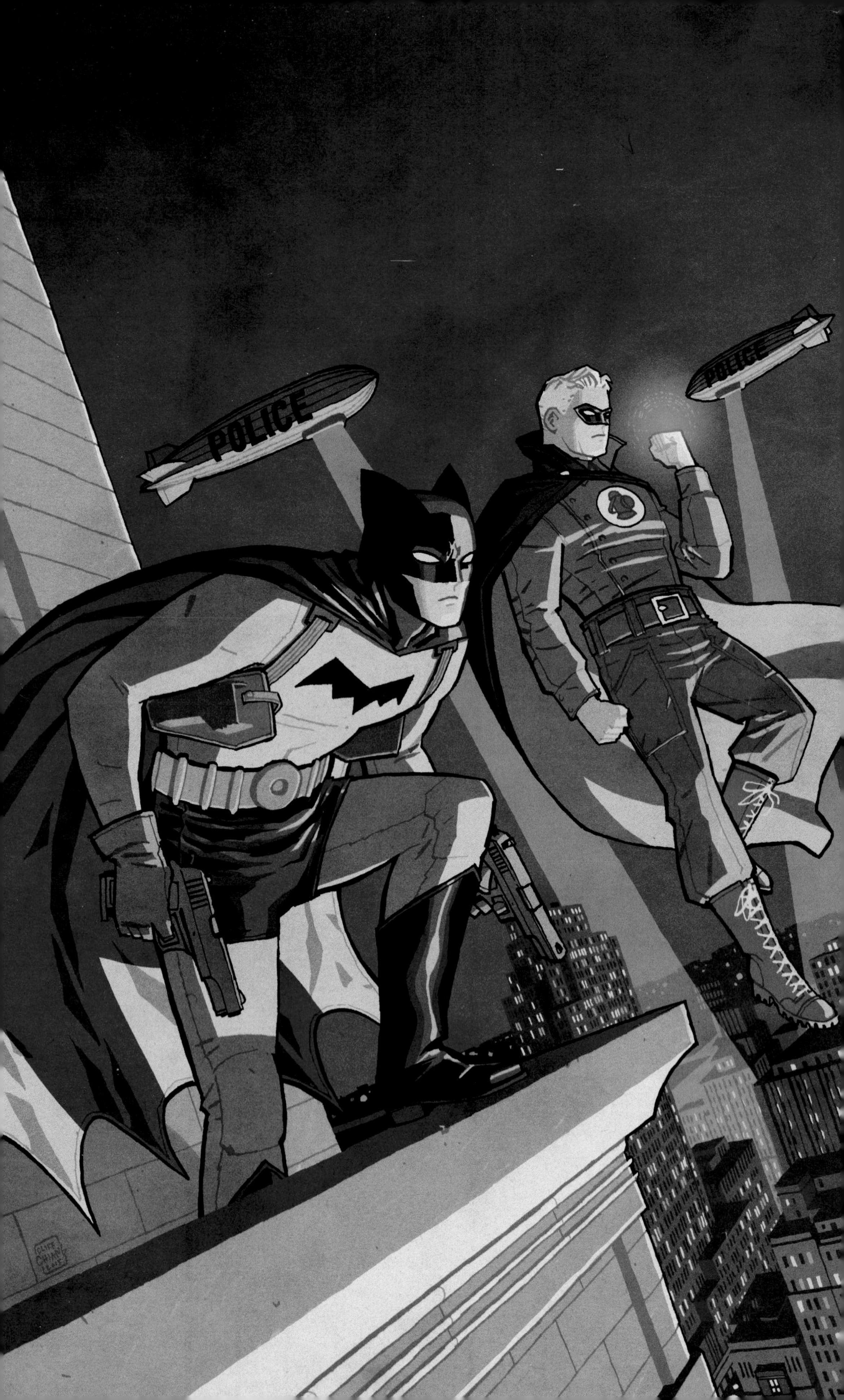
POLICE
POLICE
CLIFF
CHIANG